The Mind Incarnate

Life and Mind: Philosophical Issues in Biology and Psychology
Kim Sterelny and Rob Wilson, editors

The Mind Incarnate

Lawrence A. Shapiro

A Bradford Book
The MIT Press
Cambridge, Massachusetts
London, England

This book was set in Sabon by SNP Best-set Typesetter Ltd., Hong Kong, and was printed and bound in the United States of America.

Library of Congress Cataloging-in-Publication Data

Shapiro, Lawrence A.
  The mind incarnate / Lawrence A. Shapiro.
    p.   cm.—(Life and mind)
  "A Bradford Book."
  Includes bibliographical references and index.
  ISBN 0-262-19496-1 (hc: alk. paper)
  1. Mind and body. I. Title. II. Series.
BF161.S435   2004
128'.2—dc21

                                                    2003056117

For Athena. Wise, of course, but also loving.
And in memory of Berent Enç, whom I will miss very much.

Contents

Preface

Halfway through the twentieth century, Gilbert Ryle objected to "a doctrine about the nature and place of minds which is so prevalent among theorists and even among laymen that it deserves to be described as the official theory" (1949, p. 11). He goes on to describe this doctrine:

The official doctrine, which hails chiefly from Descartes, is something like this. With the doubtful exceptions of idiots and infants in arms every human being has both a body and a mind. Some would prefer to say that every human being is both a body and a mind. His body and his mind are ordinarily harnessed together, but after the death of the body his mind may continue to exist and function. (Ibid.)

It is this official doctrine that Ryle, "with deliberate abusiveness," labels "the dogma of the Ghost in the Machine" (ibid., pp. 15–16).

Although most philosophers of mind today probably disagree with Ryle's particular criticisms of the dogma of the ghost in the machine, they do agree that the dogma is a deplorable one. Few philosophers of mind are willing to accept that the mind is like a ghost, that "minds are not in space, nor are their operations subject to mechanical laws" (ibid., p. 11). Yet, even though philosophers no longer think of minds as supernatural things—as things that exist outside space and time—many do adhere to a conception of the mind–body relationship that seems to offer little more than a naturalized version of the ghost in the machine. According to one widely accepted doctrine, what I shall call the multiple realizability thesis, human minds are realized by human brains but can be realized in many other kinds of brains as well. Because minds can be realized in a vast variety of kinds of things, one has the sense that minds and brains are connected only loosely, and with a little tugging, or if the wind blows strongly enough, the two will go their separate ways.

The ghost in the machine can be spotted in another commonly held assumption as well. Unlike the multiple realizability thesis, which describes a synchronic relation between mind and brain (whatever constitutes the brain at the same time constitutes the mind), this second assumption concerns a *diachronic* relation between the mind and the *body*. According to what I shall call the separability thesis, although the mind and body are without question in causal interaction with each other, the mind is a fairly self-contained organ, like a stomach or kidney, whose properties and operations can be understood without having to attend much to the anatomical and physiological properties of the rest of the body. The separability thesis conceives of the mind as a fairly autonomous component residing in the body, just as a canister of film resides in a camera or, I suppose, a naturalistic ghost would reside in a machine.

I am in agreement with naturalistic approaches to understanding the mind. In my view, minds are as much a part of nature as sand on a beach or acorns on a forest floor. My worry is that naturalized ghosts are hardly better than supernatural ones. In this book I consider at length the question that the passage of Ryle's above leaves open, "How are bodies and minds harnessed together?" I work toward an answer that, I hope, ties the mind more securely to the body than either the multiple realizability thesis or the separability thesis would suggest is possible. To do so, I intend to pursue the scientific turn that has contributed so much to philosophy of mind in recent years.

Natural things can be understood through empirical means, and so it is only reasonable to expect that many of the mind's mysteries will be illuminated by the kind of empirical work cognitive psychologists, neuroscientists, psycholinguists, and other scientists of the mind conduct. To cite just a few examples of this happy marriage, philosophers have scrutinized computational theories of vision in an effort to settle questions about the role of the environment in determining the content of representational mental states. Philosophers have also drawn on findings in developmental psychology (especially research relating to the false belief task) and studies of autism to adjudicate a debate between so-called simulationists and theory theorists over the proper account of belief attribution. Finally and perhaps most conspicuously, philosophers working on the problem of consciousness have immersed themselves in neuroscience to such an extent that it is now not uncommon to find their articles appearing in scientific journals.

The goal of this book is to join some scientific work to some philosophical analysis in an effort tighten the tether between minds and bodies. Given that the mind is not like a ghost in a machine, it must inhere in the body in some other way. My intention in this book is to treat the multiple realizability thesis and the separability thesis as empirical hypotheses about the mind–brain and mind–body relationships respectively, and my aim is to evaluate the relative likelihoods of these hypotheses. I use "likelihood" in its technical sense, as having to do with the degree of support evidence provides to a hypothesis. For evidence to support a hypothesis, it must agree with the predictions the hypothesis entails. But, as Sober (1999a) notes, hypotheses cannot be tested all on their own—they must be tested against a competitor. Accordingly, I shall test the multiple realizability thesis against a thesis I call the *mental constraint thesis*, which states that there are few ways to realize the mind. Likewise, the separability thesis shall be tested against the *embodied mind thesis*, which states that bodies, in a sense to be made more specific later, are more thoroughly integrated with minds than is typically acknowledged.

The strategy in the chapters that follow is to draw forth predictions from the two pairs of competing hypotheses and to say how these predictions fare in light of the evidence. I shall have much more to say about predictions and evidence in what follows, but the basic idea is this. The multiple realizability thesis and the separability thesis make predictions about *what we can predict* about that which realizes the mind (i.e., the brain) and that which contains the mind (i.e., the body). If the former is true, it should not be possible to predict many or any properties of the mind's realizer. It should not be possible, that is, to predict, from a description of the mind's capacities, what properties the mind's realizer must possess. This, indeed, seems to be the correct prediction in cases of multiple realizability that we know to be true. If, for instance, I am asked what properties a mousetrap must possess, I am at a loss. Because mousetraps can have many different designs, can be made in many different ways, it is at least difficult if not impossible to predict from the functional property of a mousetrap (that of catching mice) what physical or structural properties a particular trap will exhibit. On the other hand, if the competitor of the multiple realizability thesis, the mental constraint thesis, is true, then from a description of the capacities of the mind it ought to be possible to predict many properties of the mind's realizer.

Similarly, the separability thesis predicts that, from a description of the mind's properties, it should not be possible to infer properties of the body. Because the body is merely a container for the mind, in the way that Tupperware is a container for last night's leftovers, facts about mental properties should cast little light on facts about the body's properties. In contrast, if the embodied mind thesis is true, it should be possible to describe with a fair amount of precision exactly what an organism's body is like, given knowledge of the organism's mind.

In the following chapters I explain in more detail why many philosophers and psychologists are committed to the multiple realizability thesis and the separability thesis. For now, however, I would like to comment on the speculative nature of what follows. Clearly, the best sort of evidence for the multiple realizability thesis would be the existence of an organism with a mind just like a human mind, but with nothing like a human brain that realizes it. Likewise, the best sort of evidence for the separability thesis would be an organism with a mind just like a human mind, but with a body that is nothing like a human body. It is unlikely that we are going to come across either sort of thing. This means that the best hope for deciding whether the theses of multiple realizability and separability are better supported than their competitors is through indirect means of the sort I suggested above. However, unlike philosophical questions about belief attribution and consciousness that have been helped along by scientific research dedicated to examining just these phenomena, there is little scientific work that is dedicated to testing the multiple realizability thesis against the mental constraint thesis. The science of artificial intelligence comes closest, I suppose, to testing the possibility of alternative designs for minds, but so far nothing produced in an AI laboratory comes close to exhibiting the capacities of a human mind. Moreover, as far as I can tell, AI research assumes that the multiple realizability thesis is true, and critics of AI like John Searle who suggest that only devices with the causal powers of a brain can have a mind are dismissed as short-sighted or chauvinistic. Fortunately, the situation is better in the case of the competition between the separability and embodied mind theses. As we will see, the new embodied cognition research program offers evidence that is clearly applicable to an evaluation of the separability thesis.

Another source of difficulty for the project I pursue in this book is the uncharacteristically casual way in which philosophers have presented and discussed the multiple realizability thesis. Typically, the thesis is motivated with examples concerning carburetors, mousetraps, or other simple devices. The unquestioned inference seems to be that because so many of the functional devices we encounter on a daily basis are multiply realizable, and because the mind itself is understood in functional terms, the mind too must be multiply realizable. But, little attention gets paid to what, in the first place, constitutes different realizations of a single functional kind. Even if philosophers are right that the kind *mousetrap* is multiply realizable, it would be valuable to have an account of the criteria by which different realizations of *mousetrap* qualify, in fact, as different. The importance of such an account only grows when one turns from simple and well-understood devices like mousetraps to systems as complex and opaque as the mind.

Below I outline the route I shall take in an effort to test the multiple realizability and separability theses against their competitors. The conclusion I reach is that the multiple realizability thesis is much less obvious than philosophers have tended to suppose. I would like to have found a stronger conclusion, but, to my knowledge, the science that is necessary to ground any stronger conclusion is simply not yet available. In any case, weak as it is, the conclusion is significant in light of the fact that most philosophers of mind have come to see the multiple realizability thesis as a virtual truism. The situation with the separability thesis is more satisfactory. I believe that evidence from the embodied cognition program makes a strong case against separability. Human minds are profoundly integrated with human bodies, to an extent that may undermine the very distinction between mind and body. Calling into question both the multiple realizability and separability theses invites the hypothesis that minds are connected to brains and bodies in a much tighter way than many philosophers have supposed.

The plan of the book is as follows. In the first chapter I talk more generally about the significance of the multiple realizability thesis, introduce several distinctions that help make its content more precise, and consider some conceptual and empirical arguments that have been made in its support. In chapter 2 I examine how some philosophers understand the idea of realization. I then offer my own analysis of what it means to say of two structures that they are the same or distinct realizations of a single kind. This analysis will prove critical in the chapters that follow, because, if correct, it suggests that many philosophers have been too liberal in their claims about multiple realizability. Some cases of multiple realizability they cite are simply trivial. The challenge facing the proponent of multiple realizability is then to demonstrate that minds are multiply realizable in a nontrivial sense.

Chapter 3 provides a discussion of various sorts of constraint. Constraints must figure importantly in an evaluation of the multiple realizability thesis, because, intuitively, the claim that a given functional kind is multiply realizable implies that there are no or few constraints on what can realize it. Conversely, if there are many or severe constraints on the physical properties that can realize it, then these constraints limit multiple realizability. Elucidating the nature of constraints and their impact on the evolution of functional traits is the goal of chapter 3.

In chapter 4 I apply the analyses of multiple realizability and constraint to the question at hand: is the human mind multiply realizable? Given our relative ignorance of how the brain produces a mind, this chapter is of necessity far more suggestive than demonstrative. Here I muster evidence from neuroscience and brain evolution in an effort to compare the likelihoods of the multiple realizability thesis and the mental constraint thesis. Although I cannot emphasize enough that until we know much more about the brain any conclusions about the multiple realizability thesis can be at best speculative, there now is evidence that organisms with humanlike minds will of necessity share many humanlike neural structures. This, of course, is just what the mental constraint thesis predicts but is counter to the predictions of the multiple realizability thesis.

In the fifth chapter I step back from the business of examining the possibility that the human mind is multiply realizable and consider more generally what (if any) challenge the possibility of multiple realizability has for the prospect of intertheoretic reduction. Philosophers have for the most part accepted multiple realizability as an obstacle to reduction and so as a justification for the claim that the special sciences are autonomous. But, I shall argue, the issues of autonomy and multiple realizability are distinct, and, in any case, reduction has nothing to fear from multiple realizability. I conclude with a discussion of why so many of the special sciences tend to take as their subject matter organisms or artifacts endowed with purposes.

Chapter 6 introduces the separability thesis via the consideration of two trends in cognitive science that downplay the significance of the body in investigations of the mind. The motivation for these trends derives from various philosophical and psychological conceptions of the mind. In response to these trends, I extract from the embodied cognition research program three senses of embodiment that, in one way or another, defy these philosophical and psychological misconceptions of mind. Then, in chapter 7, I turn to research that illustrates the various senses of embodiment introduced in chapter 6. I argue that these research programs provide evidence that is just what one would expect given the embodied mind thesis, but would be quite surprising if the separability thesis were true. Finally, chapter 8 offers some conclusions and suggestions for further research.

I have received lots of help with this project. I would like to thank the Research Committee of the Graduate School at the University of Wisconsin for the summers of support they provided me. Of great benefit to me were also the contributions of the embarrassingly named "Larry Shapiro Fan Club," the most dedicated members of which included Deborah Mower, Terry Sullivan, and Justine Wells. Several neuroscientists allowed me to probe *their* brains in the past few years: Deric Bownds, Brad Postle, and Paul Whalen. Needless to say, whatever inaccuracies present in my interpretations of brain research are entirely my fault. Scientists extraordinaire Cary and Katy Forest suffered through lots of dumb questions about physics and chemistry. The psychologist Art Glenberg deepened my understanding of and interest in the embodied cognition research program. Rob Wilson gave the penultimate draft a close read and his comments made for a much stronger final draft. Conversations with Carl Gillett, Mohan Matthen, and Tom Polger sharpened my thinking about realization. Runs with Steve Nadler provided comic relief. Thalia and Sophia made sure I never forgot about family obligations. Finally, I am especially grateful for all the time my colleagues invested in this book. Meeting regularly with me on Tuesday nights to discuss chapters and give constructive advice were Malcolm Forster, Brie Gertler, Dan Hausman, and Elliott Sober. This is a wonderful group of colleagues. Berent Enç joined us when his health permitted, and his comments on the final draft were sorely missed.

1

The Multiple Realizability Thesis: Significance, Scope, and Support

Several decades ago philosophers began to consider the possibility that the mind is multiply realizable: that it is possible for minds to be built in various distinct ways. Multiple realizability is an obvious idea when applied to things other than minds. Watches seem to be multiply realizable—a watch may be either analog or digital, for instance. Similarly, corkscrews appear to be multiply realizable—the double-lever corkscrew relies on a rack and two pinions to do its job, whereas the waiter's corkscrew makes use of a simple lever (figure 1.1).

Applied to minds, the claim of multiple realizability amounts to the thesis that what's true for watches and corkscrews is true as well for minds. For convenience, I shall call the thesis of multiple realizability when applied just to humanlike minds the *multiple realizability thesis* (MRT). If we suppose that the human mind consists of various cognitive capacities—perception, memory, language comprehension, attention, problem-solving abilities—and that these capacities in human beings are identifiably distinct from the way they might appear in other organisms (surely *human* perception, memory, language comprehension, etc. differ from similar capacities in other primates and, if present at all, in other animals), then we can speak of a uniquely human psychological profile. MRT, as I shall be using the term, is the thesis that a mind with this uniquely human psychological profile can be built in distinct ways. The claim I shall defend is that MRT is perhaps false and is in any case far from the well-supported thesis that philosophers have traditionally taken it to be.

In my effort to address the question of the truth of MRT, I shall be interested in assessing the *likelihood* of MRT. As I noted in the

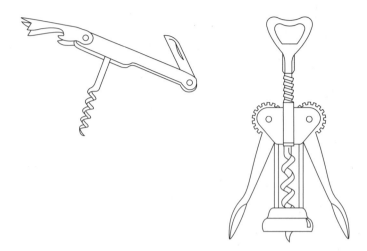

Figure 1.1
Two types of corkscrew: waiter's corkscrew (left); double-lever corkscrew (right).

preface, I intend "likelihood" in its technical sense. Likelihood is one way to measure the support that evidence provides for a hypothesis. In the case at hand, the hypothesis of interest is MRT. I shall be concerned mainly with the kinds of predictions that MRT makes, and I shall be contrasting its predictions with that of a competing hypothesis: the *mental constraint thesis* (MCT). According to MCT, humanlike minds are not multiply realizable, or, at least, many humanlike mental capacities are not multiply realizable. In the work ahead I shall be arguing that MCT and MRT, given certain background assumptions, make different predictions and that on the basis of these distinct predictions it should be possible to determine which of the two has greater likelihood. Crucially, I will *not* be trying to *prove* that MRT is true or false. Rather, I shall be considering evidence and arguments that, I think, make a plausible case that MCT is often the better supported of the two hypotheses, and so MRT is not the unimpeachable claim that so many have assumed it to be. More modestly, I hope to make evident the complexity of issues that are involved in the thesis that minds are multiply realizable.

Of course, one can believe that MRT is true but doubt that the human mind *actually* has multiple realizations (although, as we shall see, some do believe that human minds are in fact multiply realized to some degree at least). Just as something may be flammable but never actually combust, so a kind of mind may be multiply realizable although it is, in fact, never realized in more than one way. So, it is consistent with the truth of MRT that there currently exists only one kind of realization of humanlike psychology and that there never will exist another. Nevertheless, the bare possibility of multiple realizability establishes MRT as a thesis of philosophical significance.

The remainder of this chapter is dedicated to three tasks. First, I explain in more detail why philosophers have invested so much in the truth of MRT. Second, I draw some distinctions to clarify more exactly how I shall understand the scope of MRT. Finally, I critically discuss the conceptual and empirical arguments that philosophers have made in support of MRT.

1.1 The Significance of the Multiple Realizability Thesis

MRT is important for what it claims about the relationship between the mind and the brain; but more generally, multiple realizability raises issues about how various scientific theories are related to each other. In this latter context, philosophers impressed with the apparent implications of MRT for the relationship between a theory of the mind and a theory of the brain have sought to argue that the multiple realizability of, for instance, various biological kinds has profound implications for the relationship between biology and physics (e.g., Kitcher 1984; Rosenberg 1985). Whereas I will have much more to say about both MRT in particular and the implications of multiple realizability more generally in the pages to follow, a few introductory words at this time are appropriate.

Regarding the first point—the consequences of MRT for our understanding of the mind–brain relationship—it is a simplification but not an egregious one to see prior to the emergence of MRT a division among philosophers over the nature of the mind–brain relationship. On the one hand were the dualists, who conceived of minds and brains as fundamentally different kinds of substances. The brain is a physical substance and thus endowed with physical properties like mass, location, temperature, and so on. In contrast, the mind, according to the dualist, is without mass or location, and so on. It was this conception of minds and bodies that Ryle (1949) mocked with his ridicule of the "ghost in the machine." To be sure, dualists would acknowledge that goings on in the brain may be reliably correlated with happenings in the mind, but because the mind and brain are on their view so utterly different, their explanations for this correlation tended toward the mystical, the incoherent, the theistic, or the desperate.

On the other hand were the type-identity theorists (Place 1956; Smart 1959) who brushed aside centuries of dualist machinations with a simple and bold proposal: the mind and the brain are one and the same thing. On this view, the difficulty of explaining why and how events in the mind and brain exhibit such precise correlations completely vanishes. According to type-identity theorists, the idea that some mental event, say, pain, is merely correlated with a distinct event in the brain, say, the firing of C-fibers, rests on a confusion. It would be the same confusion that is obvious in the following question: why is it that whenever water is present there also is H_2O? The question is asking for an explanation of the ineluctable correlation between water and H_2O, but of course if this correlation is assumed to hold between distinct things then one has made a mistake. Water *is* H_2O. The terms "water" and "H_2O" are simply two labels that refer to one thing. It is on this model that type-identity theorists wished to think about the connection between the mind and the brain. Speaking properly, pain and C-fiber firings are not simply correlated, they are identical.

Whereas the identification of the mind with the brain provided an easy way out of the difficulties dualists confronted when trying to explain how an entity that exists outside of space could causally interact with a body in space, type-identity theorists faced a hard, and in retrospect, obvious problem of their own. As any fan of science fiction or any advocate of artificial intelligence will tell you, it is possible to build minds out of different kinds of stuff. One need go no further than the movie theater to witness minds composed of silicon chips, flocculent masses of green noodles, or gelatinous blobs of phosphorescent muck. No doubt these varieties of creatures do not in fact exist, but the examples illustrate nonetheless the coherence of the idea of humanlike minds that are not identical with humanlike brains. Unlike water, which, if it is not H_2O is not water, minds that are not brains are readily conceived. Thus, MRT is significant for the stance it offers on the relationship between mind and brain. Minds and brains, MRT teaches us, cannot stand in a relation of simple identity. Things are more complicated. Indeed, much of contemporary philosophy of mind has been devoted to developing plausible analyses of the mind–brain relationship in light of MRT. More specifically, discussions of token identity, according to which particular mental properties (e.g., my pain) are identical to particular physical properties (e.g., my C-fibers firing), take the truth of MRT and thus the rejection of type-identity theory as their starting points. At stake in these discussions is an understanding of how minds and brains are related, why minds seem to depend on brains, how mental events can cause physical events, and so on, given that "mind" and "brain" are no longer conceived of as two labels for the same thing.

I mentioned that interest in MRT has extended beyond the important but narrow topic of the mind–brain relation. This is because MRT also has consequences for how one is to understand the relation between theories of mind and theories of those biological, chemical, and physical processes on which mental events seem to depend. Prominent philosophers of science in the mid–twentieth century conceived of science as consisting of theories at various levels, where the kinds at higher levels, like psychology and economics, depend in some way on kinds in lower levels, like biology, chemistry, and, ultimately, physics. In virtue of this dependency, it would be possible, these philosophers believed, to derive laws of, say, psychology, from laws of biology, which in turn could be derived from laws of chemistry and, finally, laws of physics. The derivation of laws of a higher-level theory from laws of a lower-level theory constitutes an *intertheoretic reduction*, and it was the possibility of such reduction that promised to unify the myriad levels of science.

Appealing as this ideal of unification might seem, it effectively relegates higher-level sciences like psychology to rest stops on the road to a final destination. Psychological laws, on the unificationist's conception of science, are in principle eliminable in favor of those physical laws from which they derive. We continue to value psychology as a way to understand the mind, but only because we don't yet know enough to explain mental phenomena in physical terms. Presumably, the unificationist would hold, the days of higher-level theorizing are numbered; ideally, colleges of letters and science will one day contain only a single department of physics.

It was in response to this austere vision that Fodor (1974) developed the implications of MRT. Just as MRT prevents an identification of mental kinds and neural kinds, and so stands in the way of a reduction of mind to brain, so, more generally, does the multiple realizability of kinds in higher-level sciences challenge the dream of unification. As long as it is possible that kinds in any higher-level science are realizable in different lower-level kinds, it will be false that the higher-level kind is coextensive with a particular lower-level kind, and thus it is hopeless to try to derive higher-level laws from lower-level laws. Or, at any rate, that is the reasoning that led Fodor to see multiple realizability as a kind of salvation for higher-level sciences (but see Sober 1999b for an argument that multiple realizability need not be taken to have these consequences for reduction). So long as the multiple realizability of higher-level kinds remains a possibility, higher-level sciences must retain their autonomy. Whether this verdict is in the end correct, it is uncontroversial that philosophers have by and large *perceived* multiple realizability as securing the autonomy of higher-level sciences, and for this reason the significance of multiple realizability in philosophy of science has been immense.

1.2   The Scope of the Multiple Realizability Thesis

I have said enough, I hope, to motivate the study of multiple realizability pursued in the chapters that follow. I will now turn to clarifying the scope MRT assumes in the following chapters. Philosophers, for whatever reason, have rarely characterized MRT in precise terms. However, I believe that any evaluation of MRT must take care to draw several distinctions. Spending time now to advance these distinctions will help situate and motivate the various arguments and maneuverings in the chapters ahead.

The first distinction concerns the extent of MRT: just how much multiple realizability must one accept before proclaiming MRT to be true? For purposes of answering this question, I shall adopt with slight revisions Polger's (2002, pp. 146–147) useful taxonomy. Polger finds in the literature four conceptions of MRT:

Weak MRT: At least some creatures that are not exactly like us in their physical composition can have minds like ours.

SETI[1] MRT: Some creatures that are significantly different from us in their physical composition can have minds like ours.

Standard MRT: Systems of indefinitely (perhaps infinitely) many physical compositions can have minds like ours.

Radical MRT: Any (every) suitably organized system, regardless of its physical composition, can have minds like ours.

Polger notes that standard and radical MRT seem to receive most discussion and allegiance in contemporary philosophy of mind. In my view, these theses are prima facie incredible; and even if one does not agree with this sentiment, it is surely true that the burden falls on those who endorse them to say why they find them plausible. Weak and SETI MRT, on the other hand, are less easy to dismiss with a simple "prove it." Many might be inclined to see these hypotheses as plausible on their face. But more important, some philosophers believe that there is currently at hand evidence to support them. Accordingly, much of this book is spent defending a view about how one should interpret this evidence. In the end, I hope to have diminished significantly the support for a conception of MRT that falls somewhere between weak and standard MRT.

The label "weak MRT," while clear in its intent, remains vague. Just how "exactly like us" should qualify as *exactly like us*? As we will see in the following chapter, there are clearly some differences in realization that one should never want to claim suffice for a case of multiple realization. A moment's reflection should make obvious that vagueness is likely to permeate any characterization of MRT. After all, MRT is a thesis that requires one to talk about similarities of various sorts—similarities in kinds of realization and similarities in the kinds that are realized. I shall have much more to say about these matters in the chapters that follow. However, I think it is appropriate at this point to acknowledge that MRT is not an all-or-nothing affair. Whether one takes MRT to be true will depend on how much multiple realizability one requires (i.e., does one require weak, SETI, standard, or radical MRT?); and how much multiple realizability there is will in turn depend on how stringent one's requirements for similarities and differences in realization are. My hope is that by setting my sights on a fairly limited form of MRT—as I said, something between weak and standard MRT—and by employing a conception of similarity that seems to match the grain of description that our best sciences of the mind find useful, I will be able to challenge that statement of MRT about which one should care the most.

A second set of distinctions that an evaluation of MRT makes necessary concerns the nature of possibility. I noted above that MRT is the claim that it is possible to build a humanlike mind in different physical ways. But it is standard philosophical fare that "possible" might refer either to anything that is consistent with laws of nature or anything that is consistent with logical truth. A perpetual motion machine is impossible in the first sense but not in the second. That is, various laws of nature imply that no one will ever build a perpetual motion machine, but there is no logical contradiction in the idea of, say, a wheel that never ceases to spin. On the other hand, because triangles are by definition three-sided figures, a geometer in search of a four-sided triangle is clearly wasting her time. Such a figure is impossible not just in the first sense, but in the second as well, because the existence of a three-sided figure with four sides is logically incoherent. The first kind of possibility, because it is concerned with limits that laws of nature impose, is often called *nomological* or *physical* possibility. The second kind of possibility is known as *logical* possibility.

Given these two kinds of possibility, it should now be evident that MRT is ambiguous. Should the claim be taken to imply just the logical possibility of multiply realizable minds or, more ambitiously, the nomological possibility of such things? Pretty clearly, it must be nomological possibility that MRT assumes. This is apparent from the empirical nature of the evidence that proponents of MRT muster in its defense. In contrast, no one, as far as I know, has spent much energy trying to defend the *logical* possibility of MRT. Indeed, of the four conceptions of MRT I mentioned above, *all* are logically possible, and so whatever disagreement there is between advocates of the four types, it cannot be over the logical possibility of each type. Accordingly, if the question of the possibility of humanlike minds instantiated in nonhumanlike brains is to have any oomph, it should boil down to empirical considerations rather than claims about how to understand the concept *mind*.

There is yet a third conception of possibility that will figure prominently in my discussion of MRT. Narrower than nomological possibility is circumstantial, or historical, possibility. Circumstantial possibility recognizes the importance of initial conditions in predictions of what can happen. Some things that are nomologically possible in some places or at some times will not be nomologically possible at other places or at other times because of differences in circumstances. Thus, for instance, it may well be that life is possible only on Earth. Were this true, however, it would not be because it is nomologically impossible for life to evolve elsewhere. Presumably, life could evolve elsewhere if other planets had conditions similar to those on Earth. In saying that life is possible only on Earth, one is asserting that the initial conditions necessary for the evolution of life are present only on Earth: were they present elsewhere, life would be possible elsewhere.

In addition to the limitations on possibility that initial conditions impose, circumstantial possibility refers to limitations on what is possible as a result of historical contingencies.[2] For instance, it might now be possible for me to arrive in Chicago in time for dinner. It would take about three hours to drive to Chicago from my home in Madison, my car is working fine, and it's early in the afternoon. However, if on the way I become lost, or I run over something that punctures a tire, or I am slowed by traffic, it may become impossible for me to arrive in Chicago in time for dinner. This is an impossibility that results (we can suppose) not from conditions that are present at the start of my trip, but rather from contingencies that develop along the way.

One helpful way to illuminate further the distinction between nomological and circumstantial possibility is to consider a thought experiment

Stephen Jay Gould (1989a) suggested. Imagine, Gould requests, that the tape of life were played over again. Starting with the same initial conditions that were present at the time of the Earth's origin, if life were to evolve all over again, would the life-forms that developed bear any resemblance to the life-forms that have actually populated the Earth? Gould's answer is an emphatic "no." Because of the countless accidents involved in evolutionary processes—accidents ranging from the dramatic, such as collisions with asteroids, to the mundane but just as significant, such as the inadvertent drowning of an organism that, had it the chance, would have given birth to a new species—the odds that anything remotely resembling a human being (or any other actual organism, presumably) would evolve again are infinitesimally small. Here Gould is betting that the initial conditions by themselves leave open the possibility that many different forms of life could evolve.

In the context of MRT, Gould's claim might be put like this. Imagine that the tape of life is played over again and somewhere along its length there evolves a being with a psychological profile just like a human being's. Would the being's mind be realized in anything like the way that a human being's mind is realized? The truth of MRT requires that there be flexibility in the manner in which this new organism's mind is realized. If the tape of life were played over and over again, each time producing a being with a humanlike mind, the truth of MRT predicts that on at least some occasions the humanlike mind would be realized differently than it is realized in human beings. Like Gould's claim about the variation in life-forms that can evolve from identical initial conditions, the version of MRT in which I am interested bets that initial conditions on Earth are consistent with variation in the kinds of things that could realize a humanlike mind. In contrast, if MRT is false, one would expect to see the same kind of realization each and every time a humanlike mind evolves.

Yet, even supposing that the tape of life experiment does disconfirm MRT on Earth, it reveals nothing about the likelihood of MRT elsewhere. Just because the limited number of materials on Earth might make it impossible to build more than only a few kinds of electrical conductors, so too initial conditions on Earth might make it possible to realize humanlike minds in only a few different ways. However, all this is consistent with the possibility that elsewhere in the universe there are materials that would, if put together correctly, realize humanlike minds, just as there may well be substances capable of electrical conductance that are nowhere to be found on Earth.

My main target will be the possibility of MRT here on Earth. This is in some sense inevitable given our ignorance of the kinds of initial conditions that are necessary for the evolution of thinking things like ourselves. However, I believe that questions about the possibility of MRT just on Earth (what I shall sometimes call *terrestrial MRT*) are of sufficient interest to warrant its careful study. Is it just an accident that the human brain has the properties that it does, or could the evolution of humanlike minds result in terrestrial brains very unlike those that human beings possess? Even though limited to what can happen here on Earth, this is a question that must surely attract the interest of anyone seeking to understand why the brain has the structure it does, just as answering questions about the shape of the eye's lens would require one to understand why eye evolution has taken one course rather than another. That is, an evaluation of terrestrial MRT seems as necessary for answering some questions about the relationship between the human mind and the human brain as a study of the multiple realizability of eyes would be for answering some questions about the relationship between the capacities of the eye and anatomy of the eye.

Moreover, those who hope to build an artificial intelligence should be very curious about the prospects of terrestrial MRT. If there turns out to be good reason to believe that terrestrial MRT is true, then clearly the search for alternative ways to build a humanlike mind is not doomed from the start. Of course, if the evidence goes against terrestrial MRT, this would not show that it is impossible to build a realization of a humanlike mind that differs significantly from the brain. After all, the processes of evolution face constraints that the engineer does not. Most basically, an AI engineer approaches the problem of building a mind with the advantage of foresight. The engineer has an idea about how her finished product should behave and sets about looking for the most efficient way of realizing her goal. Evolution, on the other hand, operates without the benefit of a blueprint. The products of evolution are often poorly designed from the perspective of an engineer: they may be unnecessarily complex, they may be so constrained by earlier stages of their evolution that they can never assume a more optimal design, and so on.

Still, despite these differences between "natural" design and engineered design, AI could benefit much from considering the question "Why has nature chosen to realize a human mind in this way rather than some other?" It seems quite reasonable that the answer to this question should shape the approaches that AI researchers take toward at least some of their goals. The more the answer tends toward a rejection of terrestrial MRT—the more the answer inclines toward a sort of nomological necessity in the mind–brain relationship given the kinds of conditions present on Earth—the more reason for caution in designs that depart radically from that on which nature has settled.

There might appear to be a tension between my decision to focus on terrestrial MRT and my claim to be offering a challenge to something between the weak and standard MRTs that Polger describes. As defined, these theses do not exclude the possibility that humanlike minds can be realized in kinds of material that are not present on Earth. Indeed, SETI MRT, which falls within the range of weak and standard MRT, is quite explicit in its suggestion that minds like ours can evolve from starting conditions that differ from those on Earth. How can a challenge to terrestrial MRT be made to work against these more inclusive statements of MRT? It cannot, unless some of the arguments against terrestrial MRT are arguments about not just the circumstantial possibility of MRT but about its less confining nomological possibility as well. As we will see, it is no easy matter to determine whether the realization of the human mind is as it is because of initial conditions and historical contingencies or because nature simply cannot build a humanlike mind in more ways than one. Indeed, this is just one of many issues we will come across that has been ignored in discussions of MRT despite its obvious importance. Moreover, the muddy empirical flavor of this question suggests that it is one for the scientists to answer. For now, I shall simply claim boldly that at least some of the points I make in chapter 4 about the connection between mental and neural properties might well reflect nomological rather than circumstantial or historical possibilities. Insofar as this is true, my arguments call into question a statement of MRT that falls within the weak–standard range. If I turn out to be wrong about this, I am content to limit my challenge to terrestrial MRT, which, as I have noted, is a thesis of great interest in its own right.

1.3   Conceptual Arguments for the Multiple Realizability Thesis

In contemporary philosophy of mind, the idea that minds, or mental states, are multiply realizable emerged in the 1960s, primarily in the writings of Hilary Putnam and Jerry Fodor. The arguments Putnam and Fodor made are now part of every philosopher of mind's basic tool kit, but a close examination of their original formulation provides a useful stepping stone to a thorough examination of the claim that minds are multiply realizable. For the sake of convenience, I will group these arguments into conceptual and empirical versions, leaving discussion of the empirical arguments for the next section. I do not wish to claim that there is a sharp distinction between conceptual and empirical considerations. I use the labels merely because the evaluation of some of these arguments seems to depend less immediately on the weight of empirical evidence than does the evaluation of others. As we will see, the conceptual arguments do not work so well in support of the multiple realizability thesis. The empirical arguments seem on their face more compelling than the conceptual ones. Yet, I shall argue in the next chapter, on a reasonable analysis of how to understand the concept of *multiple realization*, even the best empirical evidence that philosophers cite on behalf of MRT is inconclusive.

1.3.1   Turing Machine Functionalism

Hilary Putnam's arguments against the identity theory (Putnam 1960; 1967) are the modern *locus classicus* of the idea that minds are multiply realizable. As I have already noted, identity theorists argued that minds and brains are strictly identical, in the same way that water is strictly identical with H_2O and lightning is strictly identical with electrical discharges. Motivating the identity theorists was a desire to characterize the mind in a way that avoided nomological danglers (Feigl 1958)—ontologically peculiar entities that fall outside the scope of physical laws. If minds or their parts consisted of nonphysical substances, then the mind's relation to the body, as well as to the rest of the world, would be irremediably mysterious. If, on the other hand, the mind simply is the brain, then the secrets of the mind, if not immediately apparent, would at least now be in a position where we could get to them. That is, mind–brain identity locates mental properties within an accessibly empirical domain.

Putnam's response to the identity theorists rests on construing the mind as a collection of Turing machine states. Turing machines are theoretical constructs (they do not actually exist because they are endowed with an infinite storage capacity) defined by two functions: one that takes inputs and states to outputs and another that takes inputs and states to other (or the same) states (Block 1978, 1980a,b). A *Turing machine table* is simply a list of instructions that defines these two functions. Turing supposed that numerals would serve as the inputs and outputs to a Turing machine. Thus, given the state of Turing machine X, a numerical input to X would cause it to produce some numerical output and then either to change state or remain in the same state. Any Turing machine that can be described by the same table that defines the operations of X is "equivalent" to X. In fact, because inputs and outputs to a Turing machine are defined purely syntactically (i.e., with no regard for what the symbolic inputs and outputs stand for), one can say that X and all Turing machines that share X's machine table are realizations of the same abstract type of machine.

Putnam's suggestion was that mental states could be conceived as analogues to Turing machine states.[3] In place of the numerals that serve as inputs and outputs to Turing machines, Putnam substituted sensory stimulations and behavior. Mental states, on this model, are defined by a machine table that specifies functional relations between sensory stimulations, states, and behavior. To be sexually jealous, for instance, is to be in a state that, given the observation of one's mate flirting with someone else, causes one to assume a threatening posture toward the individual and also to *suspect* that the mate has been or is interested in having sex with this individual, and, perhaps, to feel *humiliation* that one's mate would prefer the attention of someone else. Similarly, the mental state of humiliation receives an analysis in terms of the mental states and behavior that it will produce when combined with various sensory stimulations, and so on for all mental states.

Thus, the first step in Putnam's response to the identity theory—in the development of his idea that minds are multiply realizable—is a conception of mental states as Turing machine functional states. The next step presumably follows immediately. Just as a Turing machine table provides the means by which to classify various Turing machines as realizations of the same kind, a given mental machine table suffices to say when various physical organizations are of the same mental kind. Two physical systems are of the same mental kind when they contain states that obey the same instructions—that fall in the domains and ranges of the same functions. And, as Ned Block observes, "[i]f we could formulate a machine table for a human, it would be absurd to identify any of the machine table states with a type of *brain* state, since presumably all manner of brainless machines could be described by that table as well" (1980b, p. 178). Multiple realizability appears to follow quite naturally and immediately from the suggestion that mental states are Turing machine-functional states.

In deciding whether this argument for MRT actually works, it is important to understand its force against the identity theorists. Why not take Putnam's objection to mind–brain identity as simply a friendly amendment to the identity theory? After all, identity theorists were probably less interested in arguing for a strict identity between the mind and the brain than they were in making the mind safe for materialism. As Smart (1959) remarks in the course of considering the possibility that sensations are nonphysical, "for various reasons I just cannot believe that this can be so. That everything should be explicable in terms of physics . . . except the occurrence of sensations seems to me to be frankly unbelievable" (1959, p. 142). If, as I've claimed, the identity theorist's motivating desire was to make the mind explicable in physical terms, then Putnam's claim that minds are multiply realizable in various physical organizations gives identity theorists precisely what they want—though perhaps not for the reasons that they supposed.

Yet, it is in fact a gross misunderstanding of Turing machine functionalism to think that it is materialist in spirit. As Putnam adamantly asserts, "the functional-state hypothesis is *not* incompatible with dualism! Although it goes without saying that the hypothesis is 'mechanistic' in its inspiration, it is a slightly remarkable fact that a system consisting of a body and a 'soul,' if such things there be, can perfectly well be a Probabilistic Automaton" (1967, p. 228). Putnam's Turing machine conception of mind will not satisfy the identity theorist's desire for a materialistic characterization of mind, not because minds may be souls, but because, when equated with machine tables, there is nothing more to a mind than a complex functional relation. This functional relation may be realized in this or that substance, but mental states, according to Putnam, are not identical with that which realizes a given relation. Rather, they consist simply in the relation itself.

Comparison with David Lewis's approach to functionalism makes Putnam's account clearer. For Lewis (1969, 1978), mental states are the *occupants* of functional roles. To illustrate his position, Lewis notes that there is a particular cat, Bruce, who occupied the role (for Lewis) *my cat* (1978, p. 218). It is a contingent matter that it is Bruce who occupied this role. Had Lewis owned some different cat, it would not be Bruce who occupied the role (for Lewis) *my cat*, but this other cat. Moreover, the role *my cat*, for me, was once occupied by Roxanne. And, again, this is a contingent matter. It is quite possible that my cat, *for me*, might have been occupied by some other feline. What is not contingent is that Bruce is identical with Lewis's cat and that Roxanne is identical with my cat: Bruce is identical with the cat who occupied the role *my cat* for Lewis, and so it is necessary that Bruce is that cat, and similarly, mutatis mutandis, for Roxanne. This example demonstrates the sense in which, on the one hand, what occupies a given role is contingent, but, on the other hand, why it also makes sense to *identify*, in this case, Bruce (the occupant of *my cat*) with Lewis's cat. Bruce *is* Lewis's cat. In a similar vein, Lewis notes that it is perfectly coherent to recognize the contingency in the claim "the winning lottery number is 17" (it might have been something else) while allowing that the winning number is identical with 17 (1969, p. 233).

The lesson Lewis takes from these cases applies in the following way to mental states. Consider Othello's jealousy. Jealousy is a mental state that defines a certain role, just as *my cat* and *the winning lottery number* define certain roles. In Othello, suppose that the role jealousy describes is occupied by a cluster of neurons J_O. J_O, the occupant of the role that jealousy defines, is identical with Othello's jealousy, just as Bruce is identical with Lewis's cat and 17 is identical with the winning lottery number. It is consistent with Lewis's view that whereas J_O is the kind of brain state that is jealousy in Othello, there might be other kinds of brain states (J_P, J_Q, J_R) that are identical with jealousy in other individuals. "No mystery," Lewis remarks, "that is just like saying that the winning number is 17 in the case of this week's lottery, 137 in the case of last week's" (1969, p. 233). Thus, Lewis concludes, it is possible to be a functionalist and yet not deny that mental states are identical with physical states.

Lewis intends his characterization of functionalism as a defense of some sort of mind–brain identity theory, but it seems clear that Putnam need not endorse Lewis's view. Lewis has not provided a reason to renounce Putnam's style of functionalism; he has merely found a way to provide functionalism with room to accommodate claims of identity between mental states and brain states. Still, Putnam is within his rights to insist that it is the particular role that ought to be identified with a given kind of mental state and not the occupant of the role. After all, one can imagine Putnam arguing, what is it that Kirk and Spock share when both are jealous? They do not, by hypothesis, share a kind of brain state. And, whereas Putnam could acknowledge that whenever Kirk is jealous his brain is in state J_K, and whenever Spock is jealous his brain is in state J_S, Putnam need not agree that jealousy *is* J_K in Kirk and *is* J_S in Spock. That is, Putnam can maintain that what it is to be jealous is to be in a state that describes particular kinds of relations between inputs, other states, and outputs. Putnam can accept that the role jealousy describes is occupied by physical states in both Kirk and Spock, but he need not take the step Lewis does in identifying the jealousy of each with the occupant of the role it describes. In short, Putnam and Lewis differ over whether the relations that mental state terms refer to are, by themselves, mental states. For Putnam they are, but for Lewis they are only a means for picking out some occupant that, Lewis thinks, is the real referent of mental state terms.

Many critics of Putnam's functionalism (including Putnam in later years) have focused on the analogy Putnam draws between human minds and Turing machines (Block and Fodor 1972; Putnam 1988). However, there is a more basic difficulty with the theory. Putnam is quite clear that in suggesting that the mind is a Turing machine table he takes himself to be "advancing an empirical hypothesis" (1967, p. 226). He claims that his "strategy will be to argue that pain is not a brain state, not on *a priori* grounds, but on the grounds that another hypothesis is more plausible" (ibid.). But this raises several questions. First, in what sense is it an empirical hypothesis that the mind is a collection of relations described by some Turing machine table? This claim seems more like a stipulation on Putnam's part than an empirical hypothesis. There's no doubt that one can describe mental states in terms of their relations to sensory stimuli, other states, and behavior. Indeed, Ramsey (1931) showed that it is possible to define the theoretical terms of any theory in terms of relations between observables. In any event, because Putnam claims to be offering an empirical hypothesis, he should say something about the kind of evidence that might support the hypothesis. Whereas it is possible to imagine evidence that might bear on the question of which relations between stimuli, mental states, and behavior constitute a particular mental state, it seems completely bizarre to claim that evidence can bear on the claim that a particular mental state *is* nothing more than a relation. What experiment, for instance, might settle the dispute between Putnam and Lewis over whether jealousy refers just to a relation or to the physical state that fills the relation? This dispute seems much better suited to philosophical than empirical adjudication.

Perhaps machine functionalism is an empirical hypothesis in the following sense. It predicts that if we build a machine that realizes the mental machine table that describes our mind then this machine would have a mind just like our own. However, if this is the sense in which Putnam's hypothesis is empirical, then it seems to suffer from two shortcomings. First, it will in all likelihood not be testable within our lifetimes and may perhaps never be testable. But second and more significantly, our experience with systems simpler than the mind suggests that the hypothesis is false. Consider the relation that a mind would bear to a device, say, a computer, that has been engineered to respect the same machine table that constitutes our mind. The two systems—mind and computer—would be *functionally isomorphic*. Putnam defines this relation as follows:

Two systems are functionally isomorphic if *there is a correspondence between the states of one and the states of the other that preserves functional relations.* ... More generally, if T is a correct theory of the functioning of system 1, at the functional or psychological level, then an isomorphism between system 1 and system 2 must map each property and relation defined in system 2 in such a way that T comes out true when all references to system 1 are replaced by references to system 2, and all property and relation symbols in T are reinterpreted according to the mapping. (1975b, pp. 291–292)

With the concept of a functional isomorphism in hand, Putnam's empirical hypothesis is, on the current suggestion, that all systems functionally isomorphic to a mind are, in turn, minds.

However, we are now in a position to see why existing evidence makes this hypothesis unlikely. Computers are devices that are remarkably successful at simulating the behavior of complex systems. Moreover, a computer simulates a complex system by virtue of establishing a functional isomorphism between its own states and the states of the system it simulates. So, for instance, it is in virtue of maintaining an isomorphism between its own states and the states of a hurricane that a meteorologist can use a computer to predict the hurricane's path and force. Similarly, engineers rely on an isomorphism between a computer's states and the states of an airplane to predict how the airplane will perform in turbulent winds. One can simulate any behavior at all on a computer given a machine table description of the system to be simulated. Accordingly, the question one must now ask Putnam is this: why suppose that if we build a system that is functionally isomorphic to a mind then it would *be* a mind, given that we have built systems that are functionally isomorphic to hurricanes and airplanes but that turn out to be neither hurricanes nor airplanes? What is it about a mind that makes it the kind of thing that can be duplicated by mere functional isomorphism when functional isomorphism typically provides us with nothing more than a simulation? In short, from what evidence we have, it seems that something that satisfies a machine-functional description of a mind is no more likely to be a mind than is something likely to be a hurricane just because it satisfies a machine-functional description of a hurricane. There is simply no more reason to believe that a system functionally isomorphic to a mind can think than there is to be believe that a system functionally isomorphic to a hurricane can bend palm trees and destroy trailer parks (see also Block 1978; Searle 1980; Sober 1992).

1.3.2   Functional Analysis Functionalism

As we have just seen, "functionalism" in philosophy of mind sometimes refers to a theory of mind that identifies mental states with Turing machine functional states. Certainly Putnam was a functionalist in this sense. However, there are other ways to conceive of functional states and accordingly other kinds of functionalist theories of mind. Fodor (1968) too speaks of mental states as functional states, but for him *function* has a much richer teleological sense than its anemic mathematical cousin. For Fodor, functions are contributions toward a goal, and they become apparent in the course of a functional analysis of a system (see also Cummins 1975; Lycan 1981). The point of a functional analysis of a system is to understand how a system achieves some capacity by way of the activities of its parts. Fodor explains:

In typical cases of functional analysis . . . one asks about a part of a mechanism *what role it plays* in the activities that are a characteristic of the mechanism as a whole: "What does the camshaft do?" "It opens the valves, permitting the entry into the cylinder of fuel, which will then be detonated to drive the piston." . . . Successful functional analysis . . . requires an appreciation of the sorts of activity that are characteristic of a mechanism and of the contribution made by the functioning of each part of the mechanism to the economy of the whole. (1968, p. 113)

Functional analysis proceeds by assigning functions to the parts of a system, where these functions are better associated with purposes or goals than with mathematical operators that carry arguments from a domain onto values in a range.

If mental states are functional in this sense, the idea that minds are multiply realizable seems quite plausible. Because it is possible that various physical kinds can all exhibit the same characteristic activity, it is possible that a mind, analyzed as if it were a goal-directed system, is multiply realizable. Valve lifters, for instance, might be camshafts (understood as a kind of physical structure), but they might be other kinds of physical structures as well. What matters to whether something is a valve lifter is not that it has a particular kind of physical structure, but that it plays the role of permitting fuel to enter a cylinder in an automobile engine. As Fodor notes, "If I speak of a device as a 'camshaft,' I am implicitly identifying it by reference to its physical structure, and so I am committed to the view that it exhibits a characteristic and specifiable decomposition into physical parts. But if I speak of the device as a 'valve lifter,' I am identifying it by reference to its function and I therefore undertake no such commitment" (1968, p. 113). Physical structures, in addition to falling under a physical description, can take on a functional description in the course of a functional analysis. But, whereas physical descriptions apply to structures in virtue of their physical type, functional descriptions classify by virtue of functional contributions to a system. Multiple realizability follows as a consequence of the fact that structures that differ in physical description may play the same contributing role in the systems of which they are parts.

Yet, even if we are to accept Fodor's suggestion that the mind is functional in the sense of being defined by a goal or purpose, there remains a gap between this assumption and the conclusion that minds are multiply realizable. Fodor may be right that minds or mental states ought to be identified by their function, but this does not entail that minds or mental states are multiply realizable in physical kinds. The problem is this. Whereas there are many cases in which objects of distinct physical description may bear the same functional description, there are also cases in which a functional description may apply only to a single kind of physical object. For instance, suppose one wishes to build a machine that drills for oil through surfaces composed of extremely hard minerals. *Drill bit* is presumably a functional kind. Like *valve lifter*, it appears that one can speak of drill bits without taking on a commitment to any particular physical description of the kinds of things that can do the job of a drill bit. However, if diamonds are the only substance that in fact are hard enough to drill through very hard surfaces, then *drill bit* picks out a physical kind no less than it refers to a functional kind.

As an alternative example, suppose one wishes to build a solar cell like the kind that powers a hand calculator. To build a solar cell, one needs a substance that turns light into electricity and in which it is possible to control the flow of electrons. Existing solar cells consist of two types of silicon—n-type silicon ("n" for negatively charged) in which some of the silicon atoms have an extra electron, and p-type silicon ("p" for positively charged) in which some of the silicon atoms lack an electron. By layering n-type silicon on top of p-type silicon and exposing the resulting lattice to light, it is possible to create an electrical current. The light frees electrons, which move from the n-type silicon to the calculator, back into the p-type silicon and then up into the n-type silicon, and so on.[4] The kind *solar cell* appears to be a functional kind—it is defined as that which turns light into a controlled electrical current. But suppose that n- and p-type silicon are the only substances that exhibit the properties necessary for the construction of a solar cell. If such were the case, then "solar cell," which appears to be a functional kind, also picks out a particular type of physical structure, namely, a lattice of n- and p-type silicon atoms.

The point of these examples is not to argue that the mind, construed in the functional sense that Fodor develops, is not multiply realizable, but rather to show that adoption of a functional perspective toward the mind does not *entail* that the mind is multiply realizable. Perhaps it is; perhaps it is not. Whether it is requires empirical investigation of a sort that puts philosophers on the sidelines. Interestingly, Aristotle was sensitive to this point about limits on the multiple realizability of functional kinds, arguing (incorrectly, as it turns out) that, "if one defines the operation of sawing as being a certain kind of dividing, then this cannot come about unless the saw has teeth of a certain kind; and these cannot be unless it is of iron" (McKeon, tr. 1941).

Of course, a functionalist might respond to the above observation with the claim that functional kinds, while perhaps not always nomologically multiply realizable, are always logically multiply realizable. In other words, whereas there may be only one physical kind that fits a functional description, there are certainly many logically possible kinds that fit any given functional description. So what if diamonds are the only physically possible substance that can function in a drill that bores through hard surfaces, or if n- and p-types of silicon are physically necessary for the construction of a solar cell? We can surely *imagine* other substances from which drill bits and solar cells can be built that, although not present in the actual world, are present in logically possible worlds. This shows that minds, regardless of whether they are multiply realizable in the actual world, are multiply realizable in the logical sense.

This response seems correct. I think it would be futile to deny the logical possibility of multiple realizability. However, as I mentioned earlier, there remains the interesting question of whether minds are in *fact* multiply realizable. How could we test whether Fodor is right that minds, like valve lifters, are multiply realizable? As I argued above, the claim that minds are functional kinds does not imply that they are multiply realizable. Some functional kinds are multiply realizable, but some are not. There is nothing in Fodor's conception of functionalism that tells one way or another on the question of mind's multiple realizability.

On reflection, I think it is completely unsurprising that none of the conceptual arguments I have examined provides support for MRT. As advocates of MRT stress time and again, MRT is intended as an empirical thesis. But, this means that if one wants to confirm MRT, one should be looking not at what our concepts mean but at the world. If MRT is an empirical thesis, one should be trying to draw from it predictions that can be measured against observations. A critical discussion of the empirical support that philosophers have offered for MRT will be the business of the remainder of this chapter.

1.4   Empirical Arguments for the Multiple Realizability Thesis

If the conceptual arguments that Putnam and Fodor advance do not force us to accept MRT, perhaps their empirical arguments will do a better job. In this section I examine first a likelihood argument for MRT that Putnam (1967) makes. I then consider three lines of empirical evidence for MRT that Block and Fodor (1972) advance. The issues involved in these arguments become quite complex and untangling them all will require not only a close examination of the arguments, but also a stance on how to interpret claims of multiple realization. Because these topics can be treated separately, I will reserve discussion of the latter until the following chapter.

1.4.1   Putnam's Likelihood Argument for the Multiple Realizability Thesis

In addition to thinking that the Turing machine is the right way to conceive minds, Putnam thinks that there are independent empirical reasons for doubting the identity theory of mind. A sensible way to understand Putnam's argument is as a likelihood argument (Sober 1993). A likelihood argument is an argument that seeks to adjudicate between two competing hypotheses. It does so by considering a single body of evidence and asking of each of the hypotheses under consideration which makes the evidence more probable. The likelier hypothesis is the one that makes the evidence more probable. So, for instance, in the movie *Rounders* the girlfriend of a poker player alleges that success in poker is merely a matter of luck. The poker player, wishing to rebut this charge, points out to his girlfriend that the same players are present year after year in the World Series of Poker tournament. This is a compelling defense for reasons that a likelihood reconstruction makes clear. In essence, the poker player is asking his girlfriend to consider two hypotheses:

L: Success in poker is merely a matter of luck.

S: Success in poker is due to skill.

To decide between L and S it is necessary to consider the evidence, that is, the fact that the same people are present in the World Series of Poker tournament every year. Suppose L were true. If L were true then we would expect to see different players at the tournament every year because, by definition, luck is a matter of chance. We should no more expect to see the same faces in the tournament every year than we should expect that a single individual would pull an ace from a fair deck a hundred times in a row.

On the other hand, if S were true then the presence of the same people at the tournament every year would not be at all surprising. These players make it to the tournament every year because they are very good poker players. Happy Jack's presence in the poker tournament every year would be no more surprising than Martina Navratilova's appearance at Wimbledon every year.

Notice that likelihood and probability are two different notions. H1 is likelier than H2 when it makes an observation O more probable. This is expressed in probability theory as: $Pr(O|H1) > Pr(O|H2)$. This claim about likelihood should not be confused with a claim about the probabilities of the hypotheses given an observation—that $Pr(H1|O) >$

Pr(H2|O). To see why likelihood and probability differ, consider a third hypothesis:

T: Success in poker is due to telepathic abilities that only a very few people possess.

Hypotheses T and S appear equally likely given the fact that the same people show up in the tournament every year. That is, $Pr(O|S) = Pr(O|T)$. However, there should be no doubt that $Pr(S|O) > Pr(T|O)$. Hypothesis T is improbable to begin with, and O hardly makes it any more probable. The advantage to considering likelihood over probability is that the former focuses purely on the connection between the hypothesis and the evidence at hand. Even with no idea about the initial plausibilities of the competing hypotheses, it is still possible to assess their likelihoods.

For present purposes, we should construe Putnam (1967) as considering the following two hypotheses:

TI: The mind (construed as a collection of mental states) is type-identical with the brain.

MR: The mind (construed as a collection of mental states) is multiply realizable.

Putnam then asks us to evaluate the likelihood of these two hypotheses given observation P:

P: Pain is a mental state present in mammalian brains, reptilian brains, mollusc brains and, conceivably, extraterrestrial brains (if ETs exist).

Putnam's claim then is that $Pr(P|MR) > Pr(P|TI)$. He believes this because if mental states like pain are multiply realizable, it would not be at all surprising to find pain-feeling organisms with different brain structures. On the other hand, TI makes P improbable because, Putnam assumes, the brains of mammals, reptiles, molluscs, and ETs (should they exist) are probably very different in structure. P is probable given TI only if mammals, reptiles, molluscs, and ETs evolved similar brains independently of each other. Putnam concludes, "Thus it is at least possible that parallel evolution, all over the universe, might *always* lead to *one and the same* physical "correlate" of pain. But this is certainly an ambitious hypothesis" (1967, p. 228).

It is worth making two points about Putnam's likelihood argument. First, Putnam's line of reasoning appears to be a good argument against the identity theory, but it is not a strong argument for his Turing machine functionalism. This is because P seems to be equally probable given various kinds of functionalist theories of mind. To see this, consider two further hypotheses:

TM: The mind is a Turing machine table.

FA: The mind is functional in the sense assumed by functional analyses.

Given P, TM and FA seem equally likely because each predicts that brains of different physical organization might realize similar minds. Because P is no more or less surprising given TM or FA, it is of little help to Putnam in arguing for his version of functionalism over other versions.

Second and more important, Putnam's likelihood argument, although compelling, is not as strong as one might first suspect. Consider what makes the poker player's likelihood argument convincing. We know something about the odds of being dealt a winning poker hand. If poker were just a matter of luck, the odds that the same people would often have winning hands would be extraordinarily low. We are more likely to find winning cards in the hands of players who know what to do with the cards they've been dealt than in the hands of players who know nothing about poker. But, we know very little about the properties of the brain that make it a realization of a mind. Perhaps minds are multiply realizable, as Putnam believes. But, as I argued earlier, they may not be. Suppose one were to argue in the following way. We have the following observation:

O: Solar cells are present in all sorts of devices (calculators, satellites, watches, toys, etc.).

Now consider the following two hypotheses:

MR_S: Solar cells are multiply realizable.

TI_S: Solar cells can be built only from silicon.

Can we assert that $Pr(O|MR_S) > Pr(O|TI_S)$? I do not think so. Prior to empirical investigation of semiconductors, we simply do not know whether the myriad devices that contain solar cells offer support for MR_S

or for TI_S. If our investigation shows that there are in fact many ways to build solar cells, then we should believe MR_S. On the other hand, if scientists are unable to design a solar cell without utilizing n- and p-types of silicon, then TI_S gains support. The point is that an observation like O tells us nothing about the relative likelihoods of MR_S and TI_S. O is valuable only when combined with the information that the various devices in which solar cells appear have nothing relevantly similar in common (where "nothing relevantly similar" means something like: have no parts in common that turn light into electricity). But, of course, if one had this information then one would have already confirmed MR_S.

Similarly, why should P offer support for MR over TI unless we already know that the brains of mammals, reptiles, molluscs, and ETs are relevantly different? But if we know this then we know all we need to know to judge the relative merits of MR and TI. The conclusion to draw from this discussion is that whether minds are multiply realizable is as much a matter for empirical investigation as whether solar cells are. We cannot conclude from the observation of nonhuman organisms with mental properties that minds are multiply realizable until we take a peek inside their skulls. But, even then, we have to know what to look for.

1.4.2   Three Lines of Evidence for the Multiple Realizability Thesis

It is in this context that Block and Fodor's (1972) discussion of multiple realizability becomes relevant. Block and Fodor, rather than constructing a likelihood argument for MRT, believe that there currently exists direct evidence of multiple realizability. In particular, Block and Fodor invite us to examine "three kinds of empirical considerations" (1972, p. 238) that, they think, add up to a strong case for the multiple realizability of minds. The first line of evidence comes from studies that reveal the brain to have a very plastic structure. As Block and Fodor say, "it does seem clear that the central nervous system is highly labile and that a given type of psychological process is in fact often associated with a variety of distinct neurological structures" (ibid.). If it is true that the same psychological processes can be realized in different neurological structures, this is living proof that the mind, or at least some mental capacities, are multiply realizable. And, indeed, literature in the neurosciences seems replete with examples of such neural plasticity: people whose speech centers have developed in the right hemisphere as a result of some sort of insult to the left; the use of auditory cortex to process visual information (von Melchner, Pallas, and Sur 2000), and so on. This evidence is perhaps the best reason to think that MRT is true, but, as we'll see in the next chapter, it is not conclusive.

Second, Block and Fodor point out that convergent evolution—the phenomenon in which species evolve similar traits independently of each other—is just as likely to occur in cases of psychological traits as it is in cases of morphological and behavioral traits (1972, p. 238). They note that "if there are organisms whose psychology is homologous[5] to our own but whose physiology is quite different, such organisms may provide counterexamples to the psychophysical correlations physicalism requires" (ibid.). It is worth spending some time on this point because the issue of convergence will become significant in subsequent chapters as I develop a case for MRT's competitor—the mental constraint thesis (MCT).

Convergence involves two ideas. The first concerns the similarity of a trait (more technically, of a character state) in members of distinct species. The second idea involves an explanation of this similarity. The claim that a similar trait in two distinct species is the product of convergence means that the trait has evolved twice—once in each lineage—as a result of (presumably) similar selection pressures. The alternative hypothesis is that the trait is homologous, that is, the similarity of the trait is the result of inheritance of the trait from a common ancestor. The wings of birds and bats, for instance, are an example of convergence. They are similar traits that have evolved independently in the two lineages. In contrast to such independently derived traits—"homoplasious" traits—the wings of robins and sparrows are homologous. The similarity of these wings is a consequence of the fact that robins and sparrows are descended from an ancestor that had wings and that the lineages from which robins and sparrows descended retained this ancestral state.

Block and Fodor claim that when independent evolution results in analogous traits, it may well turn out that the traits are distinct kinds of realizations. Of course, this by itself is no *argument* that the independent evolution of analogous traits will always or even usually lead to multiple realization. It is an interesting question whether the independent evolution of analogous traits should lead us to expect that these traits will be realized in different ways. Suppose that two organisms from different species have a similar psychological trait. Further suppose that the similarity is a result of independent evolution. Does this raise the probability that the trait will be realized differently in each organism? I think the answer to this question must be "no." There is simply no reason to suppose that homoplasious traits are probably different kinds of realizations. This depends on whether the kind of trait is multiply real-iz*able* in the first place. The fact that a number of factories might produce a particular kind of drill bit is not evidence that the drill bit is realized in a number of different kinds of ways. It might turn out that diamonds are the only suitable realizer for the kind of bit in demand. If so, the number of factories that produce the bit makes no difference to the probability that the bit is multiply realized.

To illustrate the point further, suppose the psychological trait in question is vision. Block and Fodor's appeal to convergence suggests the following kind of argument. If various species have evolved vision independently then it is more probable that vision is multiply realized than if vision is a result of common ancestry. That is, one might hope convergence justifies the following:

Pr (VMR|independent evolution) > Pr (VMR|common ancestry),

where "VMR" is the claim that vision is multiply realized, "independent evolution" stands for the hypothesis that the most recent common ancestor of the two lineages lacked the observed trait, and "common ancestry" is the hypothesis that the trait shared in the two lineages is one that is present because it has been inherited from the most recent common ancestor. My claim is that evolutionary theory provides no reason to suppose that this inequality holds. It is true that vision has evolved independently in a number of lineages, and it is true that vision is realized differently in various lineages. But the latter fact is not entailed by the former. Indeed, it is also true that vision has been realized in the *same* way in a number of distinct lineages. Thus, for instance, whereas vision in some lineages is realized in a compound eye and in other lineages it is realized in a camera eye, compound eyes and camera eyes have themselves evolved independently in a number of cases. Whether the above inequality holds depends on how stingy nature is with the solutions it allows. But the stinginess of nature is an assumption that must itself be put to the test prior to making a judgment about the above inequality. In short, the two hypotheses—common ancestry and independent evolution—make no predictions about the multiple realizability of a psychological capacity without further assumptions about the extent to which nature might allow such multiple realizability.

On the other hand, the following inequality is plausible:

Pr (~VMR|common ancestry) > Pr (VMR|common ancestry).

Given that members of two distinct species have a similar psychological capacity in virtue of having inherited it from their most recent common ancestor, it is reasonable to suppose that the similarity in their psychological capacities is a result of a similarity in the realizers of the capacities. The argument for this claim depends on a parsimony consideration. If two species share the same visual capacities as a result of common ancestry, then to suppose that their visual capacities are differently realized is to suppose that at least one of these species evolved a new way to realize its visual capacities while losing the ancestral manner of realization. Thus, more evolution would be required to have the situation described by the right side of the inequality than that described on the left (see figure 1.2).[6]

So far I have been interpreting Block and Fodor as offering convergence as a hypothesis that, in their view, raises the probability of multiple realization. I think this is the correct way to understand them. However, there are other ways to understand the relation between convergence and multiple realization. In particular, and more important for my purposes, it is possible to think of convergence in a way that allows one to test MRT against its competitor MCT. Putnam must have had a similar idea, when, as we saw, he mentions parallel evolution (which is often equated with convergent evolution) as a reason that might bring one to *doubt* MRT (1967, p. 228). Putnam mentions the similarity between the octopus's eye and the mammalian eye and takes this to mark a challenge, though an extremely improbable one, to the possibility that minds are multiply realizable. I believe a likelihood argument is again the best way to understand the nature of this challenge.

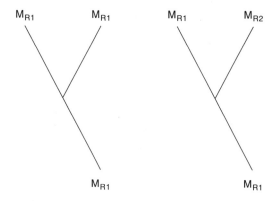

Figure 1.2
In the tree on the left, the ancestral condition consists of a mental capacity *M* realized by *R1*. The descendants also have *M* realized by *R1*. On the right, the ancestral condition is *M* realized by *R1*, but one of the descendants now has *M* realized differently, by *R2*. Thus, the tree on the right involves more evolution—the descendant on the right branch lost *R1* but gained *R2*.

As I mentioned, convergence involves two ideas: a similarity between traits and an explanation of this similarity in terms of independent evolution. If we take independent evolution to be a given, it becomes possible to make the observation of similarity in traits across species work as evidence that can test MRT against MCT. So, suppose that we are considering a trait that is similar in two species, A and B, and we know that the similarity is a result of independent evolution. The probabilities to consider are these:

(1) Pr_{IE} (A and B have similarly realized trait T | MRT); and

(2) Pr_{IE} (A and B have similarly realized trait T | MCT).

Here the "IE" subscript indicates that the probabilities are to be evaluated on the assumption that trait T has evolved independently in A and B. I claim that the first probability is less than the second. The argument is this. Suppose MRT is true of trait T. This means that there are many ways to realize T. But then it should come as a surprise that A and B, which evolved trait T independently, should realize T in the same way. On the other hand, suppose MCT is true. This means that there are few ways to realize T. If trait T has arisen independently in species A and B, and if MCT is true, there is a higher probability that T will be realized the same way in the two species.

If we think of MRT and MCT as staking out positions at opposite ends of a spectrum, a view I tend to favor, then the use of similarity observations to test MRT against MCT suggests the following. Suppose that MRT makes the claim that, for a given trait T, there are hundreds or thousands of different possible realizers. Assume further that each realization of T is as probable as another. In contrast, suppose MCT makes the claim that there are but a handful or a couple of possible realizers of T. Letting n be the number of realizers of T, MRT says that n is very large; MCT says that it is quite small. But notice that as n increases, the probability that two species will independently evolve the same trait decreases. Similarly, as n decreases, the probability that two species will independently evolve the same trait increases. Thus, the inequality between (1) and (2) will vary in size according to the number of possible realizers of a given trait, but in any event (1) will be less than (2).

If the argument above is on the right track, it is possible to understand why Putnam is impressed with the similarity of the octopus and mammalian eye. The similarity is surprising if there are many ways to build an eye, but it is just what one should expect if there are few ways to build an eye. In the same way, if minds are multiply realizable, then a similarity in the ways minds are realized (given that they have evolved independently) should cast doubt on MRT but should support MCT.

Of course, there remain many questions to answer before one can hope to apply the reasoning above in a way that will provide a meaningful evaluation of MRT. For one, more needs to be said about what, exactly, it means for something to be realized and, moreover, what it means to talk about sameness and difference in realization. Additionally, one might wonder how, given that a humanlike mind has evolved only once, it can be possible to gather the observations necessary to compare MRT to MCT. These are important issues, and ones to which I shall soon attend in the next chapter. However, before doing so, it is worth mentioning briefly the third bit of empirical evidence that Block and Fodor take to support MRT. Block and Fodor claim that "it seems very likely that given any psychophysical correlation which holds for an organism, it is possible to build a machine which is similar to the organism psychologically, but physiologically sufficiently different from the organism that the psychophysical correlation does not hold for the machine" (1972, p. 238).

It is hard to know on what Block and Fodor's faith rests regarding this point. Surely they cannot believe that AI has, even thirty years after their initial claim, come anywhere near to creating a mind that is similar in its capacities to a human mind. More bewildering still is their introduction of this claim as a "conceptual possibility" when they are presumably interested in defending the nomological possibility of MRT. In any event, whether AI offers support to MRT depends again on an assumption about how to judge sameness and difference in realizations, for smart computers confirm MRT only if their smarts are realized differently from our own. Accordingly, it is now time to consider more generally how to understand the notion of realization, as well as what makes two realizations of a type *different* types of realization.

2

The Multiple Realizability Thesis from an Empirical Standpoint

So far I have not ventured any critical comments about the nature of the realization relation. I have characterized realization as simply a kind of compositional relation. To say that watches, corkscrews, mousetraps, and so on are multiply realizable is just to say that they can be composed, or made of, different kinds of stuff. In section 2.2 I shall have much more to say about the criteria one should use in distinguishing between kinds of realization. But, before this can happen, it is important to explore the more basic question of what *realization* means. While analyses of realization have been surprisingly few, given the importance of the idea in contemporary philosophy of mind, reflection on two recent discussions—Gillett (2002) and Wilson (2001; 2004)—will help bring to light some of the more important issues and controversies surrounding realization.

2.1 Realization

A useful starting point in an analysis of the realization concept is a distinction between an R that realizes a kind K, and a C that causes a kind K. As I have already mentioned in passing, realization is intended as a synchronic relation between the realized kind and its realizer, whereas causation is most typically a diachronic relation. A realization is present simultaneously with that which it realizes and cannot be separated from it. In contrast, causes and their effects are independent events. A cause is followed by an effect and, depending on the amount of time between the cause and its effect, it is possible to imagine that a cause and its effect never exist simultaneously.

Thus, the synchronic nature of realization serves to distinguish it from causation, in at least the most familiar cases of causation. For instance, this point suffices to reject the claim that some gene (or gene complex) B realizes blue eyes despite the fact that B and blue eyes are always present together. It may be that having blue eyes is impossible without having gene B, but this is evidence only that gene B is a cause of blue eyes. The fact that gene B is present in an organism prior to the development of blue eyes, and that blue eyes can be removed from an organism without simultaneously removing gene B, shows that gene B does not realize blue eyes.

But there must be more to the realization relation than synchronicity. If it were true that everything with a shape also has a color, this would not support the claim that shape is realized by color (or vice versa). The realized kind owes its existence to that which realizes it. It is in virtue of the realizer that the realized kind exists. This *in virtue-ness* is often characterized as a species of determination: the realizer determines that which it realizes. Wilson (2001; 2004) offers a helpful discussion of some of the features philosophers often associate with this determination relation.

Wilson claims that on the standard view of realization, the realizer of a kind (or state, or property) must satisfy two constraints. He calls the first of these the *sufficiency thesis*:

Sufficiency Thesis: realizers are metaphysically sufficient for the properties or states they realize.

Second is what Wilson calls the *constitutivity thesis*:

Constitutivity Thesis: realizers of states and properties are exhaustively physically constituted by the intrinsic, physical states of the individual whose states or properties they are.

According to the first thesis, the presence of a realizer guarantees the presence of that which is realized, not, as I noted above, in a causal sense, but in the sense of making the realized kind the kind that it is. The debate about individualism that raged between philosophers of psychology in the late 1980s and throughout much of the following decade provides a useful perspective on this point. According to the individualist, facts external to an agent play no role in fixing the nature or essence of the agent's psychological state. In contrast, the externalist claims that many of an agent's mental states are the types they are because of the relationship the agent bears to features outside herself: features of either the natural environment (Putnam 1975d) or the social environment (Burge 1979).

To make concrete the difference between the views of the individualist and the externalist, consider molecularly identical twins. According to the individualist, if such twins were in molecularly distinct environments but were confronted with all the same sensory stimuli then they would share all the same beliefs. Thus, if Twin A is in a world where that which is called "water" is H_2O, and Twin B is in a world where that which is called "water" is XYZ, and supposing that the twins were unable to perceive any difference between H_2O and XYZ, the individualist would insist that Twin A's and Twin B's beliefs about water are of the same kind. The externalist denies this, arguing that because Twin A's beliefs are caused by H_2O and Twin B's are caused by XYZ, the beliefs have different contents and so are different kinds of belief.

The intricacies and epicycles surrounding this dispute are enough to drain the life energy from even the heartiest of persons, but fortunately the above suffices to illustrate the point Wilson wishes to make. Clearly it would be foolish for the individualist to claim that the external environment of an agent makes *no* difference to the agent's mental life. The individualist need not and should not deny that Twin A and Twin B both have beliefs about what each calls "water" in virtue of some causal interaction with liquids external to themselves. Were it not for the presence of liquid in their environments, Twins A and B would not, conceivably, have any beliefs about what they each call "water." So, the presence of watery stuff in each environment is a causal determinant of the twins' beliefs about (what they each call) "water." However, the composition of the watery stuff—the fact that this stuff might be either H_2O or XYZ—plays no role, according to the internalist, in making the belief of each twin the kind of belief it is.

Yet, according to the externalist, the watery stuff in the twins' environments does more than simply cause the production of a belief—it also plays a role in making the belief the kind that it is. Because Twin A's belief is caused by H_2O and not XYZ, it differs in content from Twin B's belief. It is this point that Wilson highlights, in his claim that on the standard view the realizer of a kind is metaphysically, and not merely causally, sufficient for the kind that is realized. The realizer, Wilson claims, is supposed to make that which is realized the kind that it is. For an externalist, the realizer of a mental state can include features outside an agent's head; for an individualist, the realizer of a mental state is contained wholly inside an agent's head.

It should now be apparent why the sufficiency thesis may conflict with the constitutivity thesis. This latter thesis stipulates that the realizer of a kind must be constituted by properties that exist only within the bearer of the realized property. Clearly this is a condition on realization that would please an individualist, but it is forbidden to the externalist who accepts the sufficiency thesis. As Wilson notes, if the externalist is right then it is often the case that what metaphysically suffices for a particular property is often not wholly contained in the individual in which the property is instantiated. Conversely, the intrinsic properties of an individual often fail to suffice metaphysically for a property attributed to an agent (Wilson 2004).

Wilson proceeds to offer his own account of realization—an account that abandons the constitutivity thesis in recognition of the externalist intuitions that require realizers to extend beyond the individual in which the realized property is (in part) instantiated. Also moving Wilson to contextualize the notion of realization are suspicions about the sufficiency thesis. Just as a cause suffices for an effect only in the context of certain background conditions, so too, Wilson notes, will a realizer be metaphysically sufficient for a realized property only on granting that the realizer acts within the context of a larger system. In appreciation of this point, Wilson follows Shoemaker (1981) in distinguishing the core realization of a property from the total realization of a property. The core realization suffices metaphysically for the property only when placed within the context of a larger system, which constitutes the total realization of the property. The distinction between core and total realizations provides Wilson with the tools to distinguish between realizers of varying "widths," depending on whether the total realization is contained entirely within an individual, whether the noncore part of the total realization is external to an individual, or, finally, whether the core part of a total realization is outside an individual.

Further discussion of Wilson's views on realization are unnecessary for present purposes, although I shall return to them in chapter 7 when considering the separability thesis. For now, Wilson's work is helpful for making more precise the sense of determination that realization involves. Determination is both a kind of sufficiency and a kind of constitution. Whereas Wilson sees a tension in these two elements of determination, my own inclination is to deny that the metaphysics of realization demands that realizers must confine themselves within individuals as the constitutivity thesis stipulates (Wilson ends up agreeing with this inclination). To be sure, there are philosophers—those with an individualist bent—who argue in favor of the constitutivity thesis. But these arguments tend to be methodological in spirit, in the sense that they urge adoption of the constitutivity thesis for particular explanatory purposes (e.g., to achieve explanations of greater generality, or explanations that more accurately track causal powers).[1] But these methodological concerns represent the biases or commitments of individuals and are not themselves entailed by the concept of realization. Whether a realization of a mental state, for instance, extends beyond an individual is a separate question from whether psychological explanation should assume individualism. For this reason, I see no harm in construing realization as a sufficiency relation as well as a constitution relation, where the constitution may or may not include features external to an individual.

Gillett's investigation of realization, rather than focusing on the sense of determination that realization involves, is more concerned with the relationship between the realized property, the realizing properties, and the individual that instantiates these properties. Proponents of what Gillett (like Wilson) calls the "standard" view of realization are committed to the following two theses:

(I) A property instance X realizes a property instance Y only if X and Y are instantiated in the same individual. (Gillett 2002, p. 317)

Gillett finds support for the widespread popularity of this thesis in the writings of prominent philosophers like Jaegwon Kim (1998) and Sydney Shoemaker (1999). Kim, for instance, claims that it is "evident that *a second-order property and its realizers are at the same level. . . . they are properties of the very same objects*" (1998a, p. 82; his emphasis). Kim's insistence that the same individual instantiate both the realized and realizing properties—that, as Kim puts it, the realizing and realized properties be "at the same level"—leads Gillett sometimes to characterize the standard view of realization as the "flat" view. According to the flat view, if C-fiber firings, for instance, realize pain, then in must be true of the same individual who is in pain that her C-fibers are firing. This first thesis bears some resemblance to Wilson's constitutivity thesis, for both demand that the realizer be contained within an individual.

The second of the two theses that Gillett attributes to the standard view is:

(II)   A property instance X realizes a property instance Y *only if* the causal powers individuative of the instance of Y match causal powers contributed by the instance of X (and where X may contribute powers not individuative of Y). (2002, p. 318)

Gillett again finds support for this thesis in the work of Kim (especially his causal inheritance principle). The import of the thesis appears intuitive: if C-fibers realize pain, then those causal powers that distinguish states of pain from other states—those causal powers that make pain *pain* rather than jealousy, pleasure, irritation—must belong as well to C-fiber firings. If C-fibers could not produce the behavior associated with pain or could not produce those other mental states associated with pain, then clearly C-fibers could not realize pain.

This second principle bears a strong resemblance to Wilson's sufficiency thesis. Like this thesis, Gillett's (II) asserts that the realized kind is the kind that it is in virtue of the powers of the realizing kind. Were the powers of the realizing properties not sufficient to create the powers by which the realized property is defined, it would be incorrect to identify the former properties as a realization of the latter.

However, despite the warm reception and considerable plausibility that (I) and (II) enjoy, Gillett finds both to be objectionable. Gillett complains that the standard view of realization cannot accommodate rudimentary illustrations of realization that appear throughout the sciences. Consider Gillett's example:

The example in question is that of a cut diamond "s*" which has the property of being extremely hard "H." Let us assume s* has as constituents carbon atoms "s1"—"sn," where particular carbon atoms have specific properties/relations including those of being bonded, "B1," "B2," "B3" . . . etc., and aligned, "A1," "A2," "A3" . . . etc., with other carbon atoms in a very particular way. . . . Amongst the causal powers of the diamond's hardness is that, call it "C*," of causing scratches in glass. Whilst amongst the causal powers of the bonds and relations of alignment of any particular carbon atom is the power, "CD," of causing a contiguous carbon atom to remain in a small range of its present position in certain directions, relative to other carbon atoms, even under high temperatures and forces. (2002, pp. 318–319)

We should like to say, Gillett claims, that the relations of bonding and alignment that carbon atoms bear to each other realize the hardness of the diamond. But, Gillett argues, such a claim conflicts with both (I) and (II).

In the first case, the relations of bonding and alignment are relations that belong to individual carbon atoms. Hardness, however, is a property that belongs to the diamond. Thus, the realizing properties (the relations between carbon atoms) and the realized property (hardness) are instantiated in different individuals. It is the carbon atoms that bear the relational properties of bonding and alignment to each other—the diamond does not bear these relations to anything. Similarly, it is the diamond that is hard—not the relations between carbon atoms.

Moreover, that the example violates (II) is just as clear. The diamond's property of being hard contribute to the diamond's power to scratch glass. On the other hand, the relations between carbon atoms contribute to "the power to cause a contiguous carbon atom to remain in a tight relative spatial range" (2002, p. 319).

Gillett argues that despite conflicting with (I) and (II), the diamond example describes a genuine case of realization. The relations between carbon atoms determine the hardness of the diamond in the relevant sense of determination that emerged from my discussion of Wilson's work. The relations between carbon atoms both suffice for the hardness of the diamond and constitute the hardness. Nevertheless, hardness does not belong to individual carbon atoms, and the relations between carbon atoms contribute differently to the diamond's power to scratch glass than does hardness.

Gillett is of course aware of an obvious response that advocates of the standard view might make. It is open to the proponent of standard view to "take a highly complex structure of carbon atoms, and their properties and relations, to be the realizer of H. Let us call this structural property instance "COMBO" to mark that it is a vast array of interrelated entities. If a structural property such as COMBO is taken as the putative realizer of H, concludes the response, it is no longer implausible that COMBO realizes H in a way compatible with the Flat account" (2002, p. 320). Such a response would seem to do the trick. Nothing less than the same individual that instantiates the property of being hard can also instantiate COMBO, for COMBO is, roughly, the total sum of the diamond's parts. For the same reason, COMBO contributes exactly that which hardness contributes to the scratching of glass. The response thus seems to preserve the conditions of the standard view while also accommodating Gillett's attractive intuition that it is some configuration of carbon atoms that realizes the hardness of a diamond.

Yet, Gillett argues, the COMBO response can at best serve as a temporary save of the standard view. The difficulty is that COMBO is in turn realized by some collection of properties, which is in turn realized by some more fundamental collection of properties, and so on until a most basic collection of properties—those that contemporary physics recognizes as most basic, such as spin, charm, charge, and so on—is reached. However, these most basic properties are properties not of COMBO, but of individuals like quarks and leptons, and these properties and COMBO differ in their causal powers; so once again it appears that there is a natural sense of realization that conflicts with (I) and (II).

In place of the standard, or "flat," view of realization, Gillett offers what he calls the "dimensioned" view. On this analysis: "Property/relation instance(s) *F1–Fn realize* an instance of a property *G*, in an individual *s*, *if and only if s* has powers that are individuative of an instance of *G* in virtue of the powers contributed by *F1–Fn* to *s* or *s*'s constituent(s), but not vice versa" (2002, p. 322, his italics). The dimensioned account thus allows that hardness, for example, is realized by the alignment relations of individual carbon atoms, for it is in virtue of these alignment relations that a diamond is hard. There is no worry that the relational properties of alignment and the property of hardness belong to different individuals, nor is there a concern that the causal powers of hardness differ from those of alignment. The dimensioned account seems, then, to capture a sense of realization that adherence to (I) and (II) prohibits.

There is reason to be suspicious of Gillett's representation of the "standard" view, and as well to doubt the adequacy of his dimensioned analysis of realization. Regarding the first point, there is in fact solid ground to reject (I) as an element of a standard view of realization. (I) demands that the realizing and realized properties belong to the same individual, but, as my earlier discussion of externalism suggests, many philosophers would refuse this demand. Suppose, for instance, that one agreed with externalist intuitions about the differing contents of the twins' beliefs that water is wet. The externalist claims that these beliefs differ because the twins live in distinct environments. But this must mean, then, that whatever realizes the twins' beliefs cannot be limited to the boundaries of the individual twins. The realizer of the belief "water is wet" must include features of the environment external to the twins. Insofar as (I) precludes externalist intuitions, it loses claim to be a "standard" view of realization.

Turning now to the second point, Gillett's response to the COMBO ploy points to a deficiency in his dimensioned analysis of realization. Recall that COMBO is the totality of properties and relations of carbon atoms that determine the diamond's hardness. Gillett concedes that COMBO meets conditions (I) and (II) and so appears to provide advocates of the "standard" view of realization with a scientifically plausible account of the realization of hardness. But, Gillett objects, COMBO itself must be realized by some collection of properties, which in turn must be realized by some other collection of properties, and so on until one is faced with properties like spin and charm that belong not to atoms but quarks and leptons. This is troubling for the flat view but consistent with the dimensioned account, which requires only that the powers of "higher-level" individuals are constituted by powers of "lower-level" individuals.

But the very point that Gillett relies on to defuse the COMBO defense also cuts against the dimensioned analysis, although for a different reason. Gillett's criticism of the COMBO defense depends on the fact that realizers are themselves always realized ultimately by a handful of basic properties—properties that belong to individuals that differ from those in possession of the realized properties. But if this is so, Gillett is committed to the claim that, ultimately, every property is realized in the same way. Talk of multiple realizability, on the dimensioned account, vanishes, for, it turns out, the same properties that realize, say, a digital watch also realize an analog watch (as well as everything else under—and over—the sun).

There is a flip side to this problem. In addition to ruling out the possibility of multiple realizability, Gillett's dimensioned account might also be taken to trivialize multiple realizability, distinguishing between realizations that intuitively ought to be counted as identical in kind. However, this problem becomes much more apparent after reflecting on the points that ought to be weighed in judgments of multiple realization. It is to this topic that I now turn.

2.2   Sameness and Difference of Realization

Suppose the facts I discussed in the previous chapter that Block and Fodor take to establish MRT are true: the brain is a labile organ that can respond to insult in one of its parts by reprogramming another of its parts to assume the psychological function that had occurred in the damaged part; natural selection has sculpted psychologically similar organisms from different kinds of "clay"; and AI has succeeded or will succeed in building computers that are psychologically similar to ourselves. Indeed, let's throw into this pot of evidence the discovery of ETs with a psychology much like our own. Ought we to assume, as Putnam does in his likelihood argument, that these multiple instances of minds are truly *multiple* realizations of minds? The facts are inconclusive until we can say something more general about when two things count as distinct realizations of a type.

As a starting point, it is worth noting that multiply realizable kinds are often functional kinds. As we have seen, the concept of function receives different analyses among functionalists. However, because of the doubts that I and others have expressed about Putnam's machine functionalism, I shall assume in the following that MRT is a thesis about kinds that are functional in the functional analysis sense that, in chapter 1, we saw Fodor (1968) endorsing. The functional analysis sense of function probably receives its most careful explication in the work of Cummins (1975).[2] On this conception, functions are capacities of a system, and a functional analysis involves breaking down the system into those parts or properties that contribute to the system's ability to bring about the capacity of interest.

So-called Cummins functions stand in contrast to the etiological conception of function that has been developed and discussed in the writings of Allen and Bekoff (1995), Godfrey-Smith (1993), Millikan (1984), Neander (1991), Walsh and Ariew (1996), and, originally, Wright (1973). Common to these various etiological accounts of function is the idea that the function of a system is that capacity of the system that explains why systems of that type have come into being or remain in place. So, for instance, an etiologist would claim that flight is the function of wings because it is the capacity to fly that explains why birds first evolved and continue to have wings.

For Cummins, the question of why some trait or system came to be is unrelated to talk of function. It is consistent with Cummins's account that one assign to wings the function to fly, if flight is the capacity one seeks to analyze. However, no less defensible is the decision to assign to wings the function to create particular air turbulence patterns, if it is this capacity of wings one chooses to investigate. Because my focus is on how the mind does what it does and whether there are many or just a few ways to do what the mind does, Cummins's conception of function suffices for my purposes. Of course, I do not deny that questions about why the mind evolved the properties it did are interesting,[3] or that it is often important to an investigation of some capacity to understand its purpose, for example, as in Marr's (1982) work on vision or Glenberg's (1997) work on memory. Moreover, the mental capacities on which I shall concentrate will likely be, in many cases, those that evolved because of what they do. However, my point here is just that I need no more than Cummins's conception of function to address the issues about multiple realizability with which I am concerned.

Thus, when I talk of functional kinds I shall have in mind kinds defined by some capacity, but I will not care whether the capacity by which the kind is defined is one that explains how the kind came to be. But when are two realizations the *same* type of realizations of a functional kind, and when are they *different* realizations of a functional kind? Apparently, claims of multiple realizability rest on two sorts of similarity judgments. The first judgment is that two particular, or token, realizations, X and Y, are indeed realizations of the same functional kind F. The second judgment is that X and Y are indeed different types of realization of F. For instance, if it is true that the kind *eye* is multiply realizable, it must be true of the different particular realizations of *eye* that these realizations are (i) justifiably classified as eyes and (ii) justifiably counted as belonging to distinct kinds. Likewise, if digital and analog watches are properly construed as distinct realizations of the kind *watch*, it must be that digital and analog watches, on the one hand, are the same functional kind but, on the other hand, are truly different types of realization of that functional kind. Finally, waiter's corkscrews—the kind of corkscrew that consists simply of a screw near the fulcrum end of a lever—appear to differ from double-lever corkscrews—the kind of corkscrew with two winglike appendages that stand upright as the screw descends into the cork. If one wants to claim that waiter's corkscrews and double-lever corkscrews are indeed multiple realizations of *corkscrew*, one must establish first that they are the same kind of functional thing and second that they are different types of realization of that functional kind. Same but different. This is the recipe for multiple realizability.

Before us then are two questions that any judgment of multiple realizability must first address:

1. Why count realizations X and Y as realizations of the same functional kind? and

2. Which differences between X and Y are relevant to the judgment that they are different types of realization of the same functional kind?

Intuitively, analog and digital watches provide a clear case of multiple realization. It is the kind *watch* that is being multiply realized, with the analog and digital watches each realizing *watch* in distinct ways. So, to examine the correctness of this intuition, we need to answer the following questions:

1. Why are analog and digital watches both realizations of the same functional kind?

2. Which differences between analog and digital watches are relevant to the judgment that they are different realizations of the same functional kind?

The obvious answer to the first question is this: analog and digital watches are both realizations of the same functional kind because both are watches. *Watch* is a functional kind—a kind defined by what it does—and analog and digital watches both do that which makes something a watch. But what is the function of a watch? Presumably, if analog and digital watches are both realizations of the same functional kind then they have the same defining capacity of the functional kind, whatever that may be. If they did not have the same defining capacity, then they would not realize the same functional kind and so would not be different types of realization of the same functional kind. Of course, analog and digital watches needn't share all their capacities to both count as watches. Perhaps the digital watch displays tenths of seconds and the analog watch does not. Nevertheless, in virtue of the fact that both tell time, and that telling time is (at least one of) the capacity(ies) by which watches are defined, both are watches.

Just how much difference in their capacities can realizations sustain before we no longer judge them to be realizations of the same functional kind? Is a device that fits on the wrist and tells time but also allows web access and telephone communication a realization of a watch? Is a device similar to an analog watch in all respects except for lacking a minute and second hand a realization of a watch? Both the waiter's corkscrew and the double-lever corkscrew remove a cork by pulling it from the bottle with a screw. However, if I had described the function of a corkscrew as simply that of cork removal, then the waiter's and double-lever corkscrews have the same function as the device consisting of two slender metal prongs that are slid in on either side of the cork. These prongs, which in my experience do not remove the cork from the bottle but instead cause it to fall into the wine with a muted splash, allegedly allow one to pull the cork from the bottle. Thus, if one allows fairly broad characterizations of function, such as "pulls the cork from the bottle," then the waiter's corkscrew, the double-lever corkscrew, and the two-pronged corkscrew are all the same kind of thing. However, all differ from the cork-removing device that pierces the cork with a needle and injects CO_2 into the bottle, thus *pushing* out the cork from below. But, of course, all four devices *cause the cork to rise.*

These observations suffice to make a point that is important in an evaluation of MRT but that has been overlooked in most discussions of it (but see Bechtel and Mundale 1999 for a clear appreciation of this problem). There is a certain vagueness associated with the individuation of functional kinds that may create difficulties when trying to decide whether two realizations are different types of realization of the same functional kind. Claims of multiple realizability are interesting only because they purport to show the possibility of the *same* function carried out by *different* means. As the actual capacities of the different realizations themselves differ (pulling the cork vs. pushing the cork), or as the descriptions of function become broader or narrower in scope (cork removal vs. cork pulling), verdicts about the multiple realizability of a functional kind will waver. Clearly, as the description of capacities of the realizers becomes more fine grained, one will be tempted to distinguish between them, thus increasing the apparent multiple realizability of the functional kind. Similarly, as the functional kind is described more broadly, one will be tempted to allow more variation in the capacities of realizers, thus again increasing the apparent multiple realizability of the functional kind.

There are a couple of things to say in response to these problems. First, they are problems for both critics *and* proponents of multiple realizability. Any proponent of multiple realizability should not rest her case on a tiny difference between realizations; equivalently, it would be cheating to defend multiple realizability by choosing to describe a functional kind in such gross terms that devices ordinarily construed as different functional kinds end up being the same functional kind.

Second, as Bechtel and Mundale (1999) emphasize, there is a level of description of psychological capacities and their realizers that psychologists and neuroscientists depend on to make the kinds of comparative judgments that are important for understanding how the brain realizes the mind. Whether Bechtel and Mundale are right about what this level is, the point remains that some levels of description will be better than others for understanding the relationship between the mind and the brain. I intend my challenge to MRT to be a challenge at these proprietary levels of description. For this reason, my future discussions of mental and physical properties will adopt the standard vocabulary of psychologists and neuroscientists.

It is now time to consider the second kind of similarity judgment that claims of multiple realization entail. On what basis can one say that two realizations are *different* types of realization of the same functional kind? As stated, this question seems ill formed. For reasons that will soon become clear, it makes no sense to speak of two different realizations as, simply, *different* realizations of the same kind; nor is it intelligible to say that two realizations of a functional kind are, simply, the same. No two token realizations of a functional kind are exactly identical. Whereas two corkscrews might have been produced in the same factory with the same materials by the same workers, the two will differ in some respects at some level of description. On a casual inspection they might appear to have the same dimensions, same mass, same material composition, and so on. Yet, scrutiny through a finer lens will surely reveal that their masses are not truly identical (it's unlikely that they have the exact same number of constituent atoms), nor are they exactly the same length. Perhaps, moreover, one contains traces of a substance (a microscopic bit of dirt) that the other lacks. Presumably, these are differences that don't make a difference, and to distinguish the two would constitute a cheat in one of the senses I described above. If two corkscrews that roll off the same assembly line one after the other are not identical realizations of a functional kind then nothing is.

On the other hand, two corkscrews that appear to be *different* kinds of realization of a functional kind will share *some* properties. Waiter's corkscrews *appear* to differ from double-lever corkscrews. No doubt waiter's corkscrews and double-lever corkscrews differ in more conspicuous ways from each other than they do from others of their own kind. However, it is also true that they might be made from the same materials, might have the same mass, might reflect the same wavelengths of light, and so on. Thus, sameness in some respects does not suffice to make two realizations of a kind the same kind of realization.

A natural response to these observations is to say that a waiter's corkscrew counts as one kind of realization of *corkscrew* and a double-lever corkscrew counts as another kind because they operate in different ways. Waiter's corkscrews are an instance of a *second-class lever*, that is, a lever in which the load is sandwiched between the fulcrum and the effort.[4] In contrast, the slightly misleadingly named double-lever corkscrew is really a screw attached to a double-sided rack. The depression of its "wings" causes the rotation of two pinions, which gets translated into the vertical motion of the rack that, in turn, causes the cork to rise from the bottle. Indeed, different laws govern the cork-removal operations of the two kinds of cork screws. Using the law of levers (the load multiplied by its distance from the fulcrum is equal to the force of the effort multiplied by its distance from the fulcrum) it is possible to calculate the force one needs to remove a cork from a bottle with a waiter's corkscrew if one knows the resistance of the cork and the distances of the cork and the effort from the fulcrum. This law is not applicable to the double-lever corkscrew because the double-lever corkscrew utilizes a rack and pinion mechanism. So, it might seem, waiter's corkscrews and double-lever corkscrews are different kinds of realization of *corkscrew* because they operate in different ways, as evidenced by the fact that different laws govern their operation.

Yet, as tempting as this account is of what makes different realizations different *kinds* of realization, it too is somewhat arbitrary. It is true, for instance, that both waiter's corkscrews and double-lever corkscrews remove corks by causing a screw that has been embedded in a cork to rise. If one thinks of the rising screw as the most proximate cause in the chain of causes that results in the cork's removal, then we can say that waiter's corkscrews and double-lever corkscrews share at least one causal power—one link in a chain of causes that results in a cork's removal.

Moreover, presumably the same laws that describe how a lifting force on a screw will cause a cork to rise are applicable to both kinds of corkscrew. Thus, if one wanted to distinguish the waiter's corkscrew and the double-lever corkscrew, one would have to be careful to say not that they operate completely differently—they do not, because each shares a proximate causal step—but that their operation differs at least in some of the distal causal steps by which they remove corks.

As before, these are complications that challenge any effort to say when two realizations of a functional kind are the same or different kinds of realization. They are severe but not insuperable. The first step to take in mollifying them is to concede that *same* and *different* ought to be relativized. In saying that two realizations are the same or different kind, one must say *with respect to which property* the realizations are the same or different. All corkscrews are the same with respect to the property of being able to remove corks, but corkscrews differ with respect to other properties such as mass, length, mechanism, composition, and so on. But what sorts of differences are significant when one claims that a functional kind is multiply realizable? As I already noted, waiter's corkscrews and double-lever corkscrews can be composed of similar stuff. Each, for instance, might consist mainly of steel. However, it seems odd to say that, in virtue of their similar composition, the waiter's corkscrew is more similar to the double-lever corkscrew than it is to another waiter's corkscrew that is composed of aluminum. Intuitively, we want it to turn out that the waiter's corkscrew and double-lever corkscrew are, *qua* realizations of a corkscrew, less similar to each other than each is to others of its "own kind," despite the fact that they may be made of the same stuff. Intuitively, that is, a particular waiter's corkscrew is more similar to other waiter's corkscrews than it is to a double-lever corkscrew even when its material composition is more similar to that of a given double-lever corkscrew than it is to other waiter's corkscrews.

The difficulties that arise when trying to say when or why two realizations ought to count as different realizations of the same functional kind are to be expected. It seems almost inevitable that one ends up wading into a swampy morass of problems when one starts to talk about similarity. However, my hope is that a focus on functional, or task, analysis might motivate a sensible approach to judgments about sameness and difference in realizations. Immediately in favor of such an approach is the aforementioned fact that many multiply realizable kinds are also functional kinds. Thus, it seems reasonable to suppose that judgments of sameness and difference between realizations might be relativized to those properties that make a difference to how a functional kind functions, that is, to how a functional kind actually manages to bring about the capacity (or capacities) that defines it as the functional kind that it is. It is from this perspective that functional analysis presents itself as the proper way to justify decisions about sameness and difference between realizations.

The use of functional analysis to understand the causal processes involved in the exercise of some capacity is familiar in biology, psychology, engineering, and many other disciplines. Quite simply, one begins the analysis with a description of the capacity of interest that the system under investigation possesses and then one decomposes the system into those properties that causally contribute in some way to the performance of the capacity (see Cummins 1975; Hatfield 1991; Lycan 1981). Causally contributing properties can, of course, be viewed as capacities in their own right, subject to further decomposition into properties that causally contribute to *their* performance. Of course, whereas it is a matter of the interests of the investigator to decide which of the capacities of a system to analyze functionally, it should be clear that once this decision has been made there is no interest-relativity associated with the capacity's decomposition. That is, whereas it might be up to the investigator to study a corkscrew's capacity to remove corks rather than a corkscrew's capacity to make a jingling noise, it is not a matter of the investigator's preferences which properties of the corkscrew come into play in effecting cork removal. The properties that causally contribute to the performance of a capacity must be sought through empirical means, and disagreements between investigators over which such properties play a role in the production of some capacity are subject to resolution through further experimentation.

For sake of convenience, I propose to use the name *R-property* as a label for those properties of realizations whose differences suffice to explain why the realizations of which they are properties count as different in kind. In short, two types of realization of some functional kind, like *corkscrew* or *watch*, count as different kinds of realization if (by definition) they differ in their R-properties. The question I have been considering is "Which properties of a realization are R-properties?"; and the claim emerging from this discussion is this: R-properties are those that are identified in the course of functionally analyzing some capacity. It is to functional analysis, I claim, that we should look for the identification of R-properties because it is functional analysis that uncovers those properties that causally contribute to the production of the capacity of interest. Furthermore, it is the causal properties that one should care about insofar as one's concern is with *how* some system is able to exhibit the capacity that it does.

An illustration will help at this point. As I have already noted, corkscrews can differ in all sorts of ways, but which differences ought to make a difference in judgments about multiple realization? Which, in other words, are the R-properties of a given realization of a corkscrew? Consider first two waiter's corkscrews composed of the same materials but that differ in color (one is red and the other blue). This difference justifies the claim that the two are distinct realizations of *corkscrew* only if color is an R-property, that is, a property that a correct functional analysis of cork removal identifies as causally contributing to cork removal. But it seems obvious that color does not play any role in a waiter's corkscrew's capacity to remove corks. The properties that are involved in this capacity are things like *having a rigid bar that can act as a lever, having a screw with a sharp point, having a piece that sits on the lip of the bottle and acts like a fulcrum.* Because these are the properties that causally contribute to the waiter's corkscrew's capacity to remove corks, and because the two waiter's corkscrews do not differ in these properties, they are not different realizations of *corkscrew*, or, at any rate, they are only trivially different realizations (Shapiro 2000).

Alternatively, consider two waiter's corkscrews that differ only in size—one is six inches from end to end and the other is ten. This difference might make a difference to how quickly or easily the two corkscrews do their jobs, but this difference is, so to speak, merely *quantitative* rather than *qualitative*. Both corkscrews remove corks in the same kind of way, or, at least, in a way more similar to each other than either is to the way in which a double-lever corkscrew removes corks. For this reason, I would deny that the size of the corkscrew constitutes an R-property (at least in this context).

Independently, Batterman has explored questions about multiple realizability similar to those I am now addressing. Batterman uses a pendulum to illustrate his point. Having chosen the capacity of interest—the capacity of pendulums to "all have periods (for small oscillations) that are directly proportional to the square root of the length of the rod from which the bob is hanging (2000, p. 120), Batterman asks why "are factors such as the color and (to a large degree) the constitution or microstructural makeup of the bobs irrelevant for answering our why-question about the period of the pendulums?" (ibid., p. 121). In terms I introduced, color, length, mass, composition, and so on are not among a pendulum's R-properties (relative to the capacity of a pendulum to have the kind of period pendulums have). As I understand Batterman's view, what I have been calling R-properties are comparable to the parameters across systems that cause these systems to behave in a similar way.[5] These systems may and often do diverge in a number of other parameters, but these can be irrelevant when explaining why the systems exhibit similarities in behavior. One needn't attend to the color of a bob to understand the period of a pendulum because color is a parameter that makes no difference to the arc of a pendulum. On the other hand, the length of the rod is a parameter that will explain similarities in the swinging behavior of differently colored pendulums.

Returning to the corkscrew example, it should be clear that waiter's corkscrews and double-lever corkscrews *do* qualify as different realizations of *corkscrew* because they *do* differ in their R-properties. Functional analyses of waiter's corkscrews and double-lever corkscrews turn up different R-properties. In contrast to the R-properties of a waiter's corkscrew, the R-properties of a double-lever corkscrew include having a rack and having two pinions. Waiter's corkscrews and double-lever corkscrews thus count as different realizations of *corkscrew* because the functional analysis of each reveals that each employs different mechanisms in the production of cork removal, that is, different R-properties.

My suggestion is, then, that realizations of a functional kind are the same or different with respect to their R-properties and R-properties are those that make a causal contribution to the relevant functional capacity. Naturally, questions remain. For instance, one could wonder about how to determine whether various R-properties are the same or different, and one might then have to begin to consider which properties of a property are relevant for typing properties as R-properties. For instance, if one has identified as an R-property of a corkscrew the property of having a screw with a sharp end, one might wonder whether an open-coiled screw and a closed-coil screw constitute different R-properties. Furthermore, there are questions about how to identify which properties of a functional kind are R-properties. Does having mass contribute to a corkscrew's capacity to remove corks? Presumably, a corkscrew must be massive enough to apply the force necessary to remove a cork, but not so massive that it destroys the bottle on which it perches. It sounds peculiar to talk of a corkscrew's mass as contributing to its ability to remove corks, but perhaps this is only because no one has ever thought to manufacture a corkscrew with mass less than one gram or over 1000 kilograms.

I believe that the proper thing to do at this point is to acknowledge that judgments of multiple realizability, insofar as such judgments rest on decisions about similarity, might on occasion founder on questions of function identity and property identity. However, it would be a mistake to dismiss the coherence of multiple realizability and hence MRT for this reason. There is agreement, for the most part, that analog and digital watches are different realizations of *watch*, that waiter's and double-lever corkscrews are different realizations of *corkscrew*, and so on. My goal is to say something interesting about the possibility of MRT that does not require exploiting in illicit ways the difficulties that emerge in the course of making similarity judgments. I would like, that is, to go as far as possible relying on examples of MRT that most would accept. Moreover, it is my hope that the introduction of R-properties goes a fair distance in capturing an intuitive distinction between significant and trivial cases of multiple realizability, between, say, waiter's and double-lever corkscrews on the one hand and blue and red waiter's corkscrews on the other.

Before leaving this discussion of sameness and difference in types of realization, it is worthwhile to contrast the view I have been developing with Gillett's view. Recall that Gillett objects to accounts of realization that require the realizer to have the same causal powers as the realized kind. Gillett objects to such an account, because, he thinks, science tells us that it is often the relations and properties of atoms, for instance, that causally contribute to some functional capacity, and hence realize the functional capacity, without themselves exhibiting the functional capacity. Thus, for example, the hardness of a diamond is caused by the relations and properties of a group of carbon atoms. In virtue of being arranged as they are, the carbon atoms realize hardness, but the relations and properties of the carbon atoms are not themselves hard. If we agree that hardness is realized in the relations between carbon atoms, it looks as though we must deny that a realizer has to possess the property that is individuative of the functional kind.

This may present a challenge to the way I choose to understand realization. On my view, even if it is true that the rigidity of the lever in a waiter's corkscrew can be realized in two distinct ways, this does not imply that such differently realized corkscrews should count as significantly different types of realization of *waiter's corkscrew*. Suppose, for instance, that waiter's corkscrew A is rigid in virtue of the relations and alignments of aluminum molecules and that waiter's corkscrew S is rigid in virtue of the relations and alignments of steel molecules. Suppose further that the R-properties by which aluminum molecules realize rigidity differ from those by which steel molecules realize rigidity. Neither of these facts suffice to show that A and S are different kinds of realizations of waiter's corkscrews, because it is consistent with these facts that aluminum and steel realize corkscrews in the same way despite realizing rigidity in different ways. That is, aluminum and steel realizations of waiter's corkscrews may realize rigidity in virtue of different R-properties while realizing waiter's corkscrews in virtue of realizing the same property, namely, rigidity.

Appealing to the idea of a task analysis provides insight into this case. Task analyses can consist in a number of levels, where deeper levels offer analyses of capacities at higher levels. Suppose the R-properties identified at the highest, or first, level of a task analysis of a waiter's corkscrew are things like possessing a rigid lever, having a sharp screw, and so on. At a deeper level, the task analysis would analyze each of the R-properties of the first level into other R-properties. But notice that a task analysis at this deeper level is *not* a task analysis of corkscrews, but of things like rigidity. This is evident when we consider that a task analysis that reveals how aluminum molecules produce rigidity might just as readily appear in the analysis of a clockwork as it would in the analysis of a corkscrew, assuming that a first-level task analysis of clockwork has among its R-properties things like rigidity. No doubt the task analysis of how aluminum molecules produce rigidity might differ from the analysis that shows how steel molecules produce rigidity, but this fact goes no distance toward showing that aluminum-realized-rigidity contributes differently to the capacities of a waiter's corkscrew than does steel-realized-rigidity. Hence, it is possible for realizations of rigidity to differ without this fact implying that aluminum and steel realize waiter's corkscrews in different ways. Insofar as Gillett's analysis of realization commits him to the claim that the steel and aluminum corkscrews are different kinds of realization, we part company.

2.3 Evaluating the Evidence for the Multiple Realizability Thesis

If I am right that realizations of a functional kind ought to be counted as different only when they differ in the causal properties by which they perform their defining function, then the evaluation of empirical evidence purporting to support MRT must be sensitive to this fact. All of a sudden, MRT is not as obvious as it may first have appeared. Work—hard empirical work—must be done before one can say that two realizations of a kind, even when it is obvious that the realizations differ in some of their physical properties, are in fact different kinds of realization.

Consider, for instance, a common thought experiment in philosophy of mind that is supposed to demonstrate that minds are multiply realizable (Pylyshyn 1980). Imagine that a single neuron in a brain is replaced by a silicon chip. The silicon chip, suppose, preserves the connections to other neurons in which the original neuron was involved. Intuition is supposed to tell us that this brain, though differing somewhat in its physical properties from the original brain, realizes the same kind of mind that it did before. Now suppose that the remaining neurons are, one by one, replaced by silicon chips that preserve the connections of the neurons they replace. If our prior intuition drives us to accept that a brain with a single silicon chip can realize the same kind of mind, it ought similarly to force us to accept that a brain composed of nothing but silicon can realize the same kind of mind. The conclusion of the thought experiment is that minds are multiply realizable.

But, of course, the fact that a silicon brain differs from a standard brain in its material composition does not immediately show that minds are multiply realizable. If the properties of silicon that get exercised when it embodies a mind are similar enough to the properties of standard neurons that get exercised when *they* embody a mind, then the silicon brain is only in a trivial sense a *different* realization of a mind. Let's suppose, certainly contrary to fact, that the only properties of neurons that matter to whether they can realize a mind are their electrical properties. These electrical properties figure prominently in a functional analysis of neuron function and thus are among the more important R-properties of a neuron (relative to the function of producing mental properties). In contrast, the color of a neuron, mass of a neuron, distance of a neuron from the subject's nose, and so on, never, or only at a distance far removed from the initial functional decomposition of neural functioning, receive mention in a functional analysis of a neuron. But then, if standard neurons and silicon neurons have the same electrical properties, there is no motivation for calling them distinct realizations of a neuron. The difference between standard neurons and silicon neurons, in such a case, is no more interesting relative to their contribution to psychological traits than is the difference between contributions of neurons gray in color and neurons that have been stained purple.

If this response to the silicon brain example is correct, it should lead one to question most mainstream thinking about multiple realizability. It is entirely standard in the literature to describe multiple realizability as the possibility that the same functional device can be made out of different kinds of stuff. But, why take for granted that "different kinds of stuff" amount to genuinely different R-properties? Without further argument, this facile appeal to "different kinds of stuff" may, and probably often does, provide no more than what I characterized above as a trivial sense of multiple realizability. Why count two double-lever corkscrews as different realizations of the kind *corkscrew* simply because one is steel and the other aluminum? Why count two pendulums as different realizations of *pendulum* simply because the rod of one is made of oak and the other of maple?

From this perspective, we can see why the disagreement I discussed in chapter 1 between Putnam (1967) and Block and Fodor (1972) over the significance of convergent evolution for the possibility of multiple realizability is likely to be settled in Putnam's favor. Take a familiar case of convergent evolution: the torpedo shape of the dolphin and shark. Presumably, dolphins and sharks evolved this shape independently because the streamlined shape is well adapted to quick movement through the water. But are these body shapes different realizations of the kind "streamlined shape"? According to Block and Fodor they must be, because sharks and dolphins are made out of different kinds of stuff. For instance, the shark's shape is supported by cartilage and the dolphin's by bone. However, because cartilage and bone are not the properties that get exercised in streamlining the movement of sharks and dolphins, the fact that they are composed of different matter doesn't make a difference. Cartilage and bone are not the properties that explain an organism's hydrodynamics. Likewise, if species evolve similar psychological capacities independently, we simply cannot conclude from differences in the species' neurophysiologies whether their psychological capacities have been multiply realized. This requires a careful examination of how members of each species actually achieve the psychological capacity in question—which R-properties contribute to their mental capacities.

The same point applies to Fodor and Block's claim that the plasticity of the brain supports MRT. To show that MRT is true, it is not enough to show that, for instance, the language center is sometimes in the left hemisphere and sometimes in the right. Why should left or right matter? If language is achieved in the same way by neurons in the right hemisphere as it is by neurons in the left, this lends no support to MRT. If, on the other hand, the neurons in the right hemisphere produce language through a very different set of processes from those through which neurons in the left hemisphere tend to produce language, then MRT begins to look plausible. But, again, showing this is no easy task, and, until we know a lot more about the brain, one must be very cautious in drawing conclusions about whether minds are multiply realizable from the fact that the brain is labile.

That such caution is necessary becomes even clearer on a closer examination of neural plasticity. Once one keeps in focus the two-part recipe for determining multiple realizability that I outlined above, neural plasticity is not the open and shut demonstration of multiple realizability that so many philosophers have assumed. To show that neural plasticity is an example of multiple realizability, one must show (1) that it is indeed the *same* psychological function being realized in different neural hardware; and (2) that the different neural hardware differs in its R-properties. Keeping these burdens in mind casts doubt on the support that neural plasticity brings to MRT.

One prominent sense of neural plasticity involves the ability of the brain to change as a result of experience. The brain of a violin player or a person proficient with Braille will differ in predictable ways from the brains of those who do not use their fingers for very fine discriminations (Elbert et al. 1995; Pascual-Leone and Torres 1993). The motor cortex in these specially trained individuals will have more space dedicated to representing the inputs from those fingers used in these operations than the motor cortexes of individuals not so trained. However, this standard example of plasticity does nothing to show multiple realizability for the simple reason that the brains of the trained individuals are no longer doing the same thing as the brains of untrained individuals. To be sure, just as in some contexts one might take the more precise digital watch to be of the same functional kind as an analog watch, one might take the motor cortexes of trained and untrained individuals to be "the same." But, if one's interest is in the *difference* in function between trained and untrained motor cortexes—in the finer discriminatory capacities of the violinist's or Braille reader's brains—then, as an example of multiple realizability, it has the defect of not showing a case in which it is the *same* psychological function that is being realized in two different ways. The trained brains and the untrained brains have different capacities. Insofar as this is plausible, the fact that they differ physically does not constitute a case of multiple realizability.

Another common example of neural plasticity concerns the ability of cortex to reorganize itself following section (destruction) of afferent nerves. Kaas (2000a) describes how the section of the median nerve in the thumb half of the glabrous (front) portion of a monkey's hand causes reorganization of the representation of the hand in S1 of the somatosensory cortex. Over a period of months, the portion of S1 that initially represented input from the glabrous surfaces of the thumb and first two fingers reorganizes itself so that it eventually represents inputs from the dorsal areas of these three digits. This reorganization requires that the cortex rewire itself, so that areas of S1 that were initially innervated by the median nerve are now innervated by the radial nerve that carries information from the back of the hand (see figure 2.1). Does this example of plasticity show multiple realizability? It is difficult to see how. The portions of S1 that used to represent the thumb half of the glabrous surface of the hand now do something else—they represent the thumb half of the dorsal surface of the hand. Hence, this is not a case of the same function being performed in different ways. Perhaps, however, one might interpret this as a case of multiple realization of the representation of the dorsal surface of the hand. But now a second burden comes into play. The portions of S1 that now represent inputs from the radial nerve, having before represented inputs from the median nerve, may not be representing these inputs in a way that differs significantly from the way the inputs from the radial nerve are represented in other areas of S1. That is, even if it is now true that the representation of the dorsal thumb half of the hand is represented in two places in S1 it need not be true that the two representations of the dorsal thumb half of the hand are multiple realizations of a single kind. It may well be that the dorsal thumb half is represented in the two areas in roughly the same way. If the only difference between the representations is a difference in location, and if location is itself not a property by which the representations represent the information from the radial nerve, then there is no more reason to count the two representations as multiple realizations of the kind *dorsal thumb half representation of the hand* than there is reason to deny that two pendulums are of the same type simply because they are in different locations. It appears that we have here simply a case of trivial multiple realization.

A similar complaint applies to a more dramatic kind of neural plasticity, plasticity involving changes in modality. In these sorts of cases, cortex that has the function of representing one kind of information, say, auditory, comes to represent another kind of information, say, visual.

A. Location of Map

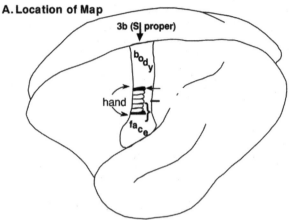

B. Representation Order

C. Normal Map

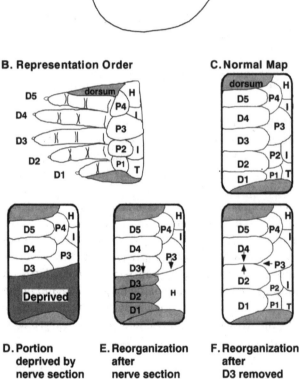

D. Portion
deprived by
nerve section

E. Reorganization
after
nerve section

F. Reorganization
after
D3 removed

Figure 2.1
(D) and (E) show the effect of destroying the median nerve, which carries information from the thumb half of the front of the hand. Portions of the somatosensory that initially represented information from the front of the hand are rewired to represent information from the back of the hand. From Kaas (2000a).

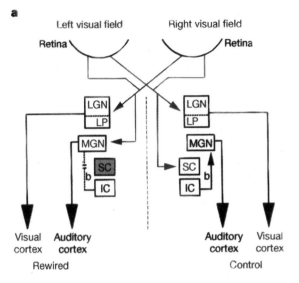

Figure 2.2
Pathway from the retina to the visual cortex. On the left side, the brachium (b) of the inferior colliculus (IC) was ablated, leading to a new pathway to the auditory cortex. From von Melchner, Pallas, and Sur (2000).

This might initially appear to be an exemplary case of multiple realizability, for it seems to involve the same function, vision, realized in two different ways. Mriganka Sur and his associates have provided some relevant studies. Sur et al. severed the connections between the brachium of the inferior colliculus and the superior colliculus to the medial geniculate nucleus in the left hemisphere of ferret neonates (see figure 2.2). This procedure caused a rewiring so that the retina sends projections to the MGN, which in turn passes along this visual information to the auditory cortex (von Melchner, Pallas, and Sur 2000, p. 872). The ferrets were then raised to adulthood, at which time Sur et al. tested the visual capacities of their right visual fields (the field now represented in the auditory cortex). Sur et al. found that rewired ferrets are indeed sensitive to light in their right visual fields and, in addition, displayed some acuity in discerning contrast in grates of light and dark bands. These findings seem to be just the sort that might tempt philosophers to conclude that minds, or at least some cognitive capacities, are multiply realizable.

But this conclusion may be too quick. Before taking Sur et al.'s work as evidence of multiple realizability, we must ask: (i) are the visual capacities of the rewired and normal ferrets the same? and (ii) are the properties by which rewired ferrets differ from normal ferrets those that cause sight in normal ferrets? The answer to the first question is "no." Although the rewired ferrets have some visual acuity in their right visual field, it is impoverished compared to the vision in their left visual fields or the vision in normal ferrets. In grating acuity tests, rewired ferrets cannot see contrast between bars in a grate that is plainly visible to normal ferrets. Moreover, normal ferrets can detect gratings at a higher frequency (a greater spatial resolution) than can rewired ferrets (von Melchner, Pallas, and Sur 2000, p. 874).

The answer to the second question, the question about how the auditory cortex processes visual information, is less clear. Nevertheless, there is evidence that the properties that matter to normal visual processing are replicated in the auditory cortex of the rewired ferrets. In normal ferrets, the auditory cortex has an organization nothing like the visual cortex (Sharma, Angelucci, and Sur 2000, p. 841). The auditory cortex of rewired adult ferrets, however, appears to be strikingly like the visual cortex of normal ferrets. For instance, both contain a two-dimensional map of visual space and both contain columns of orientation-sensitive cells.

In sum, the visual capacities of the rewired ferrets differ from those of normal ferrets, and the auditory cortexes of rewired ferrets bear a strong resemblance to the visual cortexes of normal ferrets. It seems not unreasonable to suppose that a rewired ferret sees as well as it does only to the extent that its auditory cortex resembles a visual cortex. But, if I am right about this, cross-modal plasticity, at least in this case, is poor support for multiple realizability. It affords neither a case in which the *same* function is realized in two different ways, nor a case in which the same function is realized in two *different* ways.

This discussion of neural plasticity is, I must emphasize, far from definitive. What it does, I hope, is reveal how one must think about neural plasticity *qua* evidence for MRT. It may be that there are cases of neural plasticity that do present genuine cases of a psychological capacity being multiply realized. Determining the plausibility of MRT will, no doubt, depend on the prevalence of such cases, and it is for this reason that further research on neural plasticity will figure prominently in a final evaluation of MRT.

In closing this chapter, I must say something about the final source of evidence that, in the previous chapter, we saw Fodor and Block cite in support of MRT. Fodor and Block claim that advances in AI show (or would show) that minds are multiply realizable. We are clearly in the realm of sheer speculation here. However, the arguments I just made concerning the evaluation of evidence for MRT apply here as well. An AI machine would provide an example of a significantly different realization of the mind only if it were truly, on the one hand, very similar to a mind in its psychological capacities, but, on the other, distinct in the properties by virtue of which it realized a mind. Maybe AI will succeed in building such a machine and maybe not. We cannot simply assert that it will without begging the question. Here we must simply wait and see.

2.4 Conclusion

In this chapter I have tried to motivate the need for some principle by which to judge realizations to be the same or different. Without such a principle, it is impossible to weigh the confirming force of the empirical considerations that philosophers have made in support of MRT. I have suggested that we use the idea of R-properties to decide whether two realizations of a kind ought to count as two different kinds of realization. If this idea is reasonable, then the empirical evidence Block and Fodor cite in favor of MRT is far from decisive. What we must do to decide whether minds are in fact multiply realizable is to learn something about why the brain is as it is. Which of the brain's properties are those that will be exposed in a functional analysis of psychological capacities? Could minds like ours be produced by different kinds of R-properties?

At first glance, it might appear that we simply have no evidence that could help to answer these questions. As far as we know, humanlike minds have never been realized in anything but human brains. How, then, can one hope to gather evidence about the possibility of realizing humanlike minds in other ways? How can we compare the R-properties that realize the human mind to R-properties that realize other very similar minds if there are no other very similar minds? These are good questions, and their answer will require a study of two central concepts in evolutionary biology: constraint and convergence. It is to this business that chapter 3 turns.

3

Constraints

In the previous two chapters I examined several arguments that philosophers have offered in support of MRT. The arguments that seemed most persuasive were those that mustered empirical support for MRT. These arguments moved from empirically established facts, such as the plasticity of the brain or the independent evolution of traits with similar capacities but different realizations, to the conclusion that the mind is multiply realizable. I ended chapter 2 with a discussion of how we ought to weigh empirical evidence when evaluating MRT. The central idea I developed in this discussion is that the properties by which realizations of a kind should be judged as the same or different—what I called R-properties—are those that appear in a task or functional analysis of the functional kind under investigation. Quite simply, the R-properties of a realization are those in virtue of which the realization is, in fact, able to achieve that capacity which makes it realize the functional kind that it does. Accordingly, a kind is *multiply* realizable only if it can have realizations that differ in their R-properties.

This proposal seems to capture effectively many of our intuitions about multiple realizability. Corkscrews that differ in color alone are not distinct realizations of the kind *corkscrew*, and this is because color is a causally inert property relative to the corkscrew's capacity to remove corks. However, deciding cases of multiple realizability in this manner also stirs up some surprises: corkscrews that differ in material composition may not, after all, constitute distinct realizations of the kind *corkscrew* because properties of material composition other than rigidity are as causally inert with respect to cork removal as color is. I have said that this result comes as a surprise (at least it did for me), and it runs contrary to some fairly standard illustrations of MRT, such as the silicon brain that I discussed toward the end of chapter 2. However, the concept of an R-property seems to provide a fairly clear and nonarbitrary means by which to help distinguish what I called significant cases of multiple realizability from trivial ones, and if we are left with results that occasionally run counter to intuitions then, I think, it is the intuitions that need to bend.

It is now time to consider the relevance of the preceding general discussion of multiple realizability to MRT, that is, the thesis that the *human mind* is multiply realizable. To decide whether MRT is true we must know whether, once we have identified the R-properties of the system that realizes a humanlike mind, it is physically possible that a humanlike mind may be realized in systems with vastly different sets of R-properties or whether all systems in which the mind is realized will have largely similar R-properties.

As I have already noted, part of the answer to this question depends of course on the grain at which we describe the functions of the mind. For instance, if we described a corkscrew as any device that removes corks, then the waiter's corkscrew and the double-lever corkscrew, as well as the pronged cork remover and the CO_2 cork remover, all count as corkscrews. And, because the R-properties of each of these devices differ, this characterization of a corkscrew makes it seem as though each device is, legitimately, an alternative realization of the kind *corkscrew*. But, if one describes the function of the corkscrew as *pulling* a cork from a bottle, then the CO_2 cork remover, which works by *pushing* a cork from a bottle, is no longer a corkscrew. Similarly, if a watch is anything that sits on a wrist and tells time, then digital and analog devices may both be watches. But if watches are devices that tell time to the nearest, say, hundredth of a second, then there are in fact no analog *watches*.

Like the problems concerning property identity that I discussed in the previous chapter, the problem of defining functional grain is one for which, it seems to me, there are no principled answers (Enç 2002). Accordingly, as before, I urge a pragmatic tack: one's interests and purposes should settle questions about the grain of functional description that one adopts. It seems fairly clear that if one is interested in studying corkscrews for the purpose of understanding how they work, or how to build one that is better than those already available, then the grain of functional description should be not so fine that none but a waiter's corkscrew ends up counting as a corkscrew, nor so broad that the kind *corkscrew* includes things like power drills. No doubt fixing a grain of description for the study of corkscrews is an easier job than that which faces a psychologist. It is too easy to lose sight of the fact that an effort to understand how the brain performs some mental function must follow a description of what that mental function is (a point Marr 1982 emphasized; see Shapiro 1993 and 1997 for discussion). My hope is that I can comment sensibly on the plausibility of MRT without diverging wildly from the grain at which psychologists find it useful to describe the capacities of mental components.

In this chapter, after a few brief remarks about how I understand the terms "mind," "nervous system," and "body," I shall provide a more precise statement of the thesis that will occupy this chapter and the next. Following this, I will discuss various constraints that impose themselves on systems, thereby limiting the variation the system can exhibit. This discussion of constraints together with the argument of chapter 2 concerning how to evaluate evidence for multiple realizability form the basis of a challenge to MRT. The chapter closes with several extended examples of how constraints call into question the generality of multiple realizability.

3.1 Mind, Nervous System, and Body

As I mentioned earlier, I use the term "mind" in a loose way—as a catchall for the collection of cognitive and sensory capacities that human beings possess. Thus, minds (or their components) do not have easily characterized functions. Rather, they are collections of capacities, some of which include memory, attention, language use, perception, and so on. Moreover, these capacities differ in various ways, if present at all, in different species. Important for my project is that we recognize that human cognitive capacities are sufficiently idiosyncratic to license talk of a human*like* mind.

Cognitive psychology is replete with methods for analyzing the properties of cognitive capacities, for example, dissociation experiments, reaction time experiments (see Dawson 1998), and we can rely on the research of cognitive psychologists to develop a portrait of the typical human mind. So, for instance, we know from Miller's (1956) work that a human being has a short-term memory with a capacity of roughly seven items. Likewise, Sternberg's (1969) classic reaction time experiments reveal that human beings search through items in their short-term memory store in a serial rather than parallel manner. The range of colors the typical human being is able to see as well as the range of grammars she is able to parse are other facts that contribute to a distinctively human psychological profile. These are facts about human psychology—about human minds—that, were we ever to come across organisms that resembled us otherwise, might serve as a mental fingerprint, allowing us to distinguish human minds from their minds.

I have said nothing so far about the states of mind that have perhaps received most notice in contemporary philosophy of mind. These are the folk psychological states, that is, beliefs, desires, and other propositional attitudes. Their absence in my discussion of MRT reflects my belief that an evaluation of MRT must take place within the context of our best-developed psychological theories. If the current state of knowledge about a given mental capacity contains little or no information about how it might be realized, then it seems hardly worth discussing the possibility of its multiple realizability. To date, there is simply not enough known about how propositional attitudes might be realized. Indeed, a number of prominent philosophers believe that the folk psychological states attributed to a subject do not correspond in any interesting way to structures in the subject's brain (Churchland 1981; Dennett 1981, 1991; Stich 1983). The situation with phenomenal aspects of the mental, such as feelings, sensations, and conscious awareness, is perhaps a little better (see Clark 1993), but still nowhere near the stage that would permit a meaningful discussion of whether they are multiply realizable. On the other hand, quite a bit is known about the more peripheral mental capacities, such as those involved in perception. And there is also work on more centrally cognitive capacities, like attention, that is sufficiently detailed to allow some speculation as to the possibility of their multiple realization. In sum, my focus will be on those aspects of the mind about which enough is known to venture some educated guesses about the plausibility of MRT. As we learn more about the mind these guesses will fare better or worse, and we might find that MRT is more probably true of some mental capacities than others. These are the risks one takes when removing MRT from the confines of purely philosophical discussion and placing it within a more empirically informed arena.

Just as human psychology has unique features, so too does the human nervous system. Comparative neurophysiology shows us how our nervous systems differ from the nervous systems of our nearest phylogenetic relatives. Human brains are three times larger and display greater sulcal complexity (i.e., folding) than would be predicted from the curve on which the brains of other simians fall (Martin 1990, p. 401). Among many of its distinctive features, some of which it shares with the brains of other simians, the human brain has a large cerebral cortex that is divided into two hemispheres. The human brain also contains a variety of topographic maps that represent visual, auditory, and somatosensory information. The neurons of the brain transmit information through both electrical and chemical synapses. Furthermore, neuronal axons are heavily insulated with a substance called myelin that allows signals to proceed down the length of the axon at a much faster speed than they would otherwise. The brain also seems to be modular in construction, with different areas of the brain specialized for particular tasks, for example, Broca's area for language production and the visual cortex for the production and interpretation of visual experience. There is also a characteristic amount of connectivity between neurons in the human brain, and, of course, human brains have a typical mass.

Finally, when I speak of human bodies I will usually have in mind facts about our gross morphology. Human beings walk upright on two legs, have two forward-facing eyes in their heads, and are bilaterally symmetrical. Our ears are on the sides of our heads, and we have five fingers on each hand. I mention this conception of body now, but it is not until chapters 6 and 7 that I will turn more directly to a discussion of body and mind, as distinct from brain and mind.

3.2 Refining the Thesis

The thesis I wish to explore is this: from facts about our psychology, it is possible to infer facts about the nervous system in which it is realized.

Knowledge about our psychology, that is, makes it possible to predict facts about our nervous system. This thesis competes with MRT, for if MRT is true then knowledge of our psychology tells us little or nothing about our brain. As I mentioned in chapter 1, I will understand MRT as claiming something between the weak and SETI versions of MRT that Polger (2002) describes. That is, advocates of MRT believe that the human mind can be realized in many significantly different ways. Accordingly, facts about mental properties should provide little or no information about the nervous system that realizes them. Indeed, it is for this reason that some philosophers and psychologists have denied the importance of neuroscience for psychology, arguing that neuroscience can shed no light on psychological generalizations. Fodor and Pylyshyn, for instance, claim that "all properties associated with the particular realization of the algorithm that the theorist happens to use in a particular case, is irrelevant to the psychological theory" (p. 345, 1988). This view stands opposed to MRT's competitor, the mental constraint thesis, which states that the properties of the mind predict facts about the properties of the nervous system that realizes it.

One way to make the competing claims of MRT and MCT apparent is with the aid of the concept of a morphospace. I must stress at the outset that I intend this way of illustrating the different predictions of MRT and MCT as purely heuristic. Morphospaces are a mathematical construct—a hyperspace—and it is not evident that all the various nuances of MRT and MCT can be captured within this kind of construct. Nevertheless, I believe the morphospace explication of MRT and MCT lends the disagreement between these two hypotheses a concreteness the benefits of which override concerns about the accuracy of the model.

A morphospace is simply an abstract space defined by various parameters representing the different dimensions that properties of some body type might take.[1] So, for instance, it is possible to build a morphospace that represents the different forms a cephalopod body can take given variation in the dimensions of its morphological properties. One begins with a basic cephalopod body plan and, by varying values of parameters in this plan, derives the shapes of all actual cephalopods (including those of squid, octopus, nautilus, snail, oyster, etc.). Also in this space

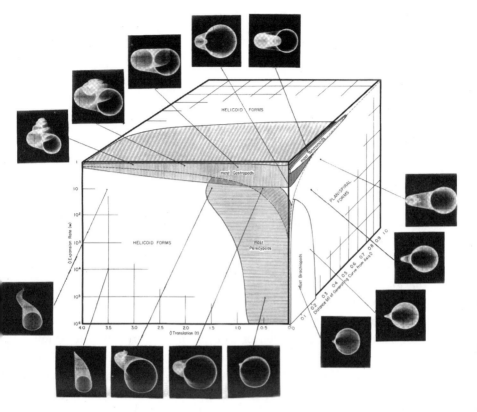

Figure 3.1
A three-dimensional space showing all possible shell forms. Outlined regions show the majority of species in four taxonomic groups. From Raup (1966).

will be the shapes of actual cephalopods that no longer exist and possible cephalopods that may eventually exist. Some of the cephalopod bodies represented in this space will never be actual, but are shapes that molluscs might have given the right evolutionary twists and turns (Conway Morris 1998).

Similarly, one could develop a morphospace limited to gastropod shells. By assuming that gastropod shells vary in four parameters,[2] Raup (1962, 1966) was able to simulate on a computer all physically possible gastropod shells. He found that almost all of the possible shell shapes have been actualized: most of the territory in gastropod shell morphospace has been filled (see figure 3.1).

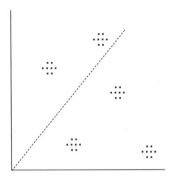

Figure 3.2
Dots represent brains in MRT space that realize humanlike minds. Dots will appear in clusters, with large distances between clusters.

For present purposes, imagine a vast multidimensional morphospace that includes all physically possible brains, where these brains realize a wide variety of different kinds of minds. Depending on our interests, we might conceive of this space as ranging over those brains that can possibly exist anywhere in the universe or just in some areas within the universe. I noted in chapter 1 that my interest would be mainly confined to an evaluation of *terrestrial* MRT, which means that we should conceive of the brain morphospace as consisting of all brains that might evolve on Earth. Surely the vast majority of the brains in this morphospace will never be actual. However, we can ask of the many points in this morphospace, which, or how many, can realize a humanlike mind, that is, a characteristically humanlike psychology. Figure 3.2 illustrates the answer that an advocate of MRT might give.

Here I have shown only the points that represent brains equipped to realize a humanlike mind. The points are clustered because, presumably, if a brain of a given type is a realization of a humanlike mind, then a brain very similar to it will also be able to realize a humanlike mind. Yet, significantly, there are clouds of points at great distances from each other.[3] This is as MRT predicts, for it illustrates the claim that very different kinds of brains can realize a humanlike mind. The further apart in morphospace two points are, the greater their variation in the dimensions that define the space. MRT can take on more or less extreme forms, with its extremeness increasing in direct proportion to the amount of

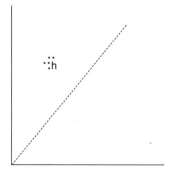

Figure 3.3
Dots represent brains in MCT space that realize humanlike minds. Dots will appear tightly packed around *h*, which represents the human brain.

territory in morphospace it allots to possible realizations of humanlike minds. In contrast, the mental constraint thesis would predict a morphospace as shown in figure 3.3. The point labeled "h" represents the human brain. In an extreme form, MCT would predict that h is the only physically possible realization of a humanlike mind. In a more liberal version, MCT would permit a cluster of points around h. As more territory in morphospace is filled with realizations of humanlike minds, the likelihood of MCT decreases.

The morphospace representations of MRT and MCT illustrate the idea that MRT and MCT are not precise doctrines. Rather, they mark regions on different ends of a continuum. Supporters of MRT think that the brain morphospace will have lots of clumps corresponding to realizers of humanlike minds. Alternatively, supporters of MCT think that there will be few such clumps.

The argument of the previous chapter bears on how one interprets distance in a morphospace. How much distance, if any, ought there to be between two brains that appear structurally identical (e.g., they consist in neurons connected in roughly the same ways) but that are composed of different kinds of material? Obviously, this depends on whether one takes material composition to be a dimension in morphospace. In practice, the morphospaces biologists construct do not typically take material composition to be a parameter of some morphotype. Raup's parameters, for instance, involve topological features of shells. This focus on the shape of shells rather than the material composition of shells makes sense if one's interest is in whether shell shape has evolved by natural selection. Indeed, an interest in morphology is often an interest in how body structure rather than body composition adapts an organism to its environment. For instance, the shapes of dolphins and sharks may be equally adaptive despite the fact that one is built of bone and the other of cartilage. For this reason, composition tends not to be a dimension in morphospace.

The dimensions in the brain morphospaces above will represent whatever properties end up being R-properties—properties by which different realizations of a mind qualify as significantly different. As I argued in the previous chapter, R-properties should be identified with those that a task analysis reveals to be making a causal contribution to the production of mental capacities. So, as in the case of the morphospace Raup describes, it is quite possible that material composition is not a dimension in the brain morphospaces above. More likely candidates for the dimensions of this space will be things like number of neurons, extent of connectivity between neurons, density of neurons, and so on. As I will discuss in the next chapter, these properties seem to be reasonable candidates for the R-properties that would distinguish one kind of realization of the mind from another.

3.3   The Argument

I hope it is immediately clear that it is an empirical question whether the brain morphospace fits the predictions of MRT better than it fits the predictions of MCT. However, this does not mean that the only way to answer the question is to find actualizations of each brain type in the morphospace and then examine the psychological properties each such brain realizes. That would, to be sure, settle the matter, but the impossibility of taking this route is obvious. Fortunately, the question of whether the properties of humanlike minds predict the nature of their realizers is an instance of a more general, and more explicitly tractable, question. The more general question concerns the relationship between structure and function. Given some function, we can ask what kind of structures are needed for the performance of the function. Given the capacity to see, for instance, one might ask about the variety of kinds of structures that are capable of seeing. Similarly, one might ask what kinds of structures enable flight, or respiration, or buoyancy, or photosynthesis, and so on. The question of interest concerns the kinds of structures that enable humanlike psychological abilities. MRT implies that these structures will vary considerably, and MCT entails the opposite. In the terms of the previous section, MRT predicts that these structures will be spread widely across the brain morphospace, and MCT predicts that they will be tightly clustered.

In answering questions about the relation between structure and function, one examines why, given some function, the structure that performs the function has one kind of organization rather than another (see Dretske 1988 for related claims about structuring causes). For instance, given that the function of some object is to see (or, more specifically, to form images), one can ask why the object contains a lens rather than not; or why it contains a spherical lens rather than a flat lens. What is it about the capacity to see that makes it true that most things that see have a lens? Why is it that organisms able to walk on the surface of water have less than a particular ratio of surface area to mass?

As shall soon become clear, it is the presence of constraints that makes it possible to predict structure from function. Nature sees to it that not just anything goes. Depending on the resources available and the laws that describe their behavior under certain conditions, there may be many, few, one, or no ways to implement some functional capacity. Whether there are many or few ways to skin a cat is clearly an empirical question (and one I do not care to explore in detail). But so too is the question of whether there are many or few ways to build a mind. In the next chapter I present some constraints that, it seems to me, suggest that realizations of humanlike minds might well share many common properties. For now, however, it is important to delve deeper into the mental constraint thesis, with special attention to the concept of constraint that features so prominently in its articulation.

3.4   Constraints

I have recommended that we understand MRT to be an empirical thesis about the nomological possibility of realizing the human mind in a non-humanlike brain and nervous system. I noted in chapter 1 that a reason for doing so is that, as a claim about logical possibility, MRT is not very interesting. There's no logical contradiction in supposing that human minds might be realized in nonhuman brains—science fiction establishes this much. Nor, however, is there any logical contradiction in supposing that organisms evolve in Lamarkian fashion, endowing their offspring with traits they acquired during their lifetimes; or that the pressure of a gas is inversely proportional to its temperature; or that water freezes at 33°F rather than 32°F (at sea level). The point is that the logical possibility of MRT, like the logical possibility of these other cases, holds little significance for what is true about the actual world (about actual minds, actual evolution, actual gases, actual compounds, etc.). For this reason, I have chosen to focus on whether minds are *actually* multiply realizable—whether it is really nomologically possible that there is more than one way to build a humanlike mind.

Surely the question of nomological possibility is the one that matters more to researchers in psychology, artificial intelligence, robotics, and so on. The assurance that there is no logical contradiction in supposing the existence of differently realized minds lends little or nothing to our understanding of the human mind. Knowledge that there are, or are not, *in physical fact* different ways of building a mind, on the other hand, is potentially quite important. Such knowledge would contribute to our understanding of how the brain is able to realize the mind; whether, and if so how, computers might realize minds; how variance in psychological abilities reflects differences in the properties of the brain; how viable the possibility of mind–brain reduction is, and so on.

Once we accept that MRT is about physical possibility, and that the route to its justification thus depends on an examination of empirical evidence, the burden to show that it is true becomes much more substantial. It is not at all obvious that humanlike minds can be built in numerous different ways. This concession by itself calls into question the use of thought experiments involving Martians, robots, the nation of

China, and silicon brains in an effort to make MRT compelling. These thought experiments establish only that MRT is a logical possibility, in the sense that it does not entail any logical contradiction. However, the thought experiments go no distance toward showing that there are, in fact, multiple ways of realizing a humanlike mind. So, once we construe MRT in a way that has significance for research about the mind, we must set aside the standard gestures that philosophers have made in its defense. Construing MRT as an empirical thesis rather than a logical one makes it a stronger claim and thus more difficult to confirm.

In considering whether MRT is true it also pays to partition its domain into natural minds and artificial minds. I mentioned this point in chapter 1, but its motivation should be clearer at this stage. The distinction I am making here is nothing more than the intuitive one between, on the one hand, minds belonging to creatures that, presumably, have evolved as a result of natural, unguided, events and, on the other hand, robots, computers, androids, and so on, that have been designed by an intentional agent. It may be that MRT is less likely to be true of natural minds than it is of artificial minds. Perhaps, that is, any natural organism with a mind like ours will also, probably, have a brain and nervous system like ours, but, in contrast, artificial minds might nevertheless display a genuine variety in morphological and neurological structure. Natural minds, because they are the result of an evolutionary process, are bound to display whatever properties are general to evolved systems. In particular, they will show the effects of constraints that impose themselves on any evolved system. Constraints are pervasive in evolution, and their presence makes it folly to portray MRT as equally plausible for natural and artificial minds.

Constraints are typically construed as limits on phenotypic variation (see, e.g., Arnold 1992; Maynard Smith et al. 1985). Not any conceivable phenotype can evolve, despite whatever fitness advantages the conceivable phenotypes might enjoy, and *constraint* is the term evolutionary biologists use to label the forces or causes that prevent some conceivable phenotypes from becoming actual. Biologists have explored extensively two types of constraints on phenotypic variability. First are those that are often labeled *universal constraints* (Maynard Smith et al. 1985); second are *historical constraints* (Gould 1989b). The distinction between these two kinds of constraint corresponds to a distinction I drew in chapter 1 between nomological and circumstantial (or historical) possibility. Universal constraints limit phenotypic variation to that which is consistent with the laws of nature. No bird will ever fly faster than the speed of light; nor will a duck with the density of lead ever be able to float. Historical constraints on phenotypic variation are those that exist as a result of features an organism has already acquired in its evolutionary history. The properties an organism has evolved in the past constrain the properties it can evolve in the future. Because historical constraints are present as a consequence of particular evolutionary histories, they tend to be taxon-specific in a way that universal constraints are not.

Maynard Smith et al. (1985) provide some examples of historical constraints. Palm trees do not branch because of the unique evolutionary history of monocotyledons. Because monocotyledons failed to evolve secondary thickening, they are unable to branch (Maynard Smith et al. 1985). Clearly, it is not nomologically impossible for trees to branch— but, given the circumstances of monocotyledons, it is impossible for them to branch. Similarly, Gould (1989b) observes that it would be very difficult, that is, involve a great number of changes, for an elephant to evolve flight because the elephant's evolutionary history "included size increase with a vengeance" (p. 517). Whereas it is not physically impossible that organisms fly, it is physically impossible for elephants, as they presently exist, to fly. Just as historical contingencies have deprived palm trees of the capacity to branch, so also have historical contingencies resulted in elephants too massive to fly.

In contrast to historical constraints that limit phenotypic variability as a result of the contingencies of evolution, universal constraints limit phenotypic variability in virtue of the physical laws that phenotypic traits, *qua* physical objects or events, must respect. As an example of a universal constraint, consider the relationship between an organism's surface area and its volume (Haldane 1928; Martin 1990). For every unit of increase in the length of an organism, the organism's surface area will expand by the square of the unit increase while its volume will increase by a power of three. This means that as organisms grow, their volume increases more rapidly than their surface area. Doubling the length of an organism, for instance, will increase its surface area fourfold while increasing its volume eightfold. As Steven Vogel colorfully puts it, "being big means having lots of inside relative to your outside; being small means having lots of outside relative to your inside" (1998, p. 42). The consequences of this nonlinear relationship between surface area and volume for phenotypic variability cannot be underestimated. It explains why small organisms are at greater risk of dehydration than larger organisms (their bigger outsides relative to their insides make them more susceptible to water loss), why big organisms can expend relatively less energy in maintaining body temperature (their smaller outsides relative to their insides reduce their heat loss), why bigger organisms have a slower metabolism than smaller organisms, why the leg bones of large animals have to be thicker in proportion to their size than the leg bones of smaller animals, and on and on.

Admittedly, this distinction between universal and historical constraints might sometimes be hard to draw. Consider the fact that respiration by diffusion is limited by body size. The small size of insects permits them to respire through the simple diffusion of oxygen and carbon dioxide through out small tubes, *tracheae*, in their bodies (Futuyma 1998, p. 526; Schmidt-Nielsen 1990). Respiration via diffusion is successful only in organisms as small as insects because, as a matter of physical law, diffusion time increases with the square of diffusion distance. Were an organism the size of a human being to respire by diffusion, it would take approximately three years for oxygen to travel from its lungs to its extremities (Schmidt-Nielsen 1990, p. 571). It is tempting to claim that it is nomologically impossible for organisms much larger than insects to respire by diffusion. However, perhaps with the "right" kind of respiratory system, diffusion could serve an important respiratory function in organisms as large as a human being. I wouldn't bet on it, but nor would I want to claim that its nomological impossibility is absolutely certain.

As I said in chapter 1, my main focus is the plausibility of *terrestrial* MRT, that is, the thesis that on Earth many significantly distinct realizers of a humanlike mind are possible. Obviously, the initial conditions present on Earth will place constraints on evolved organisms that are unique to these conditions. For instance, there are facts about the density and salinity of water, the mixture of gases in the atmosphere, the range of temperatures on land and sea, the force of gravity, and so on to which any evolved system on Earth must accommodate itself. Similarly, the initial conditions on Earth no doubt place historical constraints on the kinds of things that can realize a humanlike mind. Quite possibly, there are other planets in the universe on which there exist organisms with humanlike minds that are realized in ways that would be impossible here on Earth. Knowing nothing about conditions on other planets, however, it is hardly sensible to defend or criticize MRT on their basis. Thus, when talking about historical constraints on multiple realization, I shall have in mind historical constraints on terrestrial systems. On the other hand, there will be some occasions when evidence suggests some universal constraints on the realization of humanlike minds. These, by definition, would apply to systems anywhere.

Having drawn the distinction between historical and universal constraints and offered the reminder that I shall be focusing on terrestrial MRT, I can now say more precisely how I plan to use these ideas. Evolutionary biologists look to constraints to explain why an organism O displays the phenotype that it does. I, on the other hand, am interested in the question "Given that O has a capacity to do C, what other traits must it possess?" Whereas evolutionary biologists rely on constraints to tell a story about why something came to be the way that it is, my focus will be on what must have happened to make things the way that they are. So, one can see constraints as forward looking—as forces that fix how things will be. Alternatively, as I wish to do, one can use constraints to look backward—to explain what must have happened for things to be as they are now. Given that organisms can C, what had to have taken place to allow them to C? In effect, I shall be using constraints to inform a task analysis of a particular C, namely, a human mind.

As we shall see, universal and historical constraints often build on one another, magnifying and exacerbating the structural limitations that impose themselves on evolved systems. In schematic terms, imagine the evolution of a system that has the capacity to Y. Perhaps, as a matter of physical law, any system that is capable of Y-ing must have component R. Systems that Y are universally constrained to include within their workings component R, for without R no system could Y. Now suppose that a system that can *Y* in virtue of containing *R* must also include either of *S* or *T*, but not both. *R* by itself is not capable of bringing about *Y*, but when *R* interacts with either *S* or *T*, as well as some other pieces, the system of which it is a part can *Y*. However, whether *R* interacts with *S* or whether it interacts with *T* makes a difference to what other pieces the system will include. The system is not universally constrained to include *S*, nor is it universally constrained to include *T*, but it is universally constrained to include one or the other, and which it does in fact include will constrain "choices" among other components of the system. So, for instance, a system with *R* and *S*, in order to perform *Y*, must, perhaps, include piece *M* but not *N*, whereas a system with *R* and *T*, in order to perform *Y*, must include *N* but not *M*. The need for *M* is the consequence of a historical constraint given that the system already has *S*; likewise, mutatis mutandis, would be the need for *N*. The presence of *M* is mandated by physical law together with the historical contingencies that resulted in the system's having piece *S*.

Before tying this discussion of constraints more explicitly to MRT, it is worth returning for a moment to my claim that it is best to partition natural minds from artificial minds when evaluating MRT. I believe the presence of universal and historical constraints makes clear the utility of doing so. Whereas both natural and artificial minds are subject to both sorts of constraints, the *source* of the historical constraints that face artificial minds is often quite unlike the source of those that present themselves to natural minds. Evolved organisms tend to face constraints that an engineer need never concern herself with (Vogel 1998). Evolved creatures tend to be small in their infancy and bigger as adults. This fact requires that evolution build into its products expensive developmental equipment that, as Vogel puts it, "in effect, must transmute a motorcycle into an automobile while providing continuous transportation" (1998, p. 23). In contrast, an engineer with the task of designing an automobile is not required to design a small automobile that is capable of growing into a full-sized automobile—she simply builds the automobile to the desired size. Moreover, evolved creatures reproduce. It is costly to operate and maintain reproductive equipment, and whereas an engineer might easily design an automobile, she would no doubt have a hard time designing an automobile that could create other automobiles.[4] Finally, natural selection tends to be conservative in ways that engineers needn't be. All mammals have vertebral columns whether they run on four feet, two feet, fly through the air, or swim. It is likely that vertebral columns are not the best choice, from an engineer's perspective, for all these modes of transport. However, such conservatism is common in evolved systems. Often the evolution of a better design can occur only through an initial decrease in fitness. In such a case, selection works against optimization.[5] However, an engineered device need not get worse before getting better; it does not face the problem of having to survive while changing from some initial state to a more optimal state.

For all these reasons, the constraints that impose themselves on artificial minds may differ quite a bit from those that limit natural minds. Whereas, in the example above, it is a matter of historical whim whether a system that *Y*s contains *S* or *T*, and hence *M* or *N*, a deliberating designer might see virtues in building the system so that it incorporates *S* rather than *T*, and so *M* rather than *N*. Perhaps *S*s and *M*s are cheaper than *T*s and *N*s, or perhaps systems that include *S*s run more reliably or efficiently than systems with *T*s. In any event, deliberating designers can avail themselves of both a foresight and a hindsight to which natural selection has no access and thereby make the best of whatever constraints force themselves on a given engineering task. This does not mean that artificial minds are irrelevant to MRT. It means just that the methods I have been developing to evaluate MRT would require modification if the possibility of artificial minds were included within the scope of my study.

3.5   Constraints and the Multiple Realizability Thesis

As I suggested earlier, a useful way to think about whether MRT is true is to treat it as an instance of a more general thesis about the relation between structure and function. Is it possible from the description of some functional property to predict the properties of the structure that realizes it? As I mentioned in the preface, the answer to this question appears to be "no" when contemplating functional devices like mousetraps. If one were to ask a bunch of clever fifth graders to design a mousetrap, chances are that there will be as many distinct designs as there are students. However, suppose there were a large number of historical and universal constraints limiting the kinds of things that could successfully capture mice. In such a case, one's chances of predicting what the fifth graders would devise increases significantly. Not just any structure can successfully execute a particular capacity. Opaque materials make poor lenses, it's impossible to grasp a pencil with a fin, and just try to fly without wings. Likewise, given a lens with a certain focal length, the size of the eye has to be adjusted accordingly or else nothing will appear in focus; fingers are little use without a nervous system capable of coordinating their activity; and wings can't flap without the proper musculature. The performance of a function requires special equipment, and this special equipment can contribute to the successful completion of a function only given the existence of other equipment with which it can interact appropriately. Not just anything can see, or grasp, or fly, and this is because there are constraints that any functional design must heed.

In the chapter that follows I propose to scrutinize MRT from the perspective of an engineer. Imagine that we have been given the task of designing a humanlike mind. Given that what we are designing must, in the end, have the characteristics of a human mind, we must consider how universal and historical constraints force on us the adoption of various materials, architectures, structures, and so on, that limit the kinds of designs that will actually produce a mind. Given what our minds do, there must be some universal and historical constraints on the kinds of things that are able to realize minds. I shall be interested in the following chapter to isolate some of these constraints in order to say something about restrictions on MRT.

Before turning to some examples that will make the above discussion of constraints more concrete, it is worth pausing to remark on how the argument of chapter 2 merges with this discussion. Suppose one wished to design a kite. The function of a kite demands a design that permits flight, and so, obviously, such a design must respect those physical laws that make flight possible. These physical laws presumably dictate that the kite be made of some kinds of material but not others. Lead would be a poor choice in materials from which to build a kite, but paper, Mylar, and nylon might all be good choices. Suppose further that a single kite design would be served equally well by paper or nylon. That is, a single kite design could be realized in paper or nylon. By the argument of the previous chapter, the fact that one kite might be made of paper and another of nylon does not license the claim that these kites are multiple realizations of a single kind. The R-property of paper and nylon in virtue of which they both are able to realize kites is, it seems, identical despite the fact that paper and nylon are different physical substances. Just as it is being rigid that matters to a corkscrew's ability to remove a cork, which undermines the claim that differences in composition suffice for differences in realization, so does having a large ratio of surface area to mass make all the difference in whether a given substance will be able to realize a kite. Because it is this ratio that is relevant, and not the molecular composition of the substance realizing the ratio, differences in the material composition of a kite do not suffice to make significantly different realizations of a kite.

When one appreciates this point about how to judge differences in realization, and recognizes as well that a design for a mind must confront various constraints, the challenge to MRT becomes more apparent. How many ways can there be to build something that functions as a mind? Once we take into account the universal and historical constraints that limit variability in the realizations of mind, and acknowledge that mere differences in composition do not always constitute significant differences in realization, the class of things that can realize minds will, I suspect, be much smaller than philosophers have typically assumed.

3.6   Some Examples of Constraints on Evolved Systems

So far my discussion of constraints has been either simplistic or schematic. In this section I would like to delve deeper into the role of constraints in the evolution of systems with complex functions. In general, the more complex a system, the more constraints it will face. This is intuitive: more complex systems are those with more kinds of parts, and the more kinds of parts there are in a system the fewer degrees of freedom available for successful interaction of the parts. We saw this in the schematic example above. There may be some part R that any system capable of doing Y must have. Moreover, given that a system capable of Y has some part S, it may be that it must then also have some other kind of part *M* if it is to do *Y*. In this way, a system with many kinds of parts is more likely to face universal and historical constraints, or more likely to face greater numbers of such constraints, than a system with fewer kinds of parts. More intricate systems bring constraints on themselves. This shall become clear below.

The examples I will examine begin with a description of some capacity and then proceed to describe the various constraints that confront any system that has this capacity. I hope to make plausible that, in the context of these examples, multiple realizability of certain functional capacities is a less likely hypothesis than one that asserts that, because of the presence of constraints, these functional capacities will share many of their realizing properties. Of course, I shall be availing myself of the argument in the preceding chapter and the understanding of how to judge cases of multiple realizations that it entails.

3.6.1 Mammalian Homeostasis

Mammals, more so than any other form of life we know, are capable of maintaining a stable internal environment in the face of extreme fluctuations in the external environment.[6] It is in virtue of this tremendous capacity for homeostasis that mammals are able to thrive in many distinct geographical regions and remain active throughout diurnal and seasonal changes. But homeostasis is beneficial for a more important reason. Homeostasis makes possible a level of chemical complexity that, in turn, endows homeostatic organisms with a greater range of capacities than they would otherwise be able to have. Without homeostasis the precise regulation of chemical reactions that is necessary for certain kinds of biological complexity would be absent. Outside an environment with a constant temperature and a fixed concentration of ions, the pace of enzymatic activity would·be variable, making impossible the exact regulation of chemical reactions necessary to support biological complexity. It is this astounding capacity for homeostasis that I wish to conditionalize on, asking what properties must be present in anything that realizes such a capacity.

There are three main challenges that the environment presents to the internal stability of terrestrial organisms. First, the temperature of the environment changes as day fades into night and night gives way to day;

and as summer turns to fall, fall to winter, winter to spring, and so back to summer. Biological complexity as sophisticated as the mammal's requires that the organism somehow compensate for these changes in temperature so that it remains below the external temperature during hot periods and above the external temperature during cool periods. Second, osmosis sees to it that water will move from more dilute solutions to less dilute solutions. Because the terrestrial environment is always less dilute than the inside of a organism, the environment will do its best to pull water from an organism, drying it out and altering its concentration of ions. The enzymatic regulation of chemical reactions that maintain biological organization requires that somehow osmosis be impeded. Finally, gravity is inescapable and will do its best to flatten an organism to the Earth's surface. Because air does not by itself provide an organism with buoyancy, the organism must find its own way to resist gravity's pull.

The solution to any one of these problems—temperature regulation, chemical regulation, and spatial control—forces adjustment in the solutions to the other two. Consider first temperature regulation. Mammals rely on many mechanisms to sustain a single internal temperature. They are endothermic, meaning that they produce heat internally from a high cellular metabolic rate. Body hair serves as insulation, allowing mammals to retain this heat. By varying blood flow to blood vessels on the surface of their bodies, shivering when below the external temperature and perspiring when above it, mammals are able to balance heat production with heat loss and maintain a fixed temperature. However, endothermy has a high energy cost and thus demands that a mammal consume about ten times more food than a reptile of equal mass would require. This constrains the solution to the problem of spatial control, demanding the construction of a sophisticated locomotory apparatus that will allow the organism to move quickly and for lengthy durations so that it might hunt effectively. Of course, increased locomotory activity warms the body and thus burdens the mammal's temperature regulatory system. It also causes the organism to breathe more quickly, which aggravates water loss and so poses additional difficulties for the solution to the problem of chemical regulation.

But the solution to the problem of temperature regulation constrains the solution to the problem of chemical regulation in another way, for the production of perspiration only exacerbates the environment's osmotic pull, which promises to upset the balance of water and ions in the body. Certainly, an impermeable skin would prevent water loss, but it would at the same time prevent evaporative cooling. Another quick fix to the problem of dehydration would be to increase body size, for, as I mentioned earlier, surface area and volume are allometrically related. As the size of an organism increases, the ratio of its surface area to its volume decreases, and thus the organism becomes less vulnerable to dehydration. However, bigger organisms feel the force of gravity more so than do smaller organisms, and so locomotion becomes more costly for bigger organisms, which in turn has ramifications for energy consumption and thus for temperature regulation. The mammal meets the challenge of chemical regulation with a highly specialized kidney, which, in virtue of long loops of Henle, is able to conserve water through production of an extremely concentrated urine (Schmidt-Nielsen 1990, p. 372). By saving water in this way, the kidney makes it possible for the mammal to excrete some fluids, which in turn allows it to perspire when necessary and also to rid itself of ions that would otherwise produce a chemical imbalance.

Any organism that is to solve the problems of temperature, chemical, and spatial control with the precision to which mammals have solved it will in the end require a vast network of interrelated mechanisms. For instance, I mentioned that endothermic organisms require great quantities of energy, which in turn requires that they have a locomotory system that will make them successful hunters. A locomotory system of the sort necessary to meet the energy costs of endothermy requires muscles that must in turn be serviced by a circulatory system. Likewise, the kidney can produce a hypertonic urine only if the blood pressure in the renal artery is very high, which also places demands on the circulatory system. Greater locomotory ability also demands sophisticated sensory systems and, accordingly, a complex central nervous system to integrate sensory inputs and translate them into useful movement. Chemical regulation, in turn, demands the presence of an endocrine system that is able to detect the concentration of chemicals in the body and cause the kidney to secrete or reabsorb ions as necessary. Kemp (1982) summarizes the network of adaptations that are necessary to support homeostasis in mammals with the diagram shown here in figure 3.4.

The web of devices through which mammals maintain a stable internal environment, thus making possible greater biological complexity than is found in any nonmammalian organism, illustrates quite clearly the role of constraints in evolution. Kemp claims that the arrows in his diagram "indicate how each such structure or function depends on others for its existence" (1982, p. 312). Most generally, temperature regulation is not possible—not physically possible—without spatial control and chemical regulation. More specifically, temperature regulation in mammals is not possible without evaporative cooling, which is not possible without some sort of blood filter, which is not possible without a high metabolic rate, which requires sustained muscle action, which in turn requires improved locomotion.

As in the schematic example I discussed earlier, we see in the evolution of mammalian homeostasis a tangle of universal and historical constraints that sharply limit the number of different possible systems that can actually produce homeostasis to the degree that it appears in mammals. A system with the biological complexity of a mammal requires precisely coordinated chemical activity, which in turn requires a stable internal environment for the operation of enzymes, which in turn requires a constant temperature. Thus, biological complexity of the kind mammals exhibit requires temperature control—temperature control is a constraint on their biological complexity. Mammals regulate their temperature, as we have seen, through a host of mechanisms, but most prominent among them is endothermy. Moreover, the existence of endothermy is a historical constraint, inasmuch as it places limits on the future course of an organism's evolution. Endothermy is energetically costly, and so an endothermic organism will need some means by which to procure large quantities of energy. This has implications for the kinds of skeletal, musculature, and circulatory systems of the organism. Likewise, the fact that mammals employ evaporative cooling requires that they have some means of conserving water. Any biologically complex organism that can afford to squeeze moisture from itself must be able to

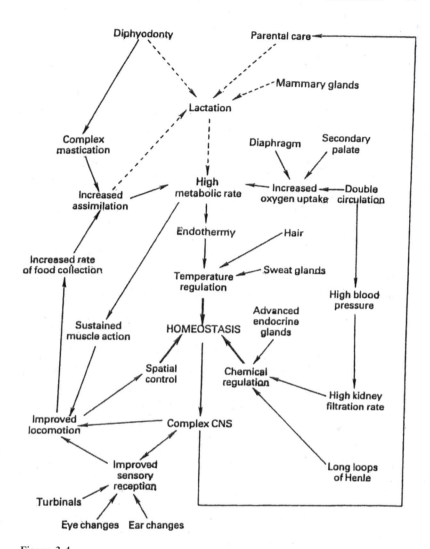

Figure 3.4
The structures and relations between them that realize mammalian homeostasis. Structures or processes at the tips of arrows depend on those things at the bases of the arrows. Dashed arrows apply in the case of juvenile mammals. From Kemp (1982).

balance its internal concentration of ions, and this requires that it evolve something like a kidney and an endocrine system, which together can monitor internal levels of ions and cause their secretion when in too much abundance or their reabsorption when they fall below a critical level.

Of course, the mammalian homeostatic system evolved over the course of millions of years, and, as Kemp notes, "[n]o single characteristic could evolve very far towards the mammalian condition unless it was accompanied by appropriate progression of all the other characteristics." Evolution of mammalian homeostasis must have been piecemeal, in fits and starts: "only a small advance in any one system could occur, after which that system would have to await the accumulation of small changes in all the other systems, before evolving a further step towards the mammalian condition" (1982, p. 313). However, one can imagine a bio-engineer charged with the task of building an organism with a mammalian-like homeostatic system. "We'll need some way of regulating temperature," the engineer explains to her team. "Endothermy will provide the best source of heat," says one expert on the team. "But that means lots of energy, which means we'll have to give the thing some means of collecting food," says another. "Sounds like it's going to be doing a lot of running around," the engineer remarks, "which means it'll overheat unless we give it some way to cool itself. How about evaporation?" "No good," says the expert in control of chemical regulation, "we can't afford the water, unless we figure out some way to concentrate the urine so that there's water to spare." A graduate student on the team pipes in, "What if we take a kidney and lengthen its loops of Henle[7]— I've been experimenting with just such a design and have a prototype ready to go...".

The team continues in this way, solving some problems but creating others until it settles into a "best fit" solution. Perhaps the solution will be identical to that which evolution discovered; perhaps it will differ radically. However, it seems clear that if the team decides initially to use endothermy as a source of heat then the historical constraints that endothermy imposes on the system will make the system more like the mammal's than it would be had the team decided on some other means of heat production. Given that a homeostatic system employs endothermy, the probability that it has other features, like a kidney with long loops of Henle, increases. But this means that the choice of an endothermic heating source *limits the multiple realizability* of a homeostatic system. Similarly, because there are numerous connections between the various components of the mammalian homeostatic system, we might just as well have conditionalized on the fact that the system has a kidney with long loops of Henle, predicting on this basis that it will also be endothermic. Whether it is possible to multiply realize a homeostatic system that exhibits the precision of the mammal's thus hinges on the extent to which any one of its more prominent parts is multiply realizable. If it is a universal constraint on systems that display a mammalian degree of homeostasis that they be endothermic, and if a homeostatic system that utilizes endothermy requires a kidney, then it is also a universal constraint on the system that it possess a kidney. My earlier schematic discussion of constraints illustrated a similar pattern of events.

However plausible this case for the limited realizability of mammalian homeostasis strikes one, I hope it serves as a vivid reminder of a point to which I have returned on several occasions—the possibility of multiple realizability rests on empirical considerations. This is clear from reflection on the tradeoffs between solutions for temperature, chemical, and spatial control. These tradeoffs arise as a result of the fact that terrestrial mammals are physical objects—semipermeable bags of chemicals—that exist in dry environments with varying temperatures but a constant gravitational field. Certainly there are no logical constraints on realizing mammalian homeostasis in numerous ways. Just as certainly there's not much of interest that follows from this fact. What is interesting—interesting for the purpose of understanding mammalian evolution, of understanding why mammals have greater biological complexity than reptiles, and so on—is how physical laws narrow the range of properties that any organism with the biological complexity of a mammal must have. To judge whether mammalian-like homeostasis is vastly, moderately, or hardly multiply realizable, one must become familiar with these physical laws and appreciate their implications for biological complexity.

3.6.2 Image-forming Eyes

As a second example of how universal and historical constraints impose a limit on the number of structures that can possibly produce some given capacity, consider image-forming eyes. The capacity of interest here is the capacity to produce a two-dimensional image from the light that objects in the environment reflect. We may conditionalize on this capacity, asking whether it will raise the probability that the structure achieving this capacity is of a particular form, or of some small number of forms. If one thinks that image-forming eyes are vastly multiply realizable, then one ought to believe that the fact that an eye can form an image carries little or no information about the structure of the eye. Clearly, one could predict that the structure is one that is capable of producing images, but belief in multiple realizability is belief that there are many different kinds of structures that can do this, and so from the fact that an image is being produced it is impossible to make predictions about the specific kind of structure that is involved. Similarly, you can predict that I possess a device that keeps time if, whenever queried, I can tell you the time. However, because time-keeping apparatuses are vastly multiply realizable—by gears and springs, quartz crystals, sand, water, shadows, geysers, and so on—my ability to tell you the time leaves you unable to predict the kind of structure I employ to keep you in the know.[8]

In thinking about designs for image-forming systems, we can suppose that our bioengineering team has been assigned the task of creating an image-forming eye. Some philosophically inclined newcomers to the team might suggest various logically possible image-forming systems, but this is unlikely to win them the respect of their more seasoned colleagues. "There's no logical contradiction in supposing that a *tree stump* can form an image," the chief engineer might impatiently reply. No—the thing to do is to learn something about optics and the nature of light, and only afterward does it make sense to consider what sorts of systems will do the required job. It could be that image-formation, like time-keeping, is an essentially unconstrained problem and thus open to myriad solutions. In fact, however, as vision experts recognize,

Eye design is fundamentally limited by the physical properties of light: it travels in straight lines, can be reflected, and varies in both wavelength (subjective hue or color) and intensity (subjective brightness). Many of the principles of design and even apparent errors we find in existing eyes reflect constraints arising directly from these physical properties of light. . . . Because of the physical laws governing the behavior of light, there are only a small number of ways to produce an eye with a usable image. (Fernald 1997, pp. 254–255)

Experts differ on what this small number of possible eye designs is, but the consensus puts the number between eight (Land 1991; Nilsson 1989) and eleven (Fernald 1997) (the higher number reflects the recent discovery of a kind of telephoto eye in a chameleon [Ott and Schaeffel 1995]). But on what are these numbers based? The science of optics recognizes various kinds of image-forming devices. Some will involve simple pinholes, others will have lenses or corneas that refract light, some will combine refraction with mirrors, some will project onto concave surfaces and others onto convex surfaces. These are differences that make a difference to optics, and thus they serve to categorize eyes into distinct optical kinds. Figure 3.5 displays eight of the basic types of eye; following that is a table describing each kind of eye and its distribution in the animal kingdom.

Note that the eyes in this diagram are categorized according to the optical principles by which they operate. There may be and in fact are molecular or cellular differences between eyes that, optically speaking, count as identical (Land and Fernald 1992). However, because the optical components and processes—lenses, mirrors, apertures, refraction, reflection—by which eyes are distinguished have similar R-properties across eyes, their differences in molecular composition are irrelevant to judgments of multiple realizability, thus making the number of distinct kinds of eyes small. Another way to put the point is this: it is optics that provides the level of description at which a clump of molecules constitutes an eye, and hence it is the science of optics that determines whether two eyes are instances of a single kind of realization or, rather, are instances of different realizations. Thus, it is a kind of category mistake to claim of two eyes that they constitute distinct types of realizations solely in virtue of molecular or cellular differences. Molecules and cells are simply not the components by which optics recognizes differences in eye designs. Relative to a task analysis of what makes one kind of eye distinct from another, molecular and cellular differences make no difference.

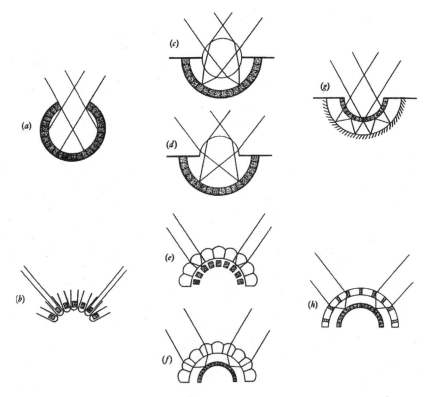

Distribution of the types of optical system shown in (a) to (h).

Type	Description	Distribution
(a)	Pigmented pit. No lens or mirror. Shadow provides some directionality. Precursor of (c), (d) and (g)	Most of the lower phyla: some coelenterates, platyhelminthes, protochordates, many annelids and molluscs. Pinhole eye in *Nautilus*
(b)	Multiple pigmented tubes. Precursor of the compound eyes (e), (f) and (h)	Sabellid tube-worms (Annelida). Probably early arthropods
(c)	Spherical lens eye	Fishes, cephalopod and some gastropod molluscs, alciopid annelids, copepod crustacean (*Labidocera*)
(d)	Corneal refraction	Terrestrial vertebrates. Most arachnids, some insect larvae, *Peripatus*, and myriapods
(e)	Apposition compound eye	Most diurnal insects and many diurnal and shallow-water crustacea. *Limulus*, trilobites, *Branchiomma* (Annelida) and *Arca* (Bivalvia)
(f)	Refracting superposition compound eye	Nocturnal insects (moths, lacewings, some beetles), some crustacea (mysids, euphausiids). Apposition version in butterflies
(g)	Simple mirror eye	*Pecten* (bivalve mollusc) and *Gigantocypris* (crustacean)
(h)	Reflecting superposition compound eye	Decapod crustacea only (shrimps, prawns, crayfish and lobsters)

Figure 3.5
Eight basic kinds of eye: (a) and (b) use shadowing; (c)–(f) use refraction; (g) and (h) use reflection. The table describes the distribution of these eyes in the animal kingdom. From Land (1991).

Some details about why there are so few possible eye designs will help to make this point clearer, I believe, and will also serve to reintroduce a concept that will play an important evidential role in my examination of MRT in the next chapter: *convergence.* There are several universal constraints on eyes that are the result of the properties light possesses. For instance, light has both wavelike and particle-like properties. Because light behaves as a wave, there is a lower limit on the size of the aperture through which it can pass before its interference with itself—a phenomenon known as diffraction—causes excessive blurring in the image it produces. In fact, the amount of blur in the image is inversely proportional to the diameter of the opening through which the light passes, and so the bigger the eye the sharper the image it can produce.[9] Indeed, it is for this reason that the compound eyes of arthropods (and a few others), which receive light through thousands of tiny tubelike *ommatidia*, can never achieve the sharpness of camera eyes. Kirschfeld (1976) calculated that a compound eye with the acuity of the human camera eye would require ommatidia so large in diameter that the eye would be one meter across.

So, bigger is better when it comes to eyes, and this explains why bigger animals tend to have better vision than smaller ones. But the particle nature of light places another kind of universal constraint on eyes. This constraint has perhaps less to do with an eye's ability to form an image than it does with an organism's ability to use the information contained in the image. The problem is this. The photoreceptors in the eye measure the intensity of the light by counting the number of light particles (photons) that hit them. More intense light will, on average, cause more hits. However, this is just an average. In fact, just as it is possible in principle to walk through a heavy rainstorm and never be hit by a drop of water, it is possible that the photons emitted by a very intense light never hit a photoreceptor.[10] On average, the heavier the rain the more likely you'll get wet, and on average the more intense the light the more likely a photoreceptor will capture photons. So, there is a statistical uncertainty associated with the photoreceptor's measure of light intensity. This uncertainty is known as photon noise, and its variance is equal to the square root of the sampled average. Hence, a photoreceptor that captures 100 photons in some unit of time will report a light intensity that can vary by as much as ten percent from the actual intensity of the light. Likewise, if the photoreceptor captures only 4 photons, it can be wrong about the intensity of the light by as much as 50 percent. This is significant, because contrasts in images stand out in virtue of differences in light intensity. These differences can be detected only when they are greater than the underlying photon noise (Nilsson 1989).

Photon noise thus places another universal constraint on eye design. For the image to be useful to the eye, the eye must somehow develop the means to boost its ability to capture photons. In fact, there are essentially three parameters that eye design can play with in order to maximize the number of photons it captures. First, the photoreceptors of some eyes will increase the time they wait before providing an average of the number of photons hitting them. Just as you are more likely to get wet the longer you stand in a rainstorm, photoreceptors that wait around a while before reporting the presence of photons are more likely to have something to report than those that are in a hurry. Another way to increase the chance of capturing a photon is to expand the receptor area. A big puddle is more likely to be hit by a raindrop than a small puddle. Likewise, wider receptors will be better at collecting photons than smaller. Finally, a third parameter that may be adjusted is the diameter of the light's entryway. The smaller the entry hole for the light, the fewer the number of photons that are likely to pass through it.

We can imagine the engineering team fiddling with these parameters. "Why not let the photoreceptors take a whole minute to collect photons, and make just a few large photoreceptive surfaces rather than a bunch of tiny ones, and expand the pupil as wide as it will go?" asks one naïve member of the team. In fact, all the solutions come with costs. For organisms that must respond quickly to fast changes in the world, a long photon-measuring period would be disastrous. Flying insects are in such a position and hence have a very brief measuring period. Nilsson, observing that a fly can respond to a flicker of more than 200 Hz (compared to a human who cannot notice flickers faster than 20 Hz) states that "a fly in a movie theater would see the 24 frames a second as if it were a slide show" (1989, p. 306).

Because its measuring periods are so brief, the fly must rely on large receptor areas to collect photons. But, the larger the receptors, the fewer of them that can be packed into a retina. Consequently, flies and other flying insects have poor visual resolution. Humans, because they have relatively big eyes through which lots of light can enter, can minimize the costs of the tradeoff between measuring period and resolution. Photon noise is inescapable—it's a consequence of the nature of light and thus places a universal constraint on the design of image-forming eyes. Unlike diffraction, which demands a single kind of solution—an aperture of sufficient diameter—photon noise can be minimized through several solutions: longer measuring periods, bigger receptors, wider aperture, or combinations of these. However, whichever solution our engineering team decides on will place historical constraints on other features of the eye. Suppose, for instance, that the engineering team decides to minimize the effects of photon noise by increasing the size of the photoreceptors. Receptor size is inversely proportional to resolution. Thus, this constrains the kind of nervous system the team must develop for processing visual information. It would be senseless to devise a nervous system capable of resolving fine visual details if the receptors are themselves oblivious to such details. Similarly, if the team decides to make the best of photon noise by widening the aperture of the eye, it will be forced to deal with the consequences of a larger eye. Bigger eyes are costly, both in terms of the energy they require and in terms of the nervous system necessary to process the greater amounts of information they collect (Nilsson 1989). In short, the universal constraint that photon noise imposes on eye design, combined with the historical constraints entailed by various solutions to photon noise, places fundamental limits on the properties that image-forming eyes will exhibit.

There is one further constraint on eye design that repays examination. It is in considering this final case that the concept of convergence comes to the fore. Let's limit the class of image-forming eyes to aquatic camera eyes. Aquatic camera eyes and terrestrial camera eyes differ slightly because the refractive index—a measure of how much some medium bends light—of water is much higher than that of air. When entering an eye from air, light needs to be bent much more to be focused than it does when entering the eye from water. Thus, terrestrial eyes focus light with both a cornea, which is responsible for two-thirds of the focusing power of the eye, and a lens. Aquatic eyes, in contrast, use just a lens for focusing light. There is also a difference in the shape of aquatic and terrestrial lenses. Aquatic eyes use a spherical lens, which focuses light on every point of the retina, whereas terrestrial eyes use a convex lens, which focuses light on just the central region of the retina.

There are two puzzles spherical lenses present. First, all spherical lenses suffer from spherical aberration: the tendency to overfocus peripheral rays so that not all portions of the image are focused on a single plane. Barring correction of spherical aberration, the resulting retinal image would be too blurry to be useful. Second, all the spherical lenses found in nature have a focal length of 2.5 radii. This means that, measured from the center of the lens, the focused image is behind the lens by a distance of 2.5 times its radius. This is puzzling because such a short focal length would require that the lens have a refractive index of about 1.66, which "is not attainable using normal biological materials like proteins" (Land 1991, p. 121). So, to put the question in the terms we have been using, what kind of lens structure ought we to predict from the facts that aquatic camera eyes produce sharp images and possess short focal lengths? Are there many kinds of lenses that can produce sharp images with a short focal length, or are there only a few (maybe just one?) solutions to such a problem?

Matthiessen, in 1877, hit on the solution to both puzzles. Matthiessen discovered that the spherical lenses in aquatic camera eyes are not made of homogenous material but instead are composed of various substances with differing refractive indices. The materials are arranged so that the lens has a high refractive index in the center and gradually weakening refractive indices toward the periphery. At its surface, the refractive index of a spherical lens is about the same as water. Because the refractive index of the lens is graded in this way, light bends not just at the surface of the lens, as it would if the lens were homogenous, but throughout the lens. This type of construction simultaneously reduces the focal length of the lens to 2.5 radii (a figure now known as Matthiessen's ratio) and, because peripheral rays now pass through a medium with a weaker refractive index than do central rays, eliminates spherical aberration (see figure 3.6).

Resorting once more to the device of an engineering team, we can imagine that the team has been assigned the task of constructing an

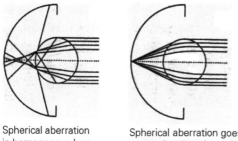

Spherical aberration
in homogenous lens

Spherical aberration goes
away when lens is graded

Figure 3.6
The lens on the left is homogenous and thus the eye suffers spherical aberration. The lens on the right is graded in the way Matthiessen discovered, thus eliminating spherical aberration. From Land and Fernald (1992).

image-forming eye for aquatic organisms. The first and most basic decision the team must make is between a camera-type eye and a compound eye. However, compound eyes, because of their extremely small lenses, are fundamentally inferior to camera eyes. Let's further suppose, then, that the person who has placed an order for aquatic image-forming eyes has demanded that the eyes have a resolution beyond that which compound eyes can attain, or, alternatively, wants the eye to be able to function in low-light conditions in which compound eyes are practically useless. "The only choice we have is a camera eye, the chief engineer grumbles." "We better start looking around for spherical lenses," she continues. "But spherical lenses produce messy images," a team member objects. "Also," another doubter chimes in, "they have such long focal lengths that the eye will practically stick out the back of the organism's head!" "What if we grade the refractive index in the lens?" says the clever graduate student. "If we make the refractive index around the edges of the sphere weaker than it is in the center, then the peripheral rays won't be overfocused. Also, with a graded index the light will continue to bend once inside the sphere, shortening the focal length!" "Hey, the kid's got a good idea," the chief engineer concedes. "Make it so!"

But, not only does the kid have a good idea, it is, for all we know, the *only* idea that has a chance of working. Whereas image-formation in water has innumerable logically possible solutions, we know from the study of those organisms that in fact produce images underwater (except for those that do so with second-rate compound eyes) that they do so with graded lenses. The upper limit on refractive indices that proteins can have makes it easy to check whether an aquatic organism uses a graded lens. If the retina of the organism's eye is 2.5 times the lens's radius from the center of the lens, the lens *must* be graded. Land and Fernald note the ubiquity of Matthiessen's ratio:

"Matthiessen" lenses have evolved at least eight times: in the fish, in the cephalopod mollusks (excluding *Nautilus*), at least four times in the gastropod mollusks (litorinids, strombids, heteropods, and some pulmonates), in the annelids (alciopid polychaetes), and once in the copepod crustaceans (*Labidocera*). . . . Interestingly, the above list does include all aquatic lens eyes of any size; none have homogenous lenses. One can conclude that there is one right way of producing such lenses, and that natural selection always finds it. (1992, p. 10)

This concludes my discussion of image-forming eyes. As with mammalian homeostasis, the point of the discussion has been to illustrate the interplay of universal and historical constraints and the consequences of this interplay for multiple realizability. The claim I have been most concerned to develop is that the possibility of multiple realizability must be evaluated on a case by case basis and cannot be decided on a priori grounds. I believe my discussion of image-forming eyes makes this point quite well. There is no saying whether image-forming eyes are multiply realizable until one knows something about optics and the nature of light. It turns out as well that one must know something about the refractive properties of proteins.

A second claim I have considered is that mammalian-like homeostasis and image-formation are, likely, not vastly multiply realizable. This is because, I have argued, the universal and historical constraints on these capacities are fairly severe. Unlike capacities like time-keeping, mouse-trapping, and cork-removal, there seem to be very few kinds of structures that can maintain homeostasis with mammalian-like precision, or that can project an image on a surface. I do not, however, wish to "go to the mat" defending this claim. To do so would be to neglect the first of the points I mentioned. Perhaps empirical investigation will uncover systems that exhibit mammalian-like homeostasis with an organization very unlike that which mammals have evolved. Similarly, just as a new kind of eye was discovered only recently, so there may be future discoveries that will suggest a far greater variety in structures that can produce images. It looks *today* as if mammalian-like homeostasis and image-formation can be realized in only a few ways. This may change.

3.7 Convergence

In closing this chapter, I wish to return to a topic that I introduced in chapter 2. Similar traits that have been derived independently in various species are known as *convergent* traits. The term calls attention to the fact that selection has caused unrelated species to converge on a similar solution to some problem. Land and Fernald's list of species that exhibit Matthiessen's ratio appears on its face to be a remarkable example of convergence.

The phenomenon of convergence is important for my purposes, because it provides evidence by which to evaluate the likelihood of MRT. The idea is simple: if there is only one way to design a structure that can do Y, then we should expect to see all organisms that can do Y to be equipped with the same kind of structure. We should, that is, expect selection to cause convergence on a particular kind of structure in distinct lineages. On the other hand, if there are many kinds of structures that can do Y, then the fact that a given organism can do Y may allow us to predict little about the nature of the structure by which it Ys. Thus, the independent evolution of similar structures makes the hypothesis of multiple realizability less likely than the alternative.

Convergence on Matthiessen's ratio is not at all surprising once one knows the relevant optics. The only way to avoid spherical aberration, without flattening the lens into something nonspherical, is to grade the refractive indices within the lens. Furthermore, grading the lens is the only way to obtain a focal length of 2.5 radii when working with proteins. But, because Matthiessen's ratio places a historical constraint on other properties of the eye, we should expect to see a cascade of convergence: eyes that converge on Matthiessen's ratio will almost certainly converge in other ways as well. Land and Fernald make just this point:

Lens construction accounts for one aspect of the remarkable convergence between fish and cephalopod eyes. The identity of Matthiessen's ratio in the two groups, itself a result of the refractive index of the dry material of the lens center, and the inevitable spherical symmetry of the image effectively dictate the eyes' shape and proportions. The presence of eye muscles can be explained from the need to stabilize the image. This need grows with image quality, if that quality is not to be compromised by blur. Similarly, the need for an accommodation mechanism is determined by eye size, in the same way that focusing becomes more critical for camera lenses as the focal length increases. Thus, many of the convergent features that seem so remarkable (Packard 1972) are inevitable, given a particular type and size of eye. (1992, p. 10)

Thus, as a result of convergence in one property, we see convergence in many. I shall sometimes refer to this phenomenon as *cascading convergence*. We shall see in the next chapter that there is convergence on several scales, and I shall try to defend the claim that cascading convergence should bring one to question the support for MRT: organisms that think like human beings probably have brains that share many of the properties of human brains.

4

Constraints on Brains

Let the tape of life be replayed. Starting with the same initial conditions that were present on Earth when life began, suppose evolution were to proceed again. Gould (1989a) claims that the products of this experiment would bear little resemblance to the creatures that have actually populated the Earth: "any replay of the tape would lead evolution down a pathway radically different from the road actually taken" (p. 51). I have a slightly different experiment in mind. Replay the tape of life, but direct the process in such a way that organisms with humanlike minds evolve. What can we predict about the "insides" of these organisms? Will their "brains" be as large as ours? Will their brains be divided into two hemispheres, and consist of neurons, and, if so, will the neurons be anything like those of which human brains are composed? Will the surfaces of their brains have the gyri and sulci that make our brains look like overgrown raisins? Will they contain topographic maps of their sensory inputs?

If MRT is correct then it seems we ought to have no expectations about the structure of the brains in these counterfactually evolved organisms. They might be as large as ours, but they might also be bigger than an automobile or smaller than a pebble. They might be roughly spherical, or they might be spread over the entire surface of the organism's body like some kind of neural spandex. Perhaps the brains are wrinkled with gyri and sulci, but on the other hand why couldn't they be smooth as marble? In fact, if MRT is correct, we should be more surprised to find that these brains resemble our own than not. After all, if there are many ways to build something that thinks, many different R-properties by which to realize humanlike psychology, it could only be a startling coincidence that the thinking organs of these counterfactually evolved organisms are very much like our own. However, not every functional system is equally multiply realizable. True, there are many different ways to build a mousetrap or a clock. These problems are relatively unconstrained. To trap a mouse, you need something that will kill, confine, or cripple it. But anything from poison to a falling piano can do this. To build a clock, you need something that moves, beeps, jumps, or drips at regular intervals. It is barely an exaggeration to say that part of the problem of building a mousetrap or clock is to figure out what *not* to use in their construction. On the other hand, some tasks are fairly constraining. Not anything can float, and this limits one's choice in life-preserver material and design. Similarly, not anything can walk on walls like a fly. The molecular adhesive forces that keep a fly from falling off a wall or ceiling are roughly proportional to the length of the fly's feet. However, because gravity works on mass, which is proportional to length cubed, increases in the length of an organism's adhesive surface cannot keep pace with the force of gravity pulling it down (McMahon and Bonner 1983; Went 1968). This sets a limit on the size of wall-walkers, Spiderman notwithstanding.

If psychological processing, like catching mice, is a relatively unconstrained problem, then it seems plausible that were the evolution of humanlike minds replayed the resulting brains might be nothing like human brains. If, on the other hand, psychological processing is a highly constraining task, like wall-walking, then it seems plausible to expect that inside the head of any organism with a humanlike mind is a brain much like the one in our own heads.

In this chapter I will consider various constraints that impose themselves on brain design. I intend to use the term "brain" in a generic (nonrigid) sense—to refer to whatever organ it is that underlies psychological processing. I will thus be exploring constraints on the construction of an organ that produces humanlike psychological capacities. In doing so, I will be providing evidence that bears on the choice between MRT and its competitor, the mental constraint thesis. MCT, recall, is the thesis that there are few distinct kinds of brains that can actually produce humanlike psychological capacities. The presence of constraints that limit the design possibilities of something that cognizes and senses like a human being supports the claim of MCT.

But what kind of evidence for MCT is there? One source of evidence comes from observations of evolutionary convergence. I ended the previous chapter with a discussion of convergence in image-forming eyes. Land and Fernald (1982) note that Matthiessen lenses—graded spherical lenses with a focal length of 2.5 radii—have evolved independently at least eight times. The convergence on such a well-defined structure supports the hypothesis that image-formation under water must face severe constraints. Were there not such severe constraints, numerous different kinds of lenses would probably have evolved: some spherical, some convex, some graded, some homogenous, some with focal lengths of 4 radii, some with focal lengths of 3 radii, and so on. The presence of such remarkable convergence makes more likely the presence of constraints, which disconfirms the possibility of multiple realizability. So, one source of evidence for MCT will be instances of neural convergence—the independent evolution of similar kinds of neural structures.

Yet, the use of convergence as a source of evidence for MCT faces an obvious limitation. As far as we know, humans are the only organisms with brains capable of humanlike mentality. So, whereas some of the traits human beings possess have been derived independently in other species, such as camera eyes, the human brain remains unique. This fact does not mean that the design of an organ capable of humanlike psychology faces no constraints, but it does mean that we cannot always rely on convergence to play the same evidential role in the discovery of these constraints as it does in the case of Matthiessen lenses.

In response to this difficulty it pays to keep in mind the following. Although human brains are unique (unlike, say, human eyes, which have analogues and homologues in many other species), human brains may nevertheless share many features with other kinds of brains as a consequence of convergent evolution. That is to say there may in fact be large numbers of homoplasies, that is, similar but independently derived traits, across a set of brains that includes the human brain. I will consider several such homoplasies in the course of this chapter. The presence of these homoplasies is significant, for they may place constraints on future evolution; the course of evolution that has led to humanlike minds may be limited in the number of routes it can travel. Shared but independently derived traits of brains may, that is, cut off some future evolutionary paths. Accordingly, if the tape of humanlike psychology were replayed then it might be true of the brains that realize this psychology that they must, of historical and universal necessity, possess many of the same R-properties of the human brain. In short, it could be that the independently derived traits human brains share with other existing brains create a cascade of convergences that would, were these other brains eventually to evolve humanlike capacities, require that they resemble human brains in many respects. Thus, the presence of neural convergences is evidence for MCT and against MRT.

Interestingly, convergence plays this evidentiary role for MCT for the same reason it causes such a problem in cladistic approaches to classification. Cladistic classification organizes species according to their degree of relatedness rather than, say, their similarity in appearance. Thus, according to cladists, birds and crocodiles belong to a more exclusive group than crocodiles and lizards because birds and crocodiles share a nearer common ancestor than do crocodiles and lizards. Likewise, despite the similarity in appearance between sharks and dolphins, dolphins are in fact classified as belonging to a group that includes apes but not sharks because apes and dolphins share a more recent common ancestor than do dolphins and sharks. The similarity in the dolphin's and shark's appearance is a result not of common ancestry, but convergent evolution. It is because of constraints on organisms that must swim quickly through water that the torpedo shape of sharks and dolphins evolved independently. Convergent evolution is thus a quicksand for the cladist—it invites the mistaken inference of common ancestry when in fact the similarities between species are due to evolution in the face of common constraints. To avoid this quicksand, cladists do well to classify on the basis of traits that have no adaptive value for an organism. Similarity in traits that are of neutral or negative adaptive value are much better evidence of common ancestry than traits that serve some function (Ridley 1986).

Studying the evolution of mammalian brains reveals several examples of convergence. Seeking an explanation for these instances of convergence will, perhaps, reveal the presence of constraints that the design for any brain with humanlike capacities must confront. Furthermore, a study of mammalian brain evolution will expose trends that the evolving brain exhibits as its psychological capacities become more sophisticated. The existence of such trends provides another valuable source of evidence for MCT: despite the fact that human brains may be unique, an appreciation of the trends in brain evolution suggests a means for predicting how brains with capacities like ours would look were the evolution of humanlike minds to be replayed.

There is an obvious need when assessing evidence of the sort I shall present to keep sharp the distinction between universal and historical constraints. Universal constraints on brain design carry more weight in an evaluation of MRT than do historical constraints. This is because universal constraints on a brain are, by definition, constraints that any brain must face. Historical constraints on a brain, in contrast, are conditional on historically contingent features of the brain. Thus, it may be true that a brain with humanlike capacities must exhibit feature X given that it evolved from a brain with feature Y, but if the ancestral brain contained feature Y for contingent reasons, that is, if the ancestral brain was not itself universally constrained to contain Y, then it may be false that any brain with humanlike capacities must exhibit feature X. To recall an example from the previous chapter, it is true that palm trees today never branch. However, we know from observation of other kinds of trees that branching is possible. The failure of palm trees to branch is not the result of a universal constraint on trees, but is a consequence of a historical constraint—of the fact that palm trees are descended from an organism that failed to evolve secondary thickening. Hence, it would be a mistake to conclude from the observation that palm trees never branch that *no* trees can branch. Similarly, one must take care when mining the evolutionary history of brains for examples of traits that all brains possess to attend to the possibility that brains exhibit these traits as a consequence of historical constraints. One must be sensitive, that is, to the difference between the following two claims: (1) All brains must possess trait X; and (2) given that a brain has trait Y, it must possess trait X.[1]

Having raised this concern to distinguish between universal and historical constraints on brain design, I must now confess that we may never be in a position to be sure that we have separated correctly the universal constraints that impose themselves on brain designs from the historical ones that reflect the idiosyncrasies of human brain evolution. We are in the position of Aristotle, who said "if one defines the operation of sawing as being a certain kind of dividing, then this cannot come about unless the saw has teeth of a certain kind; and these cannot be unless it is of iron" (Aristotle, *Physics*: Bk. II: ch. 9). If Aristotle assumed that effective saw blades must be made of iron because he did not believe that a harder metal could actually exist, then he turned out to be wrong for empirical reasons. Had the Greeks known about steel, Aristotle's utterance would no doubt have been different. Just as Aristotle's faith in iron seems charmingly quaint today, my claims about constraints on brain design might look naive tomorrow.

Accordingly, I offer the following facts about brain constraints as a challenge to advocates of MRT. I will argue that given what we know about the brain today, it seems *plausible* that any organ that exhibits humanlike psychological capacities must also possess various humanlike brain properties. I could be as wrong about what these neural properties are as Aristotle was about the necessity of iron for saws. However, if I am wrong, my mistake will be, like Aristotle's, empirical. So, if nothing else, the following exercise serves to illustrate the kinds of empirical considerations on which a proper evaluation of MRT must rest. This in itself advances discussion of MRT further than has been typical in philosophy of mind.

4.1   Sensory Systems

One useful approach to understanding the constraints that a humanlike mind places on the brain is to look first at the brain and ask "Why is it structured like *this* rather than some other way?" If MRT were true, the answer to this question would differ in an interesting way from the answer were MCT true. For, if MCT were true, the answer would be something like: "the brain has this structure rather than some other because no other structure could do what this structure does." In contrast, if MRT were true, the answer would be: "it's just a contingent matter (e.g., a historical accident) that the brain has this structure rather than some other—for other structures would serve just as well." Similarly, as I noted above, looking not just at human brains but at the brains of other organisms with whom we share some particular mental capacity M helps us to evaluate the likelihood that there is more than one way to build a brain that does M. If there is tremendous variation in the R-properties by which various species realize M, M is multiply realizable. If all brains capable of M have a similar design and this design has evolved independently in different species, this decreases the likelihood of MRT.

In this section I propose to look at the brain starting from its "outside": from where the brain makes contact with the world. It should be obvious that *what* human beings are capable of sensing must play a deep role in determining other features of human minds. We have acute vision that presents to us a colored world, we feel heat and cold and pressure, we hear distinct notes as parts of a connected melody, and so on. What machinery is necessary for these abilities? In this section I will defend the claim that humanlike perceptual capacities make the presence of certain structural properties physically necessary. I will start this defense with a discussion of some traits that are common to all sensory systems, and I will then turn to a discussion of traits particular to distinct sensory modalities.

To begin, all sensory systems have in common the following functions. First, they must be responsive to particular physical properties of a stimulus. An eye without light-sensitive elements will never see; an ear lacking something that can detect oscillations in air pressure will not hear; and so on. The very fact that different physical properties require for their detection different kinds of devices already places one, albeit only a weak, constraint on the design of sensory systems. Below we'll examine at greater length whether the detection of certain physical properties *requires* the existence of a particular kind of structure. A second function all sensory systems must perform is transduction (Ulinski 1984). Without some means of converting the properties of stimuli into a currency that the brain can process, our detection of these properties would amount to no more than a reaction—like a sunburn or chattering teeth. Properties of the stimulus must be made *accessible* to the nervous system. Finally, there is the processing of the currency into which the properties of the stimulus have been transduced.

My claim so far is that any organism with a humanlike mind will have perceptual systems consisting of receptors, transducers, and information processors. But we can say still more specific things about the structure of these systems. Given the kinds of stimuli to which human beings are sensitive, we know that the design of human perceptual abilities must include receptors capable of detecting four kinds of energy: mechanical, chemical, thermal, and electromagnetic (Kandel, Schwartz, and Jessell 2000, p. 416). Detection of these kinds of energy is necessary for vision, hearing, balance, touch, proprioception, temperature sensation, taste, and smell. Accordingly, as we shall see when we examine particular sensory systems in more detail, whatever constraints fall on receptors capable of responding selectively to these forms of energy will limit the multiple realizability of humanlike perceptual capacities.

Of course, our sensory systems do more than simply tell us that one form or another of energy is present, that is, they provide information about more than just the *modality* of the stimulus. In addition to perceiving light, sound, pressure, and so on, human beings can *locate in space* the source of the light, sound, and energy that bombards their receptors. Human beings are also sensitive to the *intensity* and the *duration* of the stimulus. These human abilities—abilities to sense the modality, location, intensity, and duration of stimuli in the world around us—are psychological abilities that force a particular kind of structure and organization on human sensory receptors.

To understand more specifically how our perceptual abilities predict particular organizations of receptors, consider first some abilities of our visual and somatosensory systems. We are able to see where in space objects are. From twenty feet we can easily discriminate between two small tacks next to each other on a bulletin board. We can discern details in acoustic tiling far above our heads. Similarly, we can locate where on our body there is pressure or heat. We can distinguish the feel of one pin prick from the feel of two pin pricks. With our fingertips we can discern details on surfaces as fine as those set in Braille. What is likely to be true about the receptors of any organism endowed with equivalent perceptual capacities?

The concept of a *receptive field* is central to understanding what makes such perceptual feats possible. The mechanoreceptors in the somatosensory system and the photoreceptors in the visual system each attend to

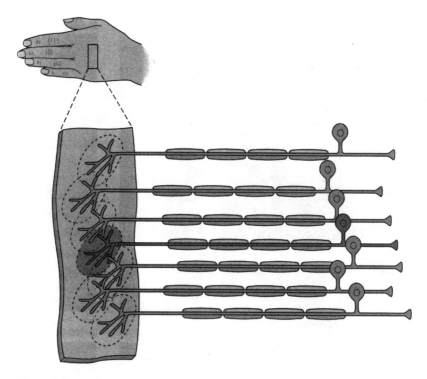

Figure 4.1
Overlapping receptive fields. From Kandel et al. (2000), p. 419.

a particular region on a sensory surface. So, for instance, although our skin appears homogenous on its surface, this homogeneity disguises a patchwork of overlapping receptive fields, each belonging to a single mechanoreceptor (see figure 4.1). Likewise, the light falling on our retinas forms a continuous image, but this continuity is digitized into discrete regions of receptivity by organizations of photoreceptors. Mechanoreceptors and photoreceptors thus have restricted regions of sensitivity. Pressure or light outside the receptive region of a receptor will not activate the receptor. But, on the other hand, two or more stimuli that fall *within* the field of a single receptor will be *indistinguishable*. Discrimination requires the excitation of distinct receptors, and it is this fact that suggests a universal constraint on perceptual systems: discrimination is inversely proportional to the size of receptive fields and directly proportional to the density of receptors.

Figure 4.2
The density and size of receptive fields in the retina determine the resolution of a visual image. From Kandel et al. (2000), p. 420.

Figure 4.2 shows the effect of variation in receptive field size and receptor density on perceptual resolution. In the first photograph, each square marks the receptive field of a single receptor. Because the receptive fields are large and the receptor density small, the resolution is poor and the image is unrecognizable. As the receptive fields decrease in size and the receptor density increases, the resolution improves until, in the final photo, the image appears as the actual scene would to a normally sighted individual.

This universal constraint on perceptual acuity—this relation between resolution, receptive field size, and receptor density—is also quite apparent in our sense of touch. Where our mechanoreceptors are densely packed and have small receptive fields, we can readily distinguish between two closely situated pressure points. Thus, holding two sharp pencils next to each other in my left hand, I can with my right index finger feel the points of each pencil. But, pressing the points against the back of my head or the back of my neck leaves me with the impression of only one point of pressure. This implies that the receptive fields of the mechanoreceptors in the tip of my index finger are smaller, and the receptors more densely packed, than they are on the back of my head or neck

To summarize my discussion of sensory systems to this point, perception requires reception, transduction, and processing. So far I have been focusing on the nature of receptors, trying to uncover those features that are likely to be found in the receptors of *any* organism with humanlike perceptual capacities. I have not yet speculated on whether the fact that these receptors must detect particular forms of energy places specific constraints on their chemical or physical nature, but I have observed facts about the nature of receptive fields that suggest the following. Were we to dissect the nervous system of any organism with powers of visual and tactile resolution that match those of a human being, we would find in its receptive surfaces a similar density of receptor cells, each with a similarly sized receptive field. This follows from the universal constraint I discussed above. *Any* perceptual system in which receptor cells are packed more loosely and endowed with larger receptive fields than they are in a human perceptual system will not match the resolving capacity of a human perceptual system. Likewise, *any* perceptual system in which receptor cells are packed more densely and endowed with smaller receptive fields will have a greater resolving capacity than a human perceptual system. Thus, if we were to come across an organism with humanlike senses of vision and touch, we could be as certain about the maximum size of its receptive fields and packing of its receptors as we could be about the rate at which it would fall were we to ungraciously push it off the top of the Empire State Building.

This fact about how the visual and somatosensory receptors must be organized in any organism with humanlike powers of visual and tactile powers of resolution serves as a fixed point from which to proceed in an examination of neural structure upstream from these receptive surfaces. At the end of chapter 3 I mentioned a phenomenon that I dubbed "cascading convergence." The idea behind cascading convergence is that convergence in one feature can lead to a cascade of convergence in other features. Land and Fernald (1992) provided one illustration in their observation that eyes that independently evolve one feature—a spherical lens—will also, if they are to produce focused images, independently evolve many other features: graded lenses, focal lengths in accordance with Matthiessen's ratio, eye muscles, accommodative mechanisms, and so on. Given the phenomenon of cascading convergence, it is worth considering whether we ought to expect a similar cascading of convergence among organisms with receptive surfaces. If any organism with the visual and tactile capacities of a human being must also have receptors with a density and field like that of a human being, what else must be true of their neural structures? Might a receptive surface like that which affords humanlike perceptual capacities trigger a cascade of other traits that any organism with humanlike perceptual capacities must have?

I have already mentioned that in addition to being able to distinguish the modality of a stimulus, human beings are sensitive to the *intensity* of a stimulus. Sounds can be loud or soft, light is bright or dim, pressure on our skin is hard or slight. So, in addition to having receptors that represent modality, anything with a humanlike mind must be equipped with receptors that can represent intensity as well. This fact of course has implications not just for the nature of receptors, but also for the process of transduction. The currency into which a receptor translates properties of a stimulus must be of a kind that can represent changes in the quantitative aspect of a stimulus. When a receptor says "more" this message must get translated as such. Again, the contrast with teeth chattering makes this point clear. Suppose that the colder the external temperature, the more my teeth chatter. But this fact does not make my chattering teeth an organ for the detection of temperature. What's lacking in my chattering teeth is a means by which to translate the effect of chattering into a currency that, when processed, can carry information about temperature. Any organism with humanlike perceptual abilities must be equipped with a mechanism that can both detect the presence of external stimuli and encode differences in the intensity of these stimuli in a way that can be used for perception.

This constraint on humanlike perceptual abilities entails that receptors for each modality must be sensitive to those properties of the modality that vary quantitatively. For sound and light, this property is amplitude. For pressure, this property is force. Receptors of sound and light must, accordingly, have a means by which to encode the amplitude of sound and light waves; mechanoreceptors must be equipped to encode facts about the force that stimuli exert on them. The behavior of a receptor must change as the strength of the stimulus to which it is sensitive varies, and facts about this change in behavior must be available to processes of perception further downstream. Here, then, is another prediction we can make about alien brains: aliens who perceive like us will have receptors that record facts about the intensities of stimuli. Variations in stimulus intensities will cause corresponding changes in their sensory receptors, and these changes will somehow be encoded for further perceptual processing.

This claim may seem like hardly more than a platitude, but its interest snowballs as we consider the kinds of cascading convergences it implies. I have already observed that human beings have the capacity to discriminate between closely spaced visual or tactile stimuli. Too close together and stimuli will fall within the receptive field of a single receptor and so will be indistinguishable. It is on the basis of empirical examinations of human discriminative capacities (a psychological trait) that we can predict the size of receptive fields and the density of receptors (a neurological trait). However, these examinations reveal another fact about the structure of our sensory systems. Consider a puzzle that my discussion of receptive surfaces raises. Imagine two receptors with receptive fields set side by side. Stimulation of these receptors will cause them to transduce a property of the stimulus (light or pressure) into a

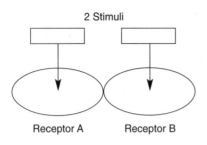

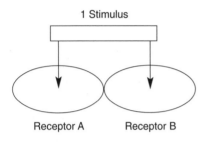

Figure 4.3
Given nonoverlapping receptive fields, it is impossible to distinguish two stimuli from one stimulus.

property that the nervous system can then process. But if this were all there were to the receptive stage of perception, how could an organism distinguish two stimuli, each of which activates one of the side-by-side receptors, from a single stimulus that is large enough to excite both receptors simultaneously? Why does the excitation of two receptors sometimes cause us to perceive two stimuli, and sometimes just one (larger) stimulus (see figure 4.3)? What's needed is some way to enhance the contrast between two distinct stimuli so that they appear as, truly, two *distinct* stimuli rather than as one larger blob.

The solution to this puzzle requires first that the receptive fields into which a sensory surface is partitioned overlap, so that the sensory surface, were we able to see the receptive fields into which it is divided, would look something like fish scales, or, better, a potato gallete. The second feature of sensory systems that have humanlike discriminative capacities is the presence of connections between neighboring receptor cells. With overlapping receptive fields and a means by which receptors can influence each other's outputs, it becomes possible to distinguish two closely situated stimuli from one larger stimulus. Let me explain how this works.

Imagine three receptor cells with receptive fields that are arranged like links on a chain. The receptive field of A overlaps with that of B, which overlaps with that of C, but the fields of A and C do not overlap. Now suppose that separate stimuli fall within the receptive fields of A and C. How, we are wondering, is it possible to sense the difference between this case and one in which a single larger stimulus falls within the receptive fields of A, B, and C? The answer involves a process that is common to sensory systems that are able to make such distinctions: lateral inhibition (Hendry, Hsiao, and Brown 1999). Indeed, the presence of lateral inhibition in sensory systems, although first predicted by Mach at the end of the nineteenth century, was later confirmed through work on the sensory system of the horseshoe crab (Hartline, Wagner, and Ratliff 1956). Here, then, is the kind of evolutionary convergence we are looking for as evidence in favor of MCT. If MRT is true, the fact that many organisms independently derived lateral inhibition as the means by which to make sensory discriminations ought to be very surprising. However, if one predicts that constraints on sensory processing make only one or few solutions to the problem of visual or tactile discrimination possible, then the finding is not at all surprising.

Simplifying a bit, lateral inhibition requires that receptor cells have the ability to dampen the activation of their neighbors (Goldstein 1989). So, returning to our example, if distinct stimuli fall within the receptive fields of A and C, then these cells will each, suppose, transduce the property to which they are sensitive (light or pressure) into some quantity of activation. B, however, will be activated as well, because B's receptive field overlaps those of A and C. Yet, because the two stimuli fall directly within the fields of A and C and only partially within B's receptive field, the strength of B's activation is less than that of A and C. Now suppose that there are connections between A, B, and C that inhibit each other in proportion to the strength of their activation. If we assign the number 100 to the activation values of A and C and assume that each inhibits its neighboring cells by ten percent of its activation value, then B will be receiving 20 units of inhibition. B too will be inhibiting A and C, but if we allow that B's excitation produces only 80 units of activation, then A and C will

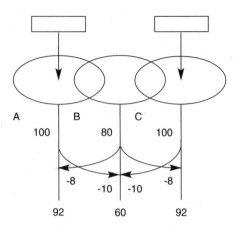

Figure 4.4
Lateral inhibition enhances contrast.

be receiving only 8 units each of inhibition from B. This means that A and C are now each reporting 92 units of activation whereas B is reporting 60 units of activation. As a result of lateral inhibition, the contrast between A and B, and between B and C, has now grown significantly—A and C's activations are roughly fifty percent greater than B's, whereas before they were only twenty-five percent greater. On the other hand, if a single stimulus were to fall within the receptive fields of A, B, and C, each receptor would produce equal numbers of activation units, and so there no longer would be a contrast between A and B or B and C. Thus, the activities of the three receptors would indicate the presence of one large stimulus rather than two distinct ones (see figure 4.4).

To summarize my discussion of sensory systems so far, I claim that, were we to dissect the sensory system of any organism with discriminative capacities like our own, we'd find that it is realized in the following way: it would have visual and tactile receptive surfaces that are partitioned into overlapping receptive fields. The receptors would be more densely packed in those parts of its body or eye that have greater resolving power. Similarly, the receptive fields in these more sensitive areas would be smaller than they would be in less sensitive areas. Finally, the receptors would be connected to their neighbors, and through these connections they would be able to dampen the activation of their neighbors.

4.2 Topographic Maps

My discussion of sensory systems has until now focused on rather peripheral processes. However, I believe that it is possible to say something about those processes that must occur further upstream from the periphery. Because, as we have been observing, one convergence can cascade into others, it should not surprise us if sensory systems that must resemble each other at the periphery must also resemble each other further up. Whereas in the previous section the inference was from a psychological capacity (sensitivity) to the realizers of this capacity, in this section the inference moves from realizer to realizer. The universal constraints that shape the realization of sensory capacities will, consequently, force on the brain other R-properties. An example of such a property is the cortical layout of sensory representations. Some neuroscientists (Kaas 1997; Radinsky 1987) have argued that evolved sensory systems will inevitably contain topographic maps of sensory surfaces.

Receptive surfaces—either skin or retina—are divided into overlapping receptive fields. In all mammals, the next-to relation that exists between receptors in these surfaces is preserved in the cortex. So, for instance, two receptors that lie next to each other on the back of a hand will project onto processing units that lie next to each other in the cortex. The maintenance of these topographic maps makes it possible, from information one can derive from the brain alone, to predict with great accuracy not only the relations between parts of an organism's body, but the sensitivity of these parts. Neuroscientists have mapped regions of sensitivity in the somatosensory cortices of mammals, and, because these maps maintain the topography of the organisms' receptive surfaces, it is possible to impose on the map a "homunculus" that represents the next-to relationships and discriminative capacities of the organisms' body surfaces. Figure 4.5 illustrates the homunculus that is predicted from recording the activity of cells in the primary somatosensory cortex of a human being. The splayed body looks odd because the size of its body parts is drawn to reflect their degrees of sensitivity. As I have explained, the more densely packed the receptor cells are in a region of the body's surface, the more sensitive that region will be. But, because the amount of cortex required to process information from various body regions is

Sensory homunculus

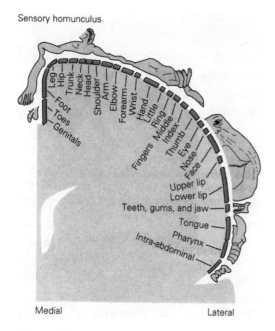

Medial   Lateral

Figure 4.5
The human sensory homunculus. From Kandel et al. (2000), p. 387.

directly proportional to the amount of information arriving from these regions, more sensitive body regions will appear much larger in proportion to the less sensitive body regions. Thus, lips, tongue, and forefinger are huge in comparison to torso, hip, and head.

The homunculi maps of perceptual sensitivity are a neat illustration of how function predicts structure. Knowing nothing more than the sensitivity of certain body parts (a psychological fact), it is possible to predict the relative amount of sensory cortex dedicated to each body part (a structural fact). The homunculi in figure 4.6 demonstrate this phenomenon. The animals are drawn to reveal the amount of somatosensory cortex dedicated to different regions of their bodies. Thus, we could rely on the drawings to produce a picture of the layout of the somatosensory cortex. The drawings tell us, roughly, how cells in the cortex will be arranged and also the volume of cells that will be present within this arrangement. But, of course, the drawings illustrate just as well a psychological fact about these organisms—the somatic sensitivities of their

Rabbit   Cat   Monkey   Human

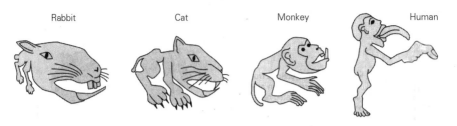

Figure 4.6
Sensory homunculi for different animals. From Kandel et al. (2000), p. 388.

body parts. We know from the drawings that the rabbit's face is the most sensitive part of its body, with its snout the most sensitive part of the face. The sensitivity of its paws is negligible in comparison to its snout. In contrast, the monkey's feet and hands are far more sensitive than its nose, and the tongue and forefinger are clearly the most sensitive parts of the human body. The important point, for my purposes, is that information about some mental property—sensitivity—predicts information about the properties of its realizer, which is just what MCT should lead one to expect.

However, my claim that constraints make it possible to predict from capacities of the mind facts about the mind's realization requires further defense. Are these constraints simply historical constraints? Does it just happen to be the case that, because all mammals are descended from a common ancestor in which sensory information was represented topographically in the brain, all mammals today have cortices in which sensory information is mapped topographically? Might not there be numerous ways to organize the cerebral cortex—ways that do not rely on a topographical representation of sensory information?

One way to answer this question is to look for convergences on topographical organization. Just as convergence on Matthiessen lenses suggests strong constraints and so limited multiple realizability of the kinds of lenses that can focus images in aquatic camera eyes, so would convergence on topographical representations of receptor sheets increase the likelihood that there are strong constraints on how sensory information must be represented if it is to endow an organism with sophisticated discriminative capacities. And, indeed, there is convergence on topographic mapping of sensory information. The homologous maps that appear in the sensory systems of mammals, birds (Clark and Whitteridge 1976; Denton 1981; Karten and Shimizu 1989; Knudsen 1980; Pettigrew and Konishi 1976; Ulinski 1984), fish (Finger 1978), and reptiles (Ulinski 1980, 1984), also appear independently in the cockroach (Dagan and Camhi 1979).

A second way to answer the question whether any brain with the sensory capacities of a human brain must have topographical mapping is to ask why topographical maps are present in the first place. Why are receptive sheets represented topographically? What is the value of topographical representations? Why did they evolve? The neuroscientist John Allman claims that topographic representations of sensory information provide for the greatest economy in brain wiring (1999, p. 39). Given the costs associated with longer cables, selection will favor those brains that minimize the length of cable connections. However, because facts about wiring economy have many interesting consequences for brain structure apart from the presence of topographic maps, it is worth devoting several sections of this chapter to a fuller discussion of brain wiring.

4.3 Brain Wiring

In my discussion of sensory systems, I have been careful to remain neutral about the physical structure of receptors and those connections between them that produce lateral inhibition. Likewise, I have not yet said anything about how there comes to be a topographic map of a receptor surface in a brain. In all organisms we know about that have evolved sensory capacities, the wires responsible for creating lateral inhibition as well as for producing a topographic representation of sensory surfaces in the brain are neurons. Clearly some sort of wiring is necessary to do what sensory systems like our own can do. The interesting question for the purpose of evaluating MRT is how must a brain be wired? Are there universal constraints on brain wiring that would lead us to predict that any organism with sensory capacities like that of a human being would have to possess a brain that is wired like a human being's? Notice too that this question can quite plausibly be generalized to other psychological capacities. Connectionist investigations of cognitive capacities strongly support the idea that among the R-properties that realize more centrally cognitive capacities like attention (Cohen, Dunbar, and McClelland 1990), learning, and memory (McClelland and Rumelhart 1986) are connections between neuronlike units. If these sorts of connections are necessary for psychological processing, then constraints on brain wiring are likely to entail facts about the realizers of at least many humanlike psychological capacities.

Nervous systems are, essentially, bundles of cables. This fact is important for understanding the constraints that bear on the design of nervous systems. Any nervous system that depends on cables to transmit information from sensory systems to a central processing brain, and back again to the muscles that move the body, will be subject to the constraints that govern cables. One of these constraints is the fact that the conductance of a cable is inversely proportional to its length but directly proportional to its diameter. This means that as nerve fibers increase in length, the speed at which they conduct their signal decreases, unless compensatory changes in their diameter are made. Another constraint on cables concerns their connections with each other. If every cable must be connected with every other cable (full interconnectedness), then adding one additional cable to a system can cause huge increases in the number of connections that must be present. In particular, if each of n units must connect to $n-1$ units, then adding one unit to a network of 10,000 units means adding 20,000 new connections to the network (10,000 connections between the old units and the new one, and 10,000 between the new unit and old ones). Furthermore, since cables have volume, full interconnectedness, or even the requirement that the connectedness between cables maintain a fixed percentage (e.g., that every cable be connected to 70 percent of other cables), entails that the addition of a single cable to the brain could result in a massive increase in the volume of the brain.

James Ringo (1991) has calculated some of the consequences of these two constraints on wiring, that is, the relationship between the length and conduction speed of a cable and that between the connectivity between cables and brain volume. Ringo asks about the costs associated with adding one calculating unit (e.g., a neuron) to a brain consisting of a particular number of calculating units, assuming full interconnectedness. His calculation makes use of the following equation:

$$V = \left[(1-c) \times y\right] + \left[2 \times c \times y\right] + \left[\left((1+V)^{1/3} - 1\right) \times c\right]$$

In this equation, V is the fractional increase in volume of the brain, y is the fractional increase in the number of cells, and c is the fraction of the brain devoted to connections, that is, the portion of the brain that consists in cables between processing units. The first term on the right-hand side of the equation represents the increase in the number of processing units; the second represents the number of new connections necessary to connect a new processing unit to every other unit; and the third term shows how much the old cables must increase in length in order to maintain their connections after the increase in brain volume resulting from the addition and connection of one new processing unit.

Ringo's equation, when applied to a 100-cm^3 brain consisting of 10,000 units to which another unit is then fully connected, reveals the following. Let c be 67 percent. This number is a conservative estimate of the percentage of human brain volume that consists of axons—the biological analogue of a cables. Interconnecting all 10,000 units requires 10,000 times 10,000 cables (1×10^8). This means that 67 percent of the brain's volume consists of 10^8 cables, which means that each cable has a volume of 6.7×10^{-7} cm^3. Given that 33 percent of the brain consists of the units to which the cables are connected (e.g., the cell bodies of neurons), adding one more unit will increase the volume by 0.0033 cm^3. The addition of the new unit also requires 20,000 new connections, which, at 6.7×10^{-7} cm^3/cable, requires an increase in brain volume of 0.0134 cm^3. Adding all this up, the addition of a new, fully connected unit will add 0.0167 cm^3 to the volume of the brain. This increase will require that the old connections increase in length to compensate for the brain's expansion, adding another 0.0037 cm^3 of volume, making for an overall increase in brain volume of 0.0215 cm^3. And, because increases in the lengths of cable will reduce their conductance speeds, processing in the brain will slow down with every additional processing unit.

Of course, although the transmission speed of information in each cable has decreased, overall there may be an increase in processing speed in the brain. With the addition of another processing unit, the brain can presumably perform more operations per second. Speed goes down between units, but, with more units available for computations, speed

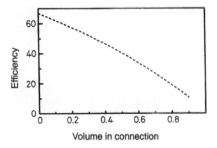

Figure 4.7
Marginal efficiency of increases in neuron number as plotted against the fraction of brain volume devoted to connection. From Ringo (1991).

may increase overall. Ringo refers to this phenomenon as a serial/parallel trade-off. But is the trade-off worth it? Employing some additional conservative assumptions, Ringo calculates that the increase in computing power that one extra computing unit brings to a brain with 10,000 units is 0.003 percent. Thus, an increase in size of about 0.02 percent buys for the brain a very small increase in power. In terms of efficiency, a measure of the percent increase in hypothetical computations per second divided by the percent increase in brain mass, the brain gains less than 15 percent (0.003/0.02). Moreover, as figure 4.7 makes clear, the efficiency of the brain will continue to decrease with continued additions of fully connected computing units. Indeed, figure 4.7 indicates that, assuming the requirement of full interconnectedness, a brain with a significant portion of its mass dedicated to connections will always *lose* in efficiency with additions to its number of computing units.

The consequence of this trade-off between computing efficiency and increases in the number of computing units is, assuming the requirement of full connectedness, yet another kind of universal constraint on brains. It is a constraint that any brain composed of computing units connected via cables must face. And, because the description of sensory systems above seems to demand the presence of cables, the constraints Ringo discusses seem bound to apply to any brain that has the perceptual capacities of a human being. But, what predictions does Ringo's analysis make about the brains we are likely to see in organisms with humanlike psychological capacities? In fact, Ringo's analysis suggests something very

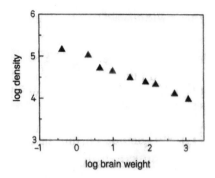

Figure 4.8
Log of cortical cell density as plotted against the log of brain weight. From Ringo (1991).

interesting about the structure that brains with humanlike capacities ought to have: they ought to be partitioned into modules.

Ringo's argument for modularity is this. In a brain in which computing units are fully connected with each other, the costs in efficiency associated with the addition of new units makes the evolution of large brains unlikely. Furthermore, when one plots cell density (the number of cells per cubic centimeter) in a brain against brain weight, one obtains the curve shown in figure 4.8. The graph in figure 4.8 shows that as cell density increases—as the number of computing units/cm^3 increases—the weight of the brain actually decreases. How could this be? This can occur only if the demand for full interconnectedness is relaxed. Because full interconnectedness makes brain growth extremely costly, we see a trend toward a decrease in percent connectedness with an increase in brain mass. It is possible to increase the number of computing units in a brain without increasing the mass of the brain if, to compensate for the increase in the number of computing units, there is a compensating decrease in the percent connectedness between units. As Ringo interprets the data in figure 4.8, they show that brain growth is accompanied by specialization (Kaas 2000b draws the same conclusion).

For my purposes, Ringo has provided a reason to expect that any evolved brain consisting of computing units and cables will, at some critical point in its growth, move from a greater to a lesser percent of interconnectedness. This move toward more limited connectedness, what Ringo refers to as specialization, is also often referred to as modularity.

Specialization, or modularity, makes a great deal of sense from a brain-designer's perspective, because "only within major groupings of neurons need there be full interconnection, while between major groupings only 'results' need to be passed" (Ringo 1991, p. 5). Indeed, Ringo goes so far as to suggest that big brains require modular specialization, and that larger modules "will be more specialized than small ones" (ibid.). There is, Ringo notes, evidence to support this suggestion: "rats, which have relatively small brains, are noted for an unspecialized cortex..., whereas monkeys are relatively large brained and have very specialized cortex.... Generally, those investigating cortical organization seem to report an increase in the number of distinct cortical areas with increasing brain size" (ibid.).

In summary, from properties that apply universally to cables, namely, the inverse relationship between cable length and conductance speed and the nonlinear relationship between increases in the number of computing units and the number of cables necessary to maintain full interconnectedness, it follows that as brains grow larger they become less efficient unless they become modular. Modularity—the division of a brain into units within which there is a high percent of interconnectedness but between which there are few connections—is something we should expect to see in any brain that has evolved, through natural selection, the complexity necessary to support humanlike psychological capacities.[2] Ringo's work suggests that if we were to open up the head of any evolved organism with humanlike psychology (or, more precisely, any such organism whose evolution has been driven mainly by selection), we should be quite unsurprised to find a brain that, like ours, consists of structurally distinct modules. Perhaps it would even be divided into hemispheres, as Ringo speculates. In any event, it would be surprising to find that it displays full interconnectedness or even a high percentage of interconnectedness. Thus, facts about cables place constraints on the number of ways to wire a brain that can do the things that human brains can do.[3] This, then, is a point in favor of MCT.

4.4   Component Placement in the Brain

A brain capable of humanlike psychological processes, if mainly the product of natural selection, will likely be divided into modules. But, if selection has operated on the placement of these modules, we can expect that there will be an order to their placement. Knowledge of constraints on component placement makes it possible to predict how modules in an adapted brain are likely to be arranged. The relevant constraint on module placement is one we encountered above: conductance speeds through a cable are inversely proportional to cable length. Because this is so, arrangements of modules that observe a "save-wire" principle will be more efficient than those that do not. Christopher Cherniak (1995) has explored the consequences of this save-wire principle on the organization of brain structure.

From the assumption that selection will favor brains in which wire lengths are minimized, Cherniak predicts that the placement of brain components will observe the following adjacency rule: "if components are interconnected, then they are positioned contiguously to each other, other things being equal" (1995, 523). The reason for this rule is obvious. If components need to communicate with each other, then the best way to minimize the lengths of wire connecting them is to situate them near or next to each other. Cherniak notes that researchers have confirmed that the placement of components in the visual systems of the macaque and the cat, as well as in the olfactory system of the rat, do indeed conform to this rule. However, to appreciate the spectacular predictive power of this rule, it is worth considering the layout of neural components in the nervous system of the lowly *C. elegans*.

Scientists have developed a complete map of the nervous system of *C. elegans*, a roundworm. *C. elegans* contains 302 neurons, clustered into 11 ganglia. The question that interests Cherniak is how, given the need to save wire, these 11 ganglia should be arranged. With no constraint on the problem, any of 11! (39,916,800) solutions is as good as any other. However, if one assumes that there has been selection for minimizing the length of cables between connected ganglia, it is possible for a computer to search exhaustively through all forty million possible component placements and calculate that placement which minimizes the amount of wire necessary to make the connections (this task took 24 hours on an SGI R4000SC workstation). Cherniak found that the "actual ganglion layout of *C. elegans* in fact requires the least total length of connecting fiber of any of the millions of possible layouts" (1995,

p. 525). It would appear that the constraints that make it beneficial to save wire make it possible to predict which, of a possible 40 million realizations, the brain of *C. elegans* will in fact adopt.

Of course, what we would like to know is whether the adjacency rule for placing interconnected neural components holds true for *H. sapiens* to the same degree as it does for *C. elegans*. Unfortunately, the magnitude of this problem is too great—we lack the resources to solve it. The human cortex has roughly 50 components. This means that there are 50! (3.04×10^{64}) possible component placement schemes. To put this number in perspective, Cherniak notes that it is "far more than the number of picoseconds in the 20-billion-year history of the universe since the Big Bang" (1995, p. 522). This fact might lead us to doubt that natural selection can optimize the amount of cable in a brain the size of our own. No matter how quickly evolution by natural selection might occur, it seems incredible that selection could possibly have sifted through the 50! potential component placement schemes in the brief period in which *H. sapiens* has evolved. However, Cherniak suggests that selection might have hit on a "quick but dirty" heuristic that leads to an approximately optimal solution. Cherniak's speculations move little beyond this suggestion; nevertheless, it is a plausible idea. Research in theory of network optimization shows that there are heuristics that generate approximately optimal solutions to component placement problems. Whereas natural selection might not have had the time to find an optimal wiring solution through a brute search method, perhaps there has been ample time for it to stumble across a heuristic that does the job well enough.

What, then, does Cherniak's work have to do with an evaluation of MRT? Like Ringo's investigation, which tells us that we should expect to find larger brains divided into modules, Cherniak's research tells us that we should expect the modules in a brain to be organized in accord with the adjacency rule. If psychologically humanlike organisms have evolved by natural selection, we should predict that their brains too are divided into modules that are arranged in accord with the adjacency rule. To revert to an image from the previous chapter, if one imagines a space consisting of all possible configurations of a nervous system—all possible arrangements of modules, for instance—my claim is that those organisms that have evolved a humanlike psychology will fall within a narrow region of this space. More precisely, they will fall within the region consisting of nervous systems that come closest to realizing the adjacency rule. Insofar as the adjacency rule provides us with a prediction about the kind of structure that selection would produce, it marks another point in favor of MCT and against MRT.

4.5   Marvelous Myelin

The inverse relationship between cable length and conductance speed goes a long way to explaining why big brains tend to be modular and why these modules tend to be arranged so that those that must communicate with each other will be adjacent to each other. However, there is another fact about cables that has interesting consequences for brain design. The conductance speed of an electrical signal in a cable is directly proportional to the cable's diameter. More precisely, conduction speed increases with roughly the square root of diameter, so that a doubling in conduction speed requires a fourfold increase in cable diameter. This constraint on conduction speed, when combined with the constraint that governs the relationship between speed and length, has interesting consequences for brain design. We have seen that the trade-off between length and speed creates a selection pressure for modularization and the adjacency of connected components. However, although modularization and adjacency alleviate to some extent the trade-off between speed and length, this cannot be the whole story behind a nervous system as efficient as our own.

Here are some facts. The diameter of axons in the brain and spinal cord leads one to expect a much slower speed for signal transmission than in fact is present. In particular, because a doubling in the rate of signal velocity demands a quadrupling in the caliber of an axon, and given the speed at which signals actually travel in these axons, we should predict that a human brain must be ten times larger than it in fact is, thus requiring the consumption of roughly ten times more food for its maintenance (Dowling 1998, p. 63). Similarly, given the speed at which signals travel through axons in the spinal cord, the spinal cord ought to be several meters in diameter (Morell and Norton 1980, p. 88). These facts raise an interesting question: why don't human beings have heads the size of weather balloons and spinal cords as thick as redwood trees?

The answer to this question should be obvious to anyone familiar with electrical circuit theory. The reason an increase in the diameter of a cable will increase the speed of the electrical signal it carries is because it reduces the internal electrical resistance of the cable. The speed of conduction is actually a function of the ratio between membrane resistance and internal resistance. The higher the ratio, the greater the velocity of the signal. Hence, one way to increase signal conductance is to decrease internal resistance by increasing cable diameter (Dowling 1998, p. 63). The problem with this solution, as we have seen, is that it requires that nervous systems grow to immense proportions to maintain an adequate transmission speed. It also requires huge energy expenditures. For instance, both frogs and squids have axons through which signals travel at 25 m/sec. The frog's axon is 12 microns in diameter, whereas the squid's is 500 microns in diameter. Not only is the squid's axon roughly 42 times larger in diameter than the frog's, but it also uses 5,000 times as much energy as the frog's (Morrell and Norton 1980, p. 88). Somehow signals in the axons in the frog's nervous system manage to match the conductance speed of signals in axons many times larger and many times more energetically costly.

Of course, given that human beings do not have weather-balloon-sized heads and frogs do not have axons 500 microns in diameter, it cannot be the case that human and frog nervous systems maintain high velocity signal transmission through an increase in cable diameter. Because, as I've mentioned, conductance speeds increase in direct proportion to the ratio of membrane resistance to internal resistance, this implies that the cables in human and frog nervous systems must have a high membrane resistance. Indeed, in all higher vertebrates, axon cables are sheathed in an insulating substance called *myelin*. It is myelin that increases membrane resistance and thus offsets the slow conduction speeds that small-caliber cables would otherwise impose on signal transmission. Morell and Newton summarize the significance of myelin: "it is impractical for a complex nervous system to lack a substance such as myelin: the energy and space requirements would both be too stringent"

(1980, p. 88). Indeed, Allman points to the lack of myelination in the brains of cephalopods as a fundamental limitation on their evolution (1999, p. 83). With no means by which to minimize the size of axons in their nervous systems, the octopus's brain cannot develop further without simultaneously becoming too large to maintain.

The significance of this discussion of myelin for my evaluation of MRT is more conditional than the points I have made so far about sensory systems, modularity, and component placement. The relationship between conductance speed and cable diameter is a relationship that applies to the transmission of *electrical* signals. Perhaps there exist other ways to carry information among the receptive fields of which sensory systems are composed. Moreover, an insulating sheath like myelin appears necessary for increased efficiency especially when the source of current is depolarization, that is, the rapid change in polarity across the axonal membrane. However, in metals current flows in a different manner. Vogel compares conductance in a solution of potassium chloride (a solution similar to that which we find in nervous systems) to that of copper wire. He calculates that "[e]qual performance would require that a copper wire a mere tenth of a millimeter across be replaced by a pipe of potassium chloride at least a foot in diameter" (1998, p. 162–163). This is because copper is nine million times more conductive than a potassium chloride solution. Thus, whether a nervous system capable of humanlike psychological abilities requires some sort of insulation around its cables will depend on how many alternative ways there are to realize signals and the cables that carry them. Perhaps metal cables cannot evolve naturally (Vogel 1998 discusses several reasons why we do not find metal in terrestrial organisms, but he is unwilling to reject the possibility that metal-containing organisms could evolve), in which case the likelihood that an insulating material like myelin will be present in the nervous system of any creature with humanlike psychological capacities increases. For now the reasonable stance to take on the need for something like myelin seems to be one of neutrality. Until more facts are in, we simply cannot say whether it is possible for an evolved system to realize a humanlike mind in a structure that lacks an insulating material.

4.6 Trends in Brain Evolution

The work of scientists like Allman (1999), Kaas (2000b), Martin (1990), and, perhaps most prominently, Jerison (1973) suggests that as brains evolve they exhibit certain trends. It is plausible that these trends are the product of cascading convergences that, as I have explained, arise from an interplay between historical and universal constraints. As a consequence of these constraints, it is tempting to infer that were the evolution of humanlike psychology to be replayed, the resulting brain would not be very unlike the brain that actually realizes the human mind.

One fairly intuitive trend in brain evolution is that toward greater size. The first organisms to populate Earth were of course very small, consisting of just one or a few cells. As evolution proceeded, organisms became larger and, as nervous systems evolved to monitor and control these larger organisms, bigger nervous systems became necessary for the monitoring and control of larger and more differentiated groups of cells. Jerison sees the correlation between body growth and brain growth as no more surprising than the correlation between body growth and the growth of other organs: "larger animals, which have generally larger organs such as livers or hearts, have to have larger brains for essentially the same reason. The nerve cells have more body to control and service" (1973, p. 16).

There are, in fact, a number of controversies about this trend for brain growth. For instance, Jerison (1973) and Martin (1990) disagree about the exponential rate at which brain growth follows increases in body size (Jerison's exponent is about 0.67 whereas Martin endorses research that suggests the exponential value to be more like 0.75). Moreover, Finlay et al. (2001) argue that growth in at least some brain structures is not, as Jerison supposes, a consequence of having more cells to keep track of. Intriguingly, they propose instead that the large isocortex of human beings is in fact an artifact or *spandrel* (Gould and Lewontin 1979) resulting from neurogenetic constraints. Human beings became so smart because they found themselves with a big brain at their disposal. However, despite these controversies about the precise allometric relationship between brain growth and body growth and the precise reason for this relationship, it is taken to be a law of brain evolution in mammals and birds (not so much reptiles and fish, which have evolved in fairly stable niches) that increases in body size will be accompanied by increases in brain size.

In addition to seeing the evolution of bigger brains as a response to a need to care for bigger bodies, Jerison (1973) hypothesizes that mammalian brains increased in size as a result of migration into a new niche. The stock from which mammals evolved had, Jerison believes, been unable to compete with reptiles for a diurnal lifestyle and thus were forced to adopt a nocturnal existence. This, in turn, led to the evolution of enhanced nocturnal senses (olfaction and audition) which then required the evolution of bigger brains in order to process the information gathered from these new senses.

Of course, were the evolution of humanlike psychology to be replayed, there is no reason to suppose that humanlike psychology would evolve as the result of the same historical contingencies. Perhaps the evolution of olfaction and audition would have evolved for reasons other than it did in our own species. For instance, olfaction and audition might have evolved not because of a losing battle for a diurnal niche, but because prey were more available at night than in day. I do not wish to claim that the evolution of auditory and olfactory senses resembling those that human beings possess can arise only through one particular sequence of historical events. The point I wish to draw from the above discussion is much more modest. Apparently, there is some correlation between what brains are capable of doing and how much brain there is available *for* the doing. Were the tape of life to be replayed with the stipulation that it produce organisms with a humanlike psychology, we should expect to see the evolution of a brain with some minimum size—some minimum number of neurons to perform the computations that create a humanlike psychology.

But because the psychological capacities of a human being require a brain of a certain minimal size, of a certain number of processing units, the evolution of such a brain will run into the kinds of constraints involving wiring and placement that I have discussed in earlier sections. As brains increase in size, as they must if they are to evolve all the capacities of a human brain, they will tend to become modular and tend to organize themselves so that modules that communicate most extensively with each other will be nearer to each other. It would also not be surprising if the replayed brain were fissured in the way that human brains are. Fissurization is a solution to the problem of packing an increasingly growing brain into a rigid container. Indeed, neuroscientists have labeled this tendency of large brains to show fissurization while small brains remain smooth *Baillarger's law*. At the present time, it is unclear whether the folds of sulci and gyri that form of the surfaces of large brains are homoplasies or homologies. Suggestively, Martin remarks, "There may be only a limited number of possible solutions for folding of the cortex as brain size increases within a skull of a particular shape and similarity of sulcal pattern may therefore tell us relatively little about phylogenetic relationships. Indeed, the obligatory folding of the cortex that accompanies increase in brain size provides one of the clearest examples of a general trend that is likely to lead to numerous cases of convergent evolution" (1990, p. 400). If Martin is right, fissurization may well be another illustration of convergence and so be another piece of evidence that the R-properties by which human brains realize human minds are not as variable as advocates of MRT suppose.

4.7 Conclusion

My goal in this chapter has been to extend the discussion of constraints I began in the previous chapter to those structures that realize human perceptual and cognitive abilities. Whereas I cannot deny that there is much we do not yet understand about how the human brain realizes the human mind, I hope to have made plausible the claim that there may well be constraints on the kind of structure that is capable of realizing a humanlike psychology. If MRT is true, we should be able to make few predictions about the properties of the organ that realizes a humanlike mind. Just as it is difficult to make specific predictions about the R-properties of something that can catch mice (must the trap have a spring? Glue? A doorway? A weight-sensitive platform? Bait?), MRT predicts that the function of a humanlike mind places few constraints on the kinds R-properties that can realize such a mind. In contrast, MCT predicts that because laws of nature curtail the number of possible ways to realize human psychological processes, there will be few ways to realize a humanlike mind. Just as the laws of optics limit the number of ways to realize an image-forming eye, so, MCT asserts, there are laws that restrict the number of ways evolution can produce an organ with the psychological capacities of a human being. Of course, the evidence in this chapter is too speculative to be more than a gesture toward the greater likelihood of MCT over MRT. Nevertheless, I submit that it marks at least a challenge to the supremacy of MRT, and in any event, places the contest between MRT and MCT in the empirical arena where it belongs.

5

Multiple Realizability and the Special Sciences

I noted in chapter 1 that one reason for philosophers' keen interest in multiple realizability is the consequences this idea appears to have for the possibility of intertheoretic reduction. It is no exaggeration to claim that since Jerry Fodor's seminal "Special Sciences" (1974) article, almost all philosophers who have thought about reduction have seen the potential for multiple realizability as a challenge or, just as likely, an insurmountable obstacle to the reducibility of higher-level sciences to lower-level sciences. Fodor (1974) himself argues that because economic and psychological kinds are multiply realizable in physical kinds, there is no prospect for reducing economics or psychology to physics. Similarly, Kitcher (1984) and Rosenberg (1985) have extended this line of reasoning in an effort to derail any suggestion that biological theories (or some parts of them) might be reducible to lower-level theories. However, there were some early dissenters to the multiple realizability argument against reduction (Enç 1983; Richardson 1979), and recently other philosophers (Kim 1992; Bickle 1998; Bechtel and Mundale 1999; Sober 1999b; Shapiro 2000; Polger 2002) have leapt from the bandwagon to cast a critical eye on the impact of multiple realizability on reductionist programs.

A proper assessment of Fodor's challenge to reduction demands careful examination of the purported goals of reductionism, of the kind of connection between terms in higher- and lower-level theories that is necessary to meet these goals, and of the extent to which reductionism, if successful, threatens the autonomy of higher-level sciences. Becoming clearer on these issues makes possible several responses to Fodor's opposition to reduction. Accordingly, after explaining the obstacle that Fodor believes multiple realizability presents to reduction, I shall examine the details necessary for its evaluation, and I shall then argue that multiple realizability does not sound the death knell to reduction that Fodor thinks he hears. In particular, there is reason to think that the truth of multiple realizability is consistent with the goals of reductionism. Some philosophers (Batterman 2000; Fodor 1997; Kim 1992) have wondered whether, and if so how, the special sciences are possible if their kinds are multiply realized in kinds of lower-level sciences. Indeed, Fodor (1997) calls this a "metaphysical mystery." In the final section of this chapter I will propose a solution to this mystery.

5.1   Fodor's Multiple Realizability Objection to Reduction

Consider two theories (or sciences), one of a higher level than the other. This talk of levels reflects several ideas. One is that a theory T_H is a higher-level theory, relative to a theory T_L, if the kind predicates of T_H name properties that are somehow made possible by or composed of the properties that the kind predicates in some T_L name. So, for instance, economics might describe properties, say, rational decisions, that are made possible by psychological properties of agents. Biology might refer to genes, which are composed of DNA. Psychologists might attribute pain to a subject, where this pain is made possible by C-fiber firings. These "made possible" and "composed by" locutions are admittedly vague, but they convey the idea that the kinds of properties that one theory talks about depend in some way on the kinds of properties that are in the domain of another theory. The latter theory is thus more basic, and so the former theory is thus of a "higher level."

Still another way to understand this talk of levels is to consider the generality of theories at various levels. Theories at higher levels have narrower scopes than theories at lower levels. The domain of objects in which there are genes is smaller than the domain of objects in which there are acids. Similarly, fewer objects have pains than have neurons. Physics, by this reasoning, is the most basic or the "lowest" science because all objects consist of physical particles and so physics spans all special domains. On the other hand, only physics has the vocabulary with which to talk about itself, for higher-level theories lack the predicates to describe physical properties. No doubt this too remains far from a precise characterization of what it means to say that one theory is of a higher level than another, but it suffices for present purposes.

Let L_H be a law in a science T_H. T_H might be psychology, for instance, and L_H might state that all organisms that are in pain will behave so as to minimize their pain. I will express this law as follows:

L_H: $P \rightarrow M$

"P" and "M" are predicates that name the properties *pain* and *behaving so as to minimize pain*. The arrow indicates that the connection between the properties P and M is a lawful one.

According to Fodor, the reduction of T_H to T_L requires that the laws of T_H be derivable from the laws of T_L. Thus, psychology reduces to, say, neuroscience only if there is some law of neuroscience, L_L, from which can be derived L_H. Psychology reduces to neuroscience *if* and only if every law of psychology follows from some law (or laws) of neuroscience. This requirement entails that for each kind predicate of T_H there is some kind predicate of T_L with which the higher-level predicate is at least coextensive. However, for reasons I will explore later, Fodor makes the more stringent demand that the so-called bridge laws by which the terms of a reduced T_H are connected to the terms of the reducing T_L express *identities*.

In sum, Fodor's conception of reduction between a higher-level theory and a lower-level theory requires that every law of T_H stand in a relation to a law of T_L like that depicted in figure 5.1. Thus, psychology reduces to neuroscience only if the properties mentioned in the law (supposing that it is one) "All organisms that feel pain behave so as to minimize their pain" are identical to properties mentioned in some law of neuroscience.

But suppose that the properties of T_H are multiply realized by properties of T_L. It could be that P can be realized in two, ten, or an infinite number of ways by properties of T_L. Similarly, there may be numerous ways to realize M in properties of T_L. This means, Fodor argues, that the laws of T_H and the laws of T_L do not refer to the same properties. Rather than the depiction in figure 5.1, the relationship between L_H and L_L is better illustrated as shown in figure 5.2. Properties P and R are not

Figure 5.1
Fodor's conception of reduction.

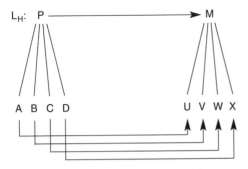

Figure 5.2
Relations between laws given the multiple realizability of higher-level kinds.

identical to properties in T_L but are instead coextensive with disjunctive collections of properties of T_L. Fodor believes that this point is a general one: for every or most properties of a given T_H, there will be at best a disjunctive collection of properties with which each is coextensive.

We are now in a position to state Fodor's argument against reduction. According to Fodor, reduction requires (i) bridge laws that assert identities between the properties named in a higher-level law L_H and the properties named in a lower-level law L_L; and (ii) the derivation of L_H from some L_L plus the bridge laws. But, the practical inevitability of multiple realizability implies that "what corresponds to the kind predicates of a reduced science may be a heterogeneous and unsystematic disjunction of predicates in the reducing science" (Fodor 1974, p. 138). Furthermore, a heterogeneous and unsystematic collection of properties is not itself a property in the reducing science. Hence, because laws reveal a connection between properties, the "bridge laws" that tie the properties of T_H

to properties of T_L are not really laws, thus violating condition (i) above. Moreover, L_L will not be a proper law because "the predicates appearing in the antecedent and consequent will, by hypothesis, not be kind predicates" (1974, p. 139). This means that L_L is not a law from which L_H can be derived, thus violating condition (ii) above. In short, the prospect of multiple realizability jeopardizes the tenability of both bridge laws and laws from which higher-level laws can be derived, and so threatens the viability of reduction.

5.2   Arguments for Strong Bridge Laws

Fodor does not say much about why reduction is an important philosophical thesis or why so many philosophers of science (e.g., Kemeny and Oppenheim 1956; Oppenheim and Putnam 1958; Nagel 1961; Schaffner 1967; Sklar 1967; Causey 1972; Enç 1976; Hooker 1981; Bickle 1998) have thought it an important task to articulate or defend accounts of reduction. Fodor mentions some features often associated with reduction, like unification, generality, and what he refers to several times as an "ontological bias," but he does not clarify what he means by these things. It *is* clear that Fodor thinks the conception of reduction he targets is the "classical" one (1974, p. 130) and the subtitle of his article, "The Disunity of Science as a Working Hypothesis," leaves little doubt that he takes himself to be responding to the defense of reduction that Oppenheim and Putnam (1958) develop.

Yet nothing is as it seems. Whereas Fodor thinks the multiple realizability argument that I presented above is successful against Oppenheim and Putnam's view, it in fact attacks a conception of reduction much stronger than that which Oppenheim and Putnam propose. In this section I explain why Fodor conceives of reduction in a way that makes it vulnerable to his multiple realizability argument. In the following section I argue that Fodor's notion of reduction is not Oppenheim and Putnam's, and that in fact Oppenheim and Putnam would be perfectly content in a world where higher-level kinds are multiply realizable in lower-level kinds, for the possibility of multiple realizability would not affect the payoffs they believe reduction can provide. The burden of this latter section is to show that a reasonable interpretation of the goals of reduction does not require that it be formulated in a way that makes multiple realizability something to be feared. This places the onus on Fodor to show why we must accept his conception of reduction.

Clearly, the assumption that does most of the work in Fodor's multiple realizability argument is that reduction requires the existence of bridge laws that express property identities. In the following, I shall refer to such bridge laws as *strong* bridge laws, to contrast them with bridge laws that express something weaker than a property identity. If a kind in T_H is multiply realized by kinds in T_L then it is not identical to any kind in T_L, and that, Fodor thinks, shows that it is not possible to construct the strong bridge laws that are necessary for T_L to reduce T_H. But why must bridge laws express identities rather than something weaker? Fodor's answer to this is that anything short of an identity "would fail to express the underlying ontological bias of the reductionist program" (1974, p. 129). His argument for this claim is as follows. Let S (a *special* science property) be a property of T_H and P (a *physical* science property) a property of T_L, and suppose we wish to derive a law about S from one about P. This requires a bridge law connecting S to P. Suppose this bridge law does not identify S and P. This, Fodor claims, means that an entity's having S would be at most causally correlated with its having P. The entity has the property S *because* it has the property P. "But," he continues, "this is compatible with a nonphysicalist ontology" (ibid., p. 129), because it is possible that S is a nonphysical property. For instance, it might be that "S" names some psychological property that is caused by some physical property but that, itself, is not physical. Accordingly, "the truth of reductionism does not guarantee the generality of physics vis-à-vis the special sciences" (ibid., p. 130).

There are several things to say about this argument. First, Fodor implies that the only alternative to strong bridge laws are bridge laws that express one-way conditionals. This is implicit in his suggestion that P is a cause of S. But this need not be the case. Famously, Nagel (1961) requires that bridge laws express biconditional relations between higher- and lower-level kinds.

Second, it is not true that if bridge laws expressed nothing stronger than conditional or biconditional relations between higher- and lower-level predicates then this would show the properties the predicates name to be at best causally correlated. It may well be that lower-level properties *realize* the higher-level properties. For instance, if a corkscrew is realized (in part) by a rigid lever, then the lever is part of a sufficient condition for the corkscrew, but it does not cause the corkscrew. Similarly, if a diamond is the only nomically possible realization of a particular kind of drill bit, then the diamond is a necessary and partly sufficient condition for the drill bit, but, again, it is not causally correlated with the drill bit. Indeed, the position that Fodor eventually defends is that instances of higher-level kinds are *token-identical* to instances of lower-level kinds (each particular instance of a higher-level kind is identical to some particular instance of a lower-level kind). But token-identity, unlike causal correlation, is a synchronic relation. Thus, the choice Fodor sees between property identity and causal correlation is not, as he suggests, exhaustive.

But what of Fodor's claim that anything short of property identity robs physics of its generality or fails to express the ontological bias of reduction? It seems clear that the ontological bias of which Fodor speaks is the view that all properties are physical properties. It is this bias that justifies hope in the generality of physics. Although special sciences apply to objects in only specially circumscribed domains, the claims of physics should hold across all domains. If some properties are not physical properties, then this generality is lost. Because this is an important claim that will prove significant in evaluating the success of Fodor's multiple realizability argument, I shall call it the *generality principle*. According to the generality principle, the truth of reductionism requires that all properties be physical properties.

However, there seems no good reason to accept the generality principle as a constraint on reduction. If, as we shall see Oppenheim and Putnam do, one takes the generality of physics to imply only that whatever can be explained by laws that cite higher-level properties can be explained by laws that cite physical properties, then the generality principle appears much too strong. Indeed, taken literally, the generality principle is inconsistent with the practice of reduction. If reduction requires that all properties be physical properties, then there is obviously no sense in trying to reduce higher-level sciences. Appearances to the contrary, the generality principle implies that the predicates of higher-level sciences just are names for physical properties, or it implies that higher-level sciences are, in some sense, radically false. Either way, if physics is general only in the sense that the generality principle describes, then reduction seems to be a nonstarter.

But Fodor has another reason to insist that bridge laws be strong. Suppose, as figure 5.2 illustrates, the connections between terms in L_H and L_L are one–many. Property P is not identical to a property in T_L, but is at best coextensive with a disjunction of properties. Still, coextension does license the inference from "$(X1 \lor X2 \lor X3 \lor \ldots \lor X_i) \to (Y1 \lor Y2 \lor Y3 \lor \ldots \lor Y_i)$" to "$P \to R$." This inference follows on the assumption that "P" is coextensive with the first disjunction and "R" with the second. Thus, one might think that at least one criterion of reduction—the derivation of higher-level laws from lower-level laws—can be satisfied without the need for property identities.

However, as I noted in the previous section, Fodor believes that L_L is not in fact a law. This is because although "X1," "X2," "X3," and so on are kind predicates of T_L, the disjunction of these predicates is not itself a kind predicate: "not all truth functions of kind predicates are themselves kind predicates" (Fodor 1974, p. 140). If the antecedent and consequent of a conditional statement do not contain proper kind predicates, the statement cannot be a law. In defense of this claim, Fodor notes that although it is a law that irradiation of green plants by sunlight causes carbohydrate synthesis, and it is a law that friction causes heat, it is not a law that (either the irradiation of green plants by sunlight or friction) causes (either carbohydrate synthesis or heat). For convenience, I will refer to this conditional statement as "C."

There is no doubting that C is a peculiar candidate for a law. However, this does not show that laws cannot have disjunctive antecedents and consequents. Perhaps the peculiarity of C is due to something other than the fact that its antecedent and consequent contain disjunctions of predicates. As Elliott Sober (1999b) remarks, it seems to be a law that water at sea level will boil when the ambient temperature exceeds 100°C. This means that water at sea level will boil when the ambient temperature is 101°C or 102°C or 103°C, and so on. In this context there appears to be no problem in allowing a disjunctive predicate into law statement.

Notice too that C is not the kind of law that is likely to play any role in a reductive project. The harsh light Fodor shines on disjunctive predicates softens noticeably when one considers disjunctions of kinds that multiply realize a single higher-level kind. Of course it is odd to claim that (irradiation by sunlight or friction) causes (carbohydrate synthesis or heat): (irradiation by sunlight or friction) does not realize anything that might figure into a higher-level generalization. In contrast, consider Putnam's (1975d) observation that "jade" in fact names two distinct minerals: jadeite or nephrite. Suppose it is a law that all jade is green, and suppose that jadeite is green in virtue of surface spectral reflectance properties J and nephrite is green in virtue of other surface spectral reflectance properties N. The law "All jade is green" thus reduces to the law "All samples of jadeite or nephrite have SSRs J or N." Perhaps this lower-level law still sounds peculiar, but, at least to my ear, it is not nearly as remarkable as the law about irradiation or friction. Moreover, there is no reason to state the law in this way. One can derive the law about jade in the following way. (1) Something is jade if and only if it is either jadeite or nephrite; (2) All jadeite has SSR J; (3) All nephrite has SSR N; (4) Anything with SSRs J or N is green; therefore, All jade is green. This appears to be a perfectly good derivation of the jade law, and, more important, it qualifies as an explanation of the jade law. In contrast, law C does not seem to explain anything.

In sum, Fodor's second reason for demanding that reduction rest on strong bridge laws is hardly compelling. His assertion that laws cannot contain disjunctive predicates receives support from a tendentious example. Once one takes note of the many laws that describe behavior above some threshold (e.g., the behavior of water above 100°C), disjunctive antecedents seem not so extraordinary. Moreover, once one considers disjunctive predicates that are "held together" by some higher-level generalization, there becomes available an explanation for why the disjunction contains exactly *this* set of predicates rather than some other. That is, laws about the color of jade will be derived from (and explained by) laws about the SSRs of jadeite and nephrite because all jade *is* jadeite or nephrite. This, I submit, takes much of the sting out of Fodor's objection to disjunctive predicates. Fodor may be right that not simply any disjunction of predicates can stand in a law, but this shows only that there is more to laws than what syntactic manipulation allows.

5.3   Unity without Strong Bridge Laws

I mentioned in the previous section that on Oppenheim and Putnam's (1958) conception of reduction, bridge laws need not express property identities. This claim raises two sorts of questions. The first is an exegetical question. Fodor certainly believes that Oppenheim and Putnam's program does rest on strong bridge laws. But is this belief justified? The second sort of question is more interesting. Do the goals that motivate Oppenheim and Putnam's defense of reductionism require the existence of strong bridge laws to tie together different sciences? In this section I say a few words in answer to the first question and then direct my attention to the second.

As I noted earlier, there is little doubt that Fodor takes his target to be the conception of reduction that Oppenheim and Putnam (1958) develop. Theirs is the only paper about reduction that Fodor cites in his attack, and in a footnote Fodor complains that Oppenheim and Putnam's conjecture that social sciences might some day be explained by physics fails to appreciate that there can be no "predicate-by-predicate reduction of economics to psychology," which is precisely what "Oppenheim and Putnam's own account of the unity of science requires" (1974, p. 323). So, to our first question: Do Oppenheim and Putnam advocate strong bridge laws?

In fact, Oppenheim and Putnam introduce several senses of reduction. One is that which Oppenheim, together with Kemeny, developed in 1956. On this earlier view, T_H reduces to T_L if and only if

(1) The vocabulary of T_H contains terms not in the vocabulary of T_L;

(2) Any observational data that T_H can explain can also be explained by T_L;

(3) T_L is at least as well systematized as T_H, where systematization is a measure of the combined strength and simplicity of the theory (Kemeny and Oppenheim 1956, p. 11).

Pretty clearly, Kemeny and Oppenheim's sense of reduction is not what most philosophers have in mind—Fodor in particular—when thinking about reduction. Indeed, rather than offering an account of reduction, it perhaps makes more sense to see Kemeny and Oppenheim as providing an account of theory *replacement*. The goal of replacement is to get rid of one theory when there is another that can do the work of the former at least as well. As an example of what I am calling replacement, Kemeny and Oppenheim discuss the reduction of biology to physics, which, if possible, would eliminate the need for biological vocabulary. Alternatively, as Schaffner (1967) notes, reduction of this sort might also include the replacement of phlogiston theory with Lavoisier's oxidation theory. In both examples, the explanatory and predictive duties of one theory are assumed by another, with a resulting gain in theoretical economy.

Of course, Fodor's multiple realizability argument has nothing to do with reduction conceived in the way Kemeny and Oppenheim articulate it. Replacement can proceed without any bridge laws at all—which would presumably be the case in the replacement of phlogiston theory with oxidation theory. Because at least some of the predicates of phlogiston theory name no properties at all, one would hope for the sake of oxidation theory that there *not* be bridge laws connecting it to these empty predicates.

The more likely focus of Fodor's attack is that which Oppenheim and Putnam call microreduction. Oppenheim and Putnam introduce microreduction by reference to *branches* of science, but it does no harm to their view to state it in the terms I have been employing. The reduction of T_H to T_L is a *microreduction* if and only if T_H is reduced to T_L in Kemeny and Oppenheim's above sense and "the objects in the universe of discourse in T_H are wholes which possess a decomposition into proper parts all of which belong to the universe of discourse of T_L" (Oppenheim and Putnam 1958, p. 407, replacing "B2" with "T_H" and "B1" with "T_L"). As an example of microreduction, Oppenheim and Putnam ask us to consider a higher-level science with multicellular organisms in its universe of discourse and a lower-level science that ranges over a universe of discourse containing single cells. "Then the things in the universe of discourse of T_H can be decomposed into proper parts belonging to the universe of discourse of T_L. If, in addition, it is the case that T_L reduces T_H at time t, we shall say that T_L *microreduces T_H at time t*" (ibid., replacing "B2" with "T_H" and "B1" with "T_L"; italics in the original).

Noticeably absent from this account of microreduction is a demand for strong bridge laws. A science of multicellular organisms may reduce to a science of single cells without having identities between the properties in the universes of discourse of each of the two sciences. Indeed, for reasons I mentioned in the previous section, it would be hard to appreciate the value of reduction were there such property identities. If properties mentioned in laws about multicellular organisms were identical to properties mentioned in laws about singular cells, this would be reason to doubt that the distinction between multicellular organisms and single cells marks an interesting or significant distinction. Or, impossibly, if *being multicellular* were identical to *being a single cell*, it is puzzling why there should be one science to describe the former and another to describe the latter. As I will soon show, the interest in reduction is in large part due to the discovery that distinct (i.e., nonidentical) properties can figure in different explanations of the *same* observations, and that laws that appear distinct at some higher level can be shown to be true "for the same reason" at a lower level.

For Oppenheim and Putnam, it is clear not only that strong bridge laws are not necessary for microreduction, but also that they have in mind a much weaker (i.e., one-way conditional) connection between predicates in the reduced and reducing theories. They claim that "[i]t is not absurd to suppose that psychological laws may eventually be explained in terms of the behavior of individual neurons in the brain; that the behavior of individual cells—including neurons—may eventually be explained in terms of their biochemical constitution; and that the behavior of molecules—including the macromolecules that make up living cells—may eventually be explained in terms of atomic physics" (1958, p. 408). As lofty as this dream may appear, the significant point is that it is not a dream in which strong bridge laws come into view. Oppenheim and Putnam even consider the possibility of microreducing such properties as "man in phone booth," where it is up to psychology to explain the "man" part of this aggregate and some physicochemical theory to explain the behavior of phone booths (1958, p. 410). Nowhere is there an indication that such a microreduction requires a strong bridge law connecting phone booths to physicochemical properties. Oppenheim and Putnam almost certainly would not wish to be committed to the view that *phone booth* is identical to some lower-level property.

In sum, it is, I think, indisputable that Fodor's multiple realizability argument attacks a conception of reduction that Oppenheim and Putnam never propose. However, one might think that Fodor is in fact correcting Oppenheim and Putnam's account. Perhaps Fodor attributes to their analysis of reduction a need for strong bridge laws because he understands that the goals Oppenheim and Putnam set for reduction can make do with nothing less (you may think your toothache will go away by itself, but I know better and that's why I made an appointment with a dentist for you). This brings us to a discussion of the goals of reduction. Surely Oppenheim and Putnam try to articulate and defend reductionism because they see some merit in the possibility of reducing one science to another. But what are the motivations for reducing one theory to another, and can these motivations be satisfied without strong bridge laws?

Oppenheim and Putnam see reduction as a means toward unification, where "unification" has two meanings that concern them. The first, weaker sense of unification is *unity of language*. Unity of language involves a connection between the terms of one science and the terms of another. As Oppenheim and Putnam note, this connection might take the form of a definition of terms in T_H by terms of T_L, where definition requires biconditionals between the predicates of the two theories. However, Oppenheim and Putnam declare that the "notion of reduction we shall employ is a wider one, and is designed to include reduction by means of biconditionals as a special case" (1958, p. 405). This confirms my claim above that Oppenheim and Putnam are not committed to strong bridge laws, and also fits with the replacement conception of reduction that Kemeny and Oppenheim defend. One way to unify the language of two sciences is simply to replace the vocabulary of one with the other.

The more interesting sense of unification that Oppenheim and Putnam wish to explore is a unity of laws. It is in this context that reduction must involve more than replacement; it must incorporate microreduction. Because microreduction is a transitive relation, a phenomenon P that is explained by laws of T_H can be explained by laws of some intermediate theory T_I, which can in turn be explained by laws of some T_L, assuming that T_H microreduces to T_I which in turn microreduces to T_L. Here, then, is a case where laws of T_H and T_I can, relative to an explanation of P, be dispensed with in favor of laws of just T_L. For Oppenheim and Putnam, this is the main meaning of unitary science. It is something to be sought because it shows how narrow domains fit within rather than outside other, broader domains.

Suppose that instead of being nested within the confines of each other, different sciences mark distinct territories. Laws that describe phenomena in one such territory, suppose, have no explanatory power in others. There is nothing a priori impossible about such a state of affairs. Consider, for instance, that the rules of baseball are not nested in the rules of football. If they were, it would be possible to rely on the football manual to explain why a runner on first must run to second if the batter hits a fair ball. The advantages of nesting are obvious in this case. If rules of baseball were nested in rules of football, complete knowledge of the latter would suffice for knowledge of the former. Whereas without nesting two manuals are necessary for explaining baseball and football phenomena, with nesting only one manual need be consulted.

For similar reasons, unitary science is an attractive prospect. The truth of Oppenheim and Putnam's sense of reduction allows one to predict from biological facts, for instance, an observation of psychology. Moreover, it allows one to explain in biological terms why some psychological law is true. Crucially, Oppenheim and Putnam's ideal of unity accounts for the generality of physics without having to subscribe to the generality principle, that is, the principle that all properties are physical properties. Recall that Fodor attributes this principle to Oppenheim and Putnam; but there is nothing in the idea of a unitary science that implies it. Reductionism can be true without the properties of more exclusive theories being identical to the properties of more inclusive theories. Absent identities, it is still possible for physics to explain why a law in the special sciences is true (as I showed in the case of the "law" about jade); and it is still possible for physics to explain all the observations that some special science explains. When Oppenheim and Putnam mention that it is possible to explain the social behavior of some insects by appeal to properties of secreted hormones (1958, p. 414), there should be no temptation to read them as claiming that a kind of social behavior *is* a chemical kind. The generality of physics means only that the social behavior of insects can be explained by laws that describe chemical behavior, and, furthermore, chemical behavior can be explained by laws that describe the behavior of atoms.

Finally, the conception of reduction that Oppenheim and Putnam advance provides for another sort of unity. Because lower-level theories, on their account, can explain why the laws of the special sciences are true, they can also tie together (unify) distinct higher-level laws. Nagel (1961) mentions an example of this sort of case. Prior to the reduction of thermodynamics to statistical mechanics, most laws about gases, Nagel tells us, "could be affirmed only as so many independent facts about gases" (1961, p. 359). The derivation of gas laws from laws in statistical mechanics changed this, opening our eyes to the fact that these "independent" laws about gases are all true as a result of the statistical properties of molecules in motion. Thus, the derivation of gas laws from statistical mechanics makes explicit why gases that obey one law will obey others as well. Furthermore, like the sense of unity I mentioned above, this kind of unification makes do without the property identities that Fodor's multiple realizability argument impugns.

As this discussion of unity and generality makes clear, for Oppenheim and Putnam explanation is the keystone of reduction. It perhaps remains an interesting question whether the predicates of two scientific levels bear the relation of identity to each other, the relation of coextension, or merely a conditional relation. However, answering this question is not necessary to pursuing a unified science.

5.4 Wherefore Autonomy?

Fodor presents his attack on reduction as a defense of the autonomy of the special sciences. Multiple realizability is a stake in the heart of reduction he claims, and with reduction dead the special sciences are safe once more. I have argued so far that Fodor attacks a conception of reduction that Oppenheim and Putnam do not hold, and so one might think there is little need to consider whether *that* kind of reduction jeopardizes the autonomy of the special sciences. However, I believe that whether reduction could succeed in either Fodor's sense or Oppenheim and Putnam's sense, there is little need to worry about the autonomy of the special sciences. This becomes clear in light of an example Putnam (1975b) develops.

Putnam asks us to imagine a board in which two holes are cut. One hole is a circle with a one-inch diameter and the other is a square with a one-inch side. There is also a cubical peg, the sides of which are just less than an inch. To be explained is the fact that the peg passes through the square hole in the board but not the circular hole. In this simple example, the "higher-level" explanation for why the peg fits through the square hole but not the circular one will mention facts about the rigidity of the peg, the rigidity of the board, the sizes of the holes, and the cross-section of the peg. "The explanation is that the board is rigid, the peg is rigid, and as a matter of geometrical fact, the round hole is smaller than the peg, the square hole is bigger then the cross-section of the peg" (1975b, p. 296).

Because the board and the peg are made up of smaller parts, it is possible to derive the observation of the peg's behavior from lower-level facts. Suppose that the peg and the board are composed of lattices of atoms. Calling the peg "system A" and the holes "region 1" and "region 2," one could, in principle, "deduce from just the laws of particle mechanics or quantum electrodynamics that system A never passes through region 1, but that there is at least one trajectory which enables it to pass through region 2" (1975b, pp. 295–296). Thus, lower-level laws are able to predict the same observations as higher-level laws. This provides for a kind of unity of science that Oppenheim and Putnam advocate.

Putnam claims that the lower-level derivation of the peg's behavior is in fact not an *explanation* of the peg's behavior. It is important to appreciate the strength of Putnam's claim: it is not simply that the lower-level derivation is not a good explanation, or not *as* good an explanation, but that it is no explanation at all. Putnam thinks this because the lower-level account fails to provide the generality that the higher-level story promises. One way to put this point is in terms of R-properties. Causally relevant in an explanation of why the peg passes through the square hole but not the round one are the kinds of properties Putnam mentions in the higher-level explanation: the rigidity of the board and peg and the dimensions of the holes and the peg. Putnam thinks that the atomic facts are not relevant—pegs composed of different materials would still, if rigid and with a cross-section just slightly less than an inch—fail to pass through the circular hole while passing through the square hole. Hold the R-properties fixed, and the atomic properties can vary in whatever way with no difference to the peg's capacity to fit through one hole and not the other.

Sober (1999b) has objected to Putnam's dismissal of lower-level explanations. He points out that one might prefer to explain the peg's behavior in terms of what I would call the R-properties, but, depending on one's interests, one could as well choose to explain the peg's behavior in terms of lower-level properties. Each kind of explanation has its own merits. The higher-level explanation is more general. If it applies to *this* peg, it will apply as well to other pegs that, despite molecular dissimilarities, have in common the same R-properties. On the other hand, scientists might choose depth over breadth. If, for instance, one wants to know how cigarette smoke causes cancer, a focus on the particular carcinogens the smoke contains seems appropriate—especially if the smoke from different kinds of cigarettes contains different kinds of carcinogens. In one context—one in which the aim of explanation is to make salient those R-properties in virtue of which molecularly distinct causes produce the same kind of effect—it is appropriate to ignore the lower-level facts. But in other contexts—those in which one's focus concerns how lower-level properties come to produce the behavior that the R-properties produce—the deep explanation is appropriate. Neither explanation is superior to the other; breadth and depth each have their own place.

Returning now to the issue of autonomy, the distinction between breadth and depth clarifies the kind of threat reduction might make to the special sciences. If the only task of the special sciences were the explanation of singular events—peg *P* going through hole *H* at time *t*—then, I think, reduction would present a real challenge to autonomy. The truth of microreduction implies that any singular event that can be explained at some higher-level can be explained by laws of all those lower levels in which the higher level is nested. In contrast, if special sciences also have as one of their goals the statement of generalizations (e.g., all pegs and boards with R-properties X, Y, and Z will behave as follows, regardless of their microstructures), then the prospect of microreduction should not conflict with autonomy. Generalizations receive expression in the predicates of the special sciences, and it is precisely the inability of lower-level sciences to "see" the properties that figure into higher-level generalizations that guarantees the endurance of the special sciences (Dennett 1981). One should fear for autonomy only if one takes a narrow and inaccurate view of the explanatory goals of the special sciences.

Fodor's suggestion that reduction jeopardizes the autonomy of the special sciences reveals an inadequate appreciation of the various explanatory goals of the special sciences. Note that even if reduction did require strong bridge laws, and even if such bridge laws were forthcoming, the special sciences would not go away. Suppose that strong bridge laws connected the predicates in the higher-level law $P \rightarrow R$ to those in the lower-level law $X \rightarrow Y$. This still would not suffice to show that T_H no longer has a claim to autonomy. Consider first of all that the higher-level law $P \rightarrow R$ remains explanatory. That P and X are identical properties does not mean that explanations involving P are no longer explanations. If the fact that all Ps are R explains why it is some Ps are also Q, then it is hard to see why the identity of P and X should in any way weaken the force of this explanation. Indeed, should we say, on discovery that P and X are identical, that all prior explanations and predictions involving P were no good, or were uninformative, or were dispensable? This would make the past explanatory and predictive successes of laws involving P miraculous. For these reasons, it is hard to understand why reductionism of even the extreme form that Fodor imagines should threaten the autonomy of the special sciences.

5.5   Multiple Realizability and the Special Sciences

I have argued that Fodor's attack on reduction goes awry because, first, he attributes to Oppenheim and Putnam a much stronger conception of reduction than they in fact propose, and second, because he unduly dismisses the possibility that laws can contain disjunctive predicates. For completeness' sake, I should note that even if Fodor's intended target was Nagel's (1961) well-known characterization of reduction,[1] in which bridge laws express biconditional relations between the predicates of T_H and T_L, he would still face the problem of justifying his claim that disjunctive predicates should not be allowed to stand on one side of the biconditional. Fodor's rejection of disjunctive predicates is no more persuasive, and perhaps even less so, in the case of biconditional relations than it is in the case of identity relations.

But even if Fodor's multiple realizability argument does not succeed for the reasons I have discussed, it does invite reflection on what some philosophers consider to be a deep mystery.[2] Fodor conveys the mystery in the following passage: "Damn near everything we know about the world suggests that unimaginably complicated to-ings and fro-ings of bits and pieces at the extreme microlevel manage somehow to converge on stable macrolevel properties. On the other hand, the "somehow" really is entirely mysterious . . ." (1997, pp. 160–161).[3] Given the multiple realizability of a higher-level kind, the mystery, as Fodor sees it, is to account for the fact that it behaves like a kind. If the various things that realize the kind are distinct, why, then, do they all behave in a way that some higher-level generalization can describe?

Kim (1992) makes the puzzle more precise. He considers an example I have already mentioned. "Jade" refers to a disjunction of kinds: a sample of jade is either jadeite or nephrite. Moreover, Kim assumes, kinds in science must adhere to the principle of causal individuation of kinds:

Kinds in science are individuated on the basis of causal powers; that is, objects and events fall under a kind, or share a property, insofar as they have similar causal powers. (1992, p. 17)

Given this principle, it is proper to distinguish jadeite and nephrite as two kinds only if they differ in their causal powers. The realizing class of a higher-level kind is a heterogeneous class just because it consists of kinds that differ in their causal powers.

In addition to the principle of causal individuation of kinds is the physical realization thesis, which states (roughly) that the properties of higher-level kinds and the nomic relationships they bear to other kinds "are due to, and explainable in terms of, the properties and causal-nomic connections among their physical 'substrates'" (1992, p. 14). In more familiar terms, Kim's claim is that higher-level kinds owe their behavior to the behavior of their realizers. Now, if, as the principle of causal individuation of kinds requires, different realizing kinds of a higher-level kind differ with respect to their causal powers, and if, as the physical realization thesis requires, the behavior of higher-level kinds is determined by the properties of their realizers, we have a succinct statement of the mystery that so intrigues Fodor. How can a higher-level kind obey regularities if its multiple and heterogeneous instances have distinct causal powers? "If pain is nomically equivalent to N, the property claimed to be wildly disjunctive and obviously nonnomic, *why isn't pain itself equally heterogeneous and nonnomic as a kind*?" (ibid., p. 15, his italics). Kim's answer is that it is: pain and other higher-level kinds are no more kinds than is jade, which is just to say they are not kinds in any scientifically useful sense.

I think there is a way out of this jam, but before I turn to it, it is worth considering Batterman's (2000) response to the mystery Fodor and Kim describe. Batterman looks to physics to shed light on the issues involved. Within physics is a technical notion known as "universality." "Universality" refers to the fact that diverse (or, in Fodor's parlance, heterogeneous) systems can display the same behavior. Often times instances of universality become apparent as systems asymptotically approach some limit. For instance, Batterman notes that the same De Moivre–Laplace limit theorem describes the behavior of a probabilistic event as the number of trials approaches infinity. Whatever the nuts and bolts of the event (whether it is rolling a given number on a die or a measurement of some quantity of a gas), one can predict that any measurement of the event, as the number of trials approaches infinity, will fit the bell curve. Interestingly, this universality abstracts from details of independent trials—it is the collective behavior of the sequence of trials that exhibits the universal behavior rather than the behavior of any particular trial.

To take another of Batterman's examples, it happens that a heterogeneous group of systems—gases, fluids, and magnets—exhibits universal behavior near critical points, where the critical point for a fluid in a container "is a point below which it is impossible to pass, by increasing pressure at fixed temperature, from the gaseous phase to the liquid phase without going through a state in which both gas and liquid are simultaneously present in the container; and above which such a transition from gas to liquid is possible without passing through a regime in which both gas and liquid are simultaneously present" (2000, p. 123). The critical point for a fluid is described with a "critical exponent," and it turns out that regardless of the molecular constitution of the fluid the same critical exponent can describe its behavior. Indeed, the same critical exponent works as well for describing "the behavior of magnets as they undergo a transition from the ferromagnetic state with positive net magnetization below the critical point, to the paramagnetic phase with zero magnetization above the critical point" (ibid.).

Universality, in the physicist's sense, is thus an analogue to the macrolevel regularities that puzzle Kim and Fodor. However—and this is Batterman's point—there is a strategy available to explain universality, and so there is a way to address the puzzle. The strategy depends on modeling the behavior of the system under investigation (whether it be a gas, fluid, or magnet) in an abstract space whose topological structure corresponds to the interactions of the system's components. This space is then transformed (renormalized) into one with fewer parameters while retaining the structure of the first space. Renormalization continues until one is left with a space in which only those interactions of the system's components that are relevant to the behavior of the system at the critical point are present in the space. Repeated application of renormalization thus distills from the system a bare bones description of just those interactions that result in its behavior at a critical point.

As I understand Batterman's approach to resolving Kim and Fodor's mystery, it depends on isolating from diverse systems various shared properties that are responsible for the universal behaviors that systems exhibit at a critical point. This is much in the spirit of my discussion of multiple realizability, where corresponding to what remains in the renormalized space of the interactions a system's components are what I call R-properties. However, it remains unclear why Batterman thinks that multiple realizability is a "kind" or "instance" of universality. Suppose it is true that the molecularly distinct kinds of systems he discusses display common behavior at a critical point and thus are subject to the renormalizing strategy of explanation. Note that most examples of multiple realizability seem not to exhibit behavior at a limit. In the examples I have used to illustrate multiple realizability—corkscrews, watches, eyes—what is the behavior of these systems at a limit? When a corkscrew successfully removes a cork, what limit does it approach asymptotically? What is its critical point? Rather than seeing multiple realizability as an instance of universality, it might be more appropriate to view universality as an instance of multiple realizability, which suggests that renormalization might be a useful tool for explaining how some heterogeneous collections of systems can display some common macrolevel behavior, but that it cannot be a tool that explains all instances of multiple realization.

In fairness to Batterman, he recognizes that the renormalization strategy for explaining universality may not by itself answer questions about the relationship between the micro- and macrolevels that concern Fodor as well as many others. Batterman concedes:

> I do not want to suggest that the mathematical apparatus of the [renormalization] analysis itself is what will provide us with an explanation of the multiple realizability of pain. I would have to know much more about the physics and microstructural makeup of the realizers. But, I do not see how any explanation would go unless it proceeds by demonstrating principled physical reasons for why most of the microstructural details of the realizers are irrelevant for the universal behavior of interest. The underlying physical theory must be able to tell us (most likely through some type of asymptotic analysis) that most (otherwise important) physical details are irrelevant. (2000, p. 133)

I of course agree with Batterman that an account of multiple realization must abstract away from irrelevant details. Indeed, I offered an account of R-properties for just this reason. Not just any difference between two realizations of a kind should suffice to distinguish the realizations as distinct in kind. My idea was to look to a task analysis of the capacity that defines a functional kind in an effort to isolate just those properties that play a role in the execution of the capacity. Such analyses abstract away from irrelevant details such as, in the case of corkscrews, color and molecular composition.

But here, Batterman and I part company. As I see it, when two realizations share their R-properties and differ only in those properties that make no difference to how they realize a given kind, they should not count as different kinds of realization. Thus, I claim, two double-lever corkscrews that differ only in color should not count as different types of corkscrew. Sameness in R-properties means sameness in kind of realization. To the contrary, however, Batterman sees multiple realization in cases of universality. On his view, fluids that behave similarly at their critical point—fluids whose critical behavior is explained by the same renormalization group—count as different realizers of this critical behavior if they differ at some microlevel. In this case, it is a difference in a property that makes no difference to their critical behavior that, on Batterman's view, makes the fluids different kinds of realizations. Similarly, he suggests that pendulums with the same period but that differ in color and mass are different kinds of realizations despite the fact that, with respect to those properties that make them subject to the law of the pendulum, they are identical. Batterman and I agree, then, that an account of multiple realization requires a distinction between properties that make a difference to the performance of a capacity and properties that don't. Yet, for Batterman, it is the properties that don't make a difference that distinguish between kinds of realizers.

Driving Batterman to this peculiar position is, I submit, his acceptance of Fodor and Kim's mystery. Fodor and Kim find it incredible that different lower-level kinds can produce behavior that is regular at a higher level. Batterman's response is to look for some property that is common across the heterogeneous collection of lower-level realizers. Sameness at the higher level is the result of "features which are stable under perturbation of the micro-details" (2000, p. 136). From my perspective, if there is some feature common to all realizers in virtue of which they are realizers of the same higher-level kind, then the realizers do not multiply realize the higher-level kind, or, as I sometimes put it, they do so in only a trivial sense. Batterman's solution to the mystery of macroregularities, seen from the position I have developed, is to deny that higher-level kinds are in fact multiply realizable in a significant sense.

But now it appears that I am left with a mystery on my hands. How can systems that share no features in common end up with the same capacities? But the bigger mystery is why this seems at all mysterious. Task analyses of two significantly different realizations of the kind corkscrew will reveal how it is that each realization is able to remove corks. Once one understands the principles by which waiter's corkscrews remove corks, and the principles by which double-lever corkscrews remove corks, what is so puzzling about how two causally distinct devices can "do the same thing"? Fodor, oddly, comes close to making the same claim: "If it weren't possible, at least *sometimes*, for quite heterogeneous mechanisms to be reliable in respect of the functional descriptions that they converge upon, new kinds of mousetraps would never work; ingenuity would fail, and mousetrap makers would be doomed to careers of fruitless self-quotation" (1997, p. 160, his italics). Of course there are different kinds of mousetraps. But, given that we can explain of each kind of mousetrap how it ends up doing what all mousetraps do, that is, respecting the generalization "live mouse in, dead mouse out" (ibid.), the only real puzzle is why Kim especially sees fit to describe macroregularities as something like voodoo science.

No doubt Kim would object at this point. On the one hand, he might respond, the waiter's corkscrew and the double-lever corkscrew could not do the same thing if they differ in their causal powers. Certainly this would be true if they shared absolutely no causal powers at all, but no advocate of multiple realizability need make a claim that strong. Indeed, functional systems like corkscrews, watches, or eyes might differ with respect to many of the distal steps whereby they perform their function while sharing a proximal step. Thus, for instance, the waiter's corkscrew and the double-lever corkscrew share a proximal stage in cork removal, namely pulling the cork from the bottle, but they differ in the sequence of steps that lead up to this proximal event. True, if one were to individuate corkscrews only by their most proximal effect—the removal of the cork from the bottle— then waiter's corkscrews and double-lever corkscrews would not differ. However, this is not a method of individuation that is at all standard in sciences that describe the behavior of systems. Camera and compound eyes differ despite having (roughly) the same capacity. Analog and digital watches differ despite the fact that both tell time.

Alternatively, Kim might object that the kind *corkscrew*, or *eye*, or whatever other kind that truly allows of multiple realization, cannot be a proper scientific kind precisely because of this fact. This is the claim he makes about jade.[4] However, this is just to deny the undeniable: that there are multiply realizable kinds in the special sciences that behave in lawlike ways. Here the mystery might seem to recur. How can generalizations be true of a kind that is realized by a diversity of distinct kinds? The answer, once more, is that this is possible because causally distinct systems are capable of the same effects. When generalizations range over these effects, they range too over the heterogeneous collection of systems that produce these effects.

I suspect Kim is thinking about "internal" generalizations to the exclusion of "external" generalizations. The distinction is rough but illuminating. Kim's doubts about generalizations over multiply realizable kinds assume that such generalizations must have the form "All *SK*s are also *I*," where *SK* is a multiply realizable kind in some special science and *I* is a fact about the innards of *SK*, that is, *SK*'s microstructure. Thus, Kim is looking for a law about jade of the form "All jade is *X*," where *X* is some microstructural fact about jade. As things turn out, however, "jade" is a label for both jadeite and nephrite, and so no such generalization is forthcoming. Similarly, if one hoped for a generalization about some common microstructure that all eyes share, given that eyes are genuinely multiply realizable, then one will probably be disappointed. The diversity of eyes makes finding generalizations like "All eyes are *X*," where *X* is some microstructural fact about eyes, improbable.[5] This is just what one should expect if a kind is multiply realizable in a significant sense.

However, consider generalizations of the form "All *SK*s are also *E*," where *SK* is again a multiply realizable kind but now *E* is a fact about processes or relations into which *SK* enters. It should not be surprising to find a multiply realizable kind entering into such generalizations given that many multiply realizable kinds—those of interest to special sciences like psychology and biology—are defined by their effects. If a diversity of kinds all produce similar effects, it is no wonder that this diversity of kinds might enter into the same "external" generalizations. Thus, whereas "internal" generalizations about eyes might be hard to find, it is not at all difficult to uncover "external" generalizations. "All eyes allow for the detection of distal objects by the reflection or occlusion of light" is a particularly obvious example. Similarly, there may exist generalizations about the kinds of environments in which eyes are likely to evolve. These generalizations would be possible because of what eyes do, rather than because of what eyes are made of.

My suggestion that generalizations over multiply realizable kinds will tend to be external rather than internal—will be true in virtue of similarities in what multiply realizable kinds do rather than in what they are made of—hints at an answer to a question that is perhaps too obvious to have received much notice. Why are so many of the special sciences, for example, biology, psychology, sociology, economics, interested in domains that range over living things? The answer, I submit, is that living things are the products of processes that are effect-sensitive, and, similarly, they are things that engage in activities that are effect-driven. Generalizations about biological and psychological phenomena can focus on what biological and psychological kinds do, because these things have evolved precisely because of what they do rather than because of what they are made of. Natural selection is oblivious to what things are made of so long as the effects of these things are fitness enhancing. Likewise, sociology and economics can focus on group behavior and rational decision making because there are things to be said about what groups do and what decisions are rational that need not mention the composition of the group or the underlying processes that make rational decision making possible. Thus, it is only appropriate that so many of the special sciences that deal in multiply realizable kinds have domains that range over kinds defined by their effects.

In sum, the mystery that has tantalized Fodor, Kim, Batterman, and others—the question how multiply realizable kinds can engage in lawful behavior—dissipates once one recognizes that many generalizations concern what kinds do rather than what kinds are made of. Recognition of this fact also goes some distance toward explaining why so many of the special sciences are concerned with living things and their activities. Living things are composed of traits that have been selected for what they do, and living things participate in activities that have purposes. For these reasons, the generalizations of the special sciences are especially at home in the biotic world.

6

Disembodied Minds

So far the focus of this book has been on MRT. I have offered a sustained examination of the multiple realizability thesis, arguing that whether the human mind is multiply realizable is ultimately an empirical question. In treating MRT as an empirical hypothesis, I have looked to various sources of evidence in an effort to weigh its likelihood against a competing hypothesis: the mental constraint thesis. The widespread occurrence of similar designs in independently evolved sensory systems is one fact that ought to be surprising given MRT, but it is just what one would expect given MCT. Similarly, convergences in brain wiring are curious given the hypothesis that there are many ways to design a brain, but they are exactly what one would predict given the belief that there are constraints on the realization of mental properties. In further support of MCT, I argued that it is possible to *explain* why there are various convergences in sensory and neural architecture. Physical laws that apply to the design of, say, sensory systems and brains, constrict the space of physically possible solutions. In short, the presence of constraints on the number of designs that are capable of performing the functions of a human mind lowers the probability that minds are multiply realizable, which in turn suggests that mind–brain reduction is not the lost cause that so many have recently supposed.

The constraints I have considered have been constraints on realization. Realization, as I have noted, is a synchronic relationship between the realizer and that which is realized. To say that, for instance, a corkscrew can be realized by a rack and pinions is to say that a gadget composed of a rack and pinions is, in some sense, a corkscrew. The rack and pinions do not *cause* the corkscrew: they are the corkscrew. Holding in one hand a waiter's corkscrew and in the other hand a double-lever corkscrew, you are holding two realizations of *corkscrew*. You are not holding two things that cause corkscrews.

Constraints on realization are limits on the kinds of things that can synchronically determine a functional kind. Depending on the severity of such constraints, some functional kinds might have many different kinds of realizers; other functional kinds might have just a few. Chapter 4 was all about the kinds of constraints that realizers of a humanlike mind must respect. It was an effort to say something in support of MCT, which, in contrast to MRT, claims that constraints make it possible to predict properties of the brain from facts about properties of the mind.

Whereas my efforts so far have been in search of an answer to the question "In what way must a humanlike mind be realized?" another question of interest is: "What kind of *body* must an organism with a humanlike mind possess?" This is the question I will be exploring in this chapter and the next. Like the question about realization, this new question can also be stated in terms of prediction. From facts about the mind, what is it possible to predict about the body? However, unlike the question about realization, the answer to this question leaves open the possibility that properties of the body, in addition to realizing some mental properties, stand in a diachronic relationship to mental properties. MCT predicts that, for instance, mental property M must be realized by structure N. But, one can also wonder, is it possible to make claims like "if an organism has mental property M, its body must have property B"? This claim, unlike the one about realization, allows that the relation between B and M is diachronic rather than synchronic. Surprisingly, much research in cognitive science has proceeded as if the mind can be investigated in isolation from the body; as if psychology need not pay attention to anatomy and physiology. If this is true, then it would appear that properties of the mind make no or few predictions about properties of the body. This is the naturalistic version of the ghost in the machine dogma I mentioned in the preface.

One might dramatize this way of construing the mind–body relationship by supposing that someday the SETI project scores a hit, and we find ourselves conversing with extraterrestrials on some distant planet. Suppose further that, from all that we can tell, the extraterrestrials have minds just like human minds. What do they look like? Can their bodies consist in amorphous puddinglike blobs of slimy material? Can they have masses of tentacles surrounding a large, hexagonally shaped eye? Might they be whale-sized, carrying themselves about on hundreds of legs, like centipedes? Or, if they think like human beings, must they have bodies like human beings?

Corresponding to MRT is a thesis I shall call the *separability thesis* (ST). According to ST, from knowledge of mental properties it is impossible to predict properties of the body. Hence, a humanlike mind can exist in bodies with very different properties. Corresponding to MCT is a thesis I shall call the *embodied mind thesis* (EMT). According to EMT, minds profoundly reflect the bodies in which they are contained—so much so that an investigation of the mind would reveal much about the body. Whereas a proponent of ST would venture no predictions about the bodies of the extraterrestrials I mentioned above, a supporter of EMT would predict that, were we ever to encounter such a being, we should expect it to look very much like a human being.

As I understand ST and EMT, they are logically independent of MRT and MCT. It is logically possible that a mind could be realized in a number of different kinds of structures, but that all of these structures are contained in similar sorts of bodies. Similarly, it is logically possible that there is only one or a few ways of realizing a humanlike mind, but that these few types of realizations can exist in many different sorts of bodies. However, despite the logical independence of these theses, there are probably empirical facts that bind the theses together in rather tight ways. Although it is an empirical question, my bet is that if MCT is true, ST is false. If there are but a few ways to realize a humanlike mind, probably there are but a few kinds of bodies that could contain such a mind. This is because the realizer of the mind must interact with a body, and no doubt there are constraints on the kind of body with which a particular kind of realization is able to interact. Though the analogy is crude, just as one could predict from the properties of a Volkswagen Beetle engine that the vehicle that contains it is not a large truck, so one should be able to predict from the properties of the human mind's realizer that the body that contains it is not like a whale's.

On the other hand, the relationship between MRT and EMT is not as obvious. Are there empirical reasons to think that if there are many ways to realize a mind then we should not be able to predict properties of the body from study of the mind? It may be that the mind has the properties it does in large part because of the kind of body through which it interacts with the world. If this is true, then, despite the fact that mind is multiply realizable, we should expect to see organisms that have similar mental properties to have similar bodies as well. Of course, this requires that the nature of the mind's realizer does not place significant constraints on the kind of body that contains it. Whether this is plausible, like every other question regarding multiple realization, boils down to empirical considerations.

I propose to examine the competition between ST and EMT from the perspective of a recent research program: embodied cognition (henceforth EC). In calling EC a research program, I wish to contrast it with well-defined fields, possessing clearly articulated subject matters, methods, goals, and results. There are no or few journals dedicated to EC, no textbooks that spell out its basic tenets, no departments of EC, and no or few faculty positions that list EC as an area of specialization. Rather, "embodied cognition" is a label useful for whatever unity it imposes on work deriving from a variety of fields: psychology, linguistics, artificial intelligence, artificial life, robotics, neuroscience, cognitive science, and philosophy.

The work in these fields to which the EC label applies concerns, generally, the contribution an organism's body makes to its sensory and cognitive abilities. Becoming more specific about what's new and interesting about EC will be one of the tasks of this chapter. However, my main focus will be on the implications of EC research for deciding between ST and EMT. If the most that EC research can show is that the body and mind influence each other, then this will be of little consequence to an investigation of the plausibility of ST. ST, as I construe it, does not deny that there is causal interaction between the body and mind. The fact that the state of one's stomach can produce a feeling of hunger, or that one's desire to sit down causes one's body to bend in particular ways, is not in dispute. Additionally, it is completely trivial that visual perception, for instance, implies that the body has eyes.

The more interesting questions involve the extent to which bodies permeate minds. One might suppose that methodological solipsism is true (Fodor 1980). On this view, one can completely disregard facts about bodies when endeavoring to understand how the mind works. Alternatively, one might think that the kind of body one has makes no difference to the concepts one develops or the manner in which one represents features of the world. The embodied cognition program is of interest because it claims to reveal connections between bodies and mind that are much more profound than many researchers in cognitive science and AI have appreciated. The interest in the dispute between ST and EMT lies in an investigation of these unsuspected connections between body and mind rather than in the obvious sorts of interaction that I mentioned above.

In this chapter I lay out two prevalent views in cognitive science that minimize or neglect altogether the significance of the body in shaping the mind. According to the first view, *body neutrality*, the mind is like a computer program; just as a computer program can be specified without reference to features of the hardware that runs it, so is it unnecessary to attend to properties of the body to understand the workings of the mind. The second view, one that I call *envatment*, holds that the mind, like the proverbial brain in a vat, is an entity distinct from the body and has as its function the processing of signals *from* the body and the computation and transmission of signals back *to* the body. These are the views that many researchers in EC are reacting to. In this chapter I also present three claims that one can distill from the research that EC theorists have amassed.[1] I explain how these claims serve as responses to body neutrality and envatment and discuss how they bear on the debate between ST and EMT. In the following chapter I address more directly the impact of work in EC on this debate.

6.1   Disembodied Cognition

A natural way to approach an understanding of EC is to look at those principles or views to which it is reacting. If what's new about EC is the emphasis on embodiment, then what does it mean to think about cognition without embodiment? This means different things to researchers in EC, and I shall discuss two of the more prominent views in this section. We will then be in a position to see how the claims of EC contrast with those of more traditional cognitive science.

6.1.1 Body Neutrality

One sense of disembodiment receives expression in a foundational assumption of cognitive science: that the mind is a computer program instantiated in the brain. It is this assumption that has launched countless efforts to reveal the algorithmic processes that, cognitive scientists believe, constitute mentality. It is difficult to say who was the first to identify the mind with a computer program. Surely Turing (1950) has some responsibility for this widespread view. It was he who made the audacious suggestion in 1950 that within fifty years an appropriately programmed computer could imitate human thinking sufficiently well to fool any interrogator most of the time. This bet of Turing's makes explicit a commitment to the idea that minds could somehow be captured as programs. Newell and Simon (1976) too, in equating the human ability to solve problems with the same kind of symbol manipulation that takes place in a digital computer, led many to look on human minds as computer programs.

The idea of mind-as-program is no less overt in the early philosophical work on functionalism. I described some of this work in chapter 2, where I discussed how Putnam's machine functionalism might lead to a belief in MRT. According to the functionalist, mental states are relations between inputs, other states, and outputs (Block 1978). Significantly, a functionalist like Putnam identifies mental states with these *patterns* of relations, and not with the relata. Mental states are the cracks between the bricks. Just as particular chess games can be described abstractly, as sequences of moves, so too, many functionalists believe, it is possible to describe minds abstractly, as collections of states defined by relations between inputs, other mental states, and outputs. A particular chess game has an existence apart from the actual board and pieces on which it might be played; and likewise, according to the functionalist, a particular mind has an existence outside the given hardware in which it might be instantiated.

In chapter 1 I criticized this view of mind, agreeing with Searle (1980) that a formal description of rules and state transitions might suffice to produce a simulation of a mind, but could not be all there is to a mind. However, my interest here is not in criticizing the equation of mind with computer program, but in exploring the sense in which this equation makes the mind disembodied. One way in which it does so should already be clear. There is a sense, as I noted above, in which chess games exist apart from any actual board and pieces. This is because chess is a formal system (Haugeland 1981), that is, a system that can be exhaustively described in terms of some well-defined pieces, starting positions, and allowable moves, each of which is definable "abstractly." Because chess is a formal system, it is possible to talk about formally equivalent instances of any particular chess game. Thus, it makes sense to say of two games played one hundred years apart, in different countries and on different boards, that they are tokens of the same game. Any particular type of chess game, C, is medium-independent insofar as any system that has pieces that can be interpreted as chess pieces and that can be interpreted as making the moves that pieces in game C make is an instance of C. Indeed, one need not even have a board and pieces to play chess, as is evident by the fact that games can be played by email correspondence. Thus, it makes sense to say that characterizations of chess games can remain silent about the kinds of things that might implement them.

But, of course, these properties that make possible a disembodied description of a chess game also make possible a disembodied description of any formally describable system. Accordingly, if the mind is a program, or, equivalently, a formal system, then it too is disembodied. Mental states are analogous to chess pieces, and the starting positions in chess are analogous to the states of a mind at birth.[2] Analogous to the rules of chess are psychological laws that describe how mental states interact with other mental states, inputs, and outputs. Such a system, just like chess, can be described in a medium-independent manner. Thus, the functionalist believes, it is possible to say of two minds, one realized in silicon and the other in neurons, that they are tokens of the same mental type. Minds are abstract in the same way chess games are abstract. The disembodiment of the mind seems to follow directly from conceiving the mind as a program.

It is important at this point to be clear about what, in the functionalist's account of mind, is objectionable to EC theorists. I noted that viewing the mind as a computer program, as a sequence of rule-prescribed transitions between formally defined states, has encouraged many cognitive scientists to distinguish minds from the matter in which they are realized. However, although this does lead to a picture of mind as a disembodied thing (see Searle's 1980 charge that those who think minds are computer programs are in fact dualists!), it is not yet apparent why a functionalist account of mind must ignore facts about bodies. Consider the fact that one can continue to think of the mind as a computer program and yet also believe that some of the inputs and outputs that define particular mental states are inputs and outputs from and to bodies. That is, it is consistent with functionalism that a mental state like pain is the mental state it is because of various relations between stubbing one's *toe* and *wincing*, both of which are properties of a body. The mind may be a program, but if some of the inputs and outputs that serve to define mental states are bodily states, then a functionalist can coherently maintain a view of minds as programs while insisting that a science of the mind cannot afford to ignore the properties of bodies.

This suggestion that minds are programs but that reference to bodies remains an important element in an understanding of the mind reveals a tension in functionalism. On the one hand, minds, because they consist in computational *relations* between various things, are disembodied. On the other hand, because the relata that stand in these relations might partly consist of properties of the body, a functionalist cannot define particular mental states without mentioning bodily states. Although I have not yet said anything about what role EC theorists assign to the body in their investigations of mind, one can imagine a functionalist denying the charge that they ignore, neglect, or in any other way diminish the significance of bodies in their conception of mind. Bodies are important, a functionalist might insist: it is by reference to bodies that mental states can be defined at all.

Nevertheless, I think there is a solid reason that EC researchers ought to find disagreeable the mind-as-program equation. The offending features of this equation become clear against the background of a criticism that Block (1978) levels at functionalism. Block describes what he calls the *problem of the inputs and the outputs*. The problem arises from the very tension I noted in the previous paragraph. Functionalists define mental states as relations between inputs, other states, and outputs. But this means that a mental state counts as a particular kind of mental state—say, pain—in virtue of the particular kinds of inputs that produce it and the particular kinds of outputs that it, in turn, produces. A mental state is a pain state if and only if it is caused in the *right* way and produces the *right* kind of behavior. But how, Block wonders, is it possible to define what's "right" about the input and output without saying either too little or too much about the body of the organism? If inputs and outputs are described too abstractly, as, say, simply inputs and outputs, then it is consistent with functionalism that complex systems like the economy of Bolivia, as Block suggests, might have pain states. After all, Bolivia's economy has internal states, and many of these states might be defined in terms of their relations to inputs and outputs, and it may well be possible to pair the relations between inputs, states, and outputs of the Bolivian economy to those that define some mind. Thus, to preclude the absurd conclusion that the economy of Bolivia feels pain, one must be more explicit about which inputs and outputs make a particular state a state of pain rather than some other state (e.g., a state of high inflation).

So, without some detail about the nature of the inputs and outputs, functionalism is too liberal: it ends up attributing mental states to systems that clearly do not have them. But, Block argues, at the moment one starts adding enough detail to curtail this profligacy, functionalism becomes too chauvinistic:

Functionalists tend to specify inputs and outputs in the manner of behaviorists: outputs in terms of movements of arms and legs, sound emitted and the like; inputs in terms of light and sound falling on the eyes and ears. . . . [t]his conception is chauvinist, since it denies mentality to brains in vats and to paralytics. But the chauvinism inherent in Functional descriptions runs deeper. Such descriptions are blatantly *species-specific*. Humans have arms and legs, but snakes do not—and whether or not snakes have mentality, one can easily imagine snake-like creatures that do. . . . The variety of possible intelligent life is enormous. Given any fairly specific descriptions of inputs and outputs, any high-school-age science-fiction buff will be able to describe a sapient sentient being whose inputs and outputs fail to satisfy that description. (1978, pp. 294–295, italics in the original)

Simply put, Block is pointing out that any embodiment of inputs and outputs is too much embodiment for the functionalist to admit. Once one tries to specify inputs and outputs in terms that limit minds to the sorts of systems that might legitimately have them, too many of these end up not having them. Put in terms of embodiment, Block's dilemma is this: if minds are disembodied, they are everywhere; if embodied, they are too rare.

Block, in my view, has presented a cogent criticism of functionalism. However, as I argue below, research in EC puts a significantly different spin on the second horn of Block's dilemma. As Block presents matters, embodiment entails chauvinism. Minds, Block seems to think, could be present in bodies and brains that bear no physical resemblance to human bodies and brains. He suggests that brains in vats might have minds, as well as organisms with snakelike bodies and creatures existing only in the fantastic worlds of science fiction. If Block's claim is only that states like pain can be present in organisms with bodies and brains that differ substantially from those of human beings, then EC theorists need not disagree. However, if he means to suggest that the kind of body one has makes no difference to the kind of mind one has—that brains in vats, snakelike organisms, and creatures of science-fiction might all have the same kind of mind—then, I think, he needs to reevaluate his claim in light of investigations in EC.[3] If it is chauvinistic to think that only humanlike bodies and brains can have humanlike minds, then many EC theorists are unabashed chauvinists.

I noted that Block's criticism of functionalism suggests a reason EC theorists reject the mind-as-program view. Yet, it may seem that Block has in fact provided a reason for EC researchers to, if not embrace, then at least tolerate functionalism. Block has pointed out that any specification of the inputs and outputs that define mental states is chauvinistic because it restricts attributions of minds to just those organisms with bodies or brains of a particular sort. This sounds like something that an EC theorist would assert: the structure of the mind depends in some profound way on the properties of the body. Why, then, do EC researchers try to distance themselves from the functionalist conception of mind?

I think the simplest answer to this question is that functionalists almost always go the route of the first horn in Block's dilemma: they insist on highly abstract characterizations of inputs and outputs. Functionalism rests in part on the intuition that identically minded organisms can be physically distinct. But, for this to be possible, the program that constitutes the mind cannot specify its inputs and outputs in language that commits the functionalist to particular types of bodies.[4] If functionalism commits one to anchoring minds in particular sorts of bodies then it fails, in the functionalist's eyes, to provide the abstract characterization of minds that functionalists developed in response to the identity theory. Functionalism's great promise lay in its suggestion that it is possible to investigate minds at a level of description that makes unnecessary an appreciation of the bodies and brains in which they are implemented. So, whereas there might be statements of functionalism that an EC researcher could find copacetic, it is certainly in the spirit of functionalism that the mind be investigated without regard for the body or brain that houses it.

So, the first sense of disembodiment to which EC is a reaction is the idea that the mind is a program that can be characterized in abstraction from the kind of body/brain that realizes it. I shall refer to this view of how the body stands in relation to the mind as *body neutrality*. According to body neutrality, characteristics of bodies make no difference to the kind of mind one possesses. The same kind of mind can exist in bodies with very distinct properties because the relata whose relationships define mental states can be described in language that abstracts away from particular sorts of bodies.

6.1.2 Envatment

Whereas the sense of disembodiment I have called body neutrality arises from a theory about what the mind *is*—a pattern of interactions between inputs and outputs that are defined at a high level of abstraction—a second sense of disembodiment emerges from a prevalent view in cognitive science about what the mind *does*. According to this view, the task of the mind is to accept inputs from sensory organs, process these inputs and compute actions on their basis, and transmit instructions that will cause the body to act accordingly. The mind, on this view, fills the middle place in what roboticists refer to as a "sense-think-act" cycle (Clark 1999).

Roboticist Rodney Brooks's discussion of Shakey nicely illustrates the mind's responsibilities in this sense-think-act cycle (Brooks 1991a). Shakey was a mobile robot built in the late 1960s at the Stanford Research Institute. Shakey inhabited several specially designed rooms, around which were placed brightly colored blocks, platforms, and wedges. Depending on the task assigned to Shakey via a teletype, Shakey would move blocks from one room to another, position ramps in front of platforms so that it could push a block onto a platform, steer around blocks and other obstacles that stood in its way, and so on (Copeland 1993).

Of present interest is how Shakey accomplished its various feats. Shakey's primary sensor was a black-and-white television camera. With this camera, Shakey would transmit images to an offboard computer, which would then analyze the images and encode symbolic descriptions of the features in the image, for example, walls, blocks, and ramps. This symbolic description of Shakey's environment was then sent to a planning program, called STRIPS, which would rely on the description in order to compute a sequence of actions. These action instructions were then transmitted back to Shakey, which then acted accordingly.

I mentioned that Shakey's environment was specially designed for it. To ease its encoding of the environment into a symbolic description that could then be analyzed into a representation that STRIPS could process, the walls of the rooms had dark baseboards that made the boundaries between floor and walls conspicuous and the use of corners for purposes of orientation possible. Also, the surfaces of the blocks were painted different colors to highlight their edges and thus simplify the identification of their shapes. Lighting in the rooms was carefully controlled, and in an effort to avoid obscured views of objects, the number of blocks and wedges present was small (Brooks 1991a, p. 1228). Despite all these handicaps, each of Shakey's movements would still require about an hour of computation, and it could take Shakey days to move a block from one room to another (Copeland 1993, p. 86).

Consider now the sense in which the "thinking" Shakey does is disembodied. There is, of course, a literal sense in which Shakey's thinking is disembodied: it takes place in a computer that is separate from Shakey. Of course, this only makes explicit what would still be true if Shakey carried its computer on its back: Shakey's "brain" is distinct from Shakey's body. It's the body that moves about collecting information and acting on the environment; it's the brain that processes information and calculates instructions for action. Indeed, Shakey's "mind" is just like a brain in a vat. If one could replicate the sensory images that Shakey collected with its TV camera and could send these to Shakey's offboard computer, the computer would operate exactly as it would if the messages had come from Shakey's body. Shakey's body takes care of the sensing and acting parts in the sense-think-act cycle, but Shakey's thinking takes place somewhere else. The existence of Shakey's body is incidental to the processing that Shakey's "brain" performs.

In his excellent discussion of embodiment, John Haugeland (1995) articulates another way to understand the sense in which minds, when portrayed as filling the middle part of a sense-think-act cycle, are disembodied. Haugeland begins his discussion of embodiment with an analysis of systems and components. Such a discussion is necessary because Haugeland wishes to investigate whether it makes sense to talk of "partitioning off" the workings of the mind from features of the body and environment (1995, p. 211), as it might make sense to do so in a description of Shakey's psychology. Whether this is possible depends on whether it is appropriate to conceive of the mind as a self-contained piece of a larger system, of which the body is another such piece.

Leaving out some of the details, Haugeland defines the components of a system as those parts that are "relatively independent and self-contained" (1995, p. 212). So, for instance, a resistor in a television is a distinct component because it "does not interact with the rest of the system except through its circuit connections. . . . nothing that happens outside of it affects anything that happens inside, or vice versa, except by affecting the currents in those connections" (ibid.). The two wires by which the resistor is connected to other components of the television constitute its sole interface with these other components. That the resistor's interface with other components is well defined is crucial to its being a single component. Through its narrow interface, the resistor is able to influence other components in the system while remaining isolated from the behavior of its surrounding components.

In contrast to this well-defined component of a television, Haugeland asks us to imagine dividing the television into components in the following way: "assuming the set is roughly cubical, divide it into ten equal slices along each axis, to yield a thousand smaller cubes, of which the entire set exactly consists" (1995, p. 212). One such cube might contain "half a transistor, two thirds of a capacitor, several fragments of wire, a small triangle of glass from the picture tube, and a lot of hot air" (ibid.). Such a cube does not count as a proper component of the television, "even though a thousand equally crazy 'pieces,' put together *exactly* right, would make up a TV set" (ibid.), because "the surfaces separating them are not proper interfaces" (ibid., p. 213). Each cubical piece of the television connects to its neighboring pieces in extremely complex ways, requiring precise alignment, as is evident from the difficulty one would have in removing one such piece and replacing it with another so that the television would not lose any of its functionality. The fact that one could replace a broken resistor with hardly any effort speaks to the simplicity and precision of its interface, which in turn suggests that it does indeed constitute a component of the television.

It would be misleading to suppose that components must be spatially localized. As Haugeland recognizes, corporations, universities, and governments are divided into units and departments; there is no reason to expect that these units and departments will be spatially isolated in distinct buildings or offices. The members of a learning support service, for instance, might be spread around a university, occupying space that is shared by members of other departments. More dramatically, "as more and more business is conducted via worldwide communication networks, the physical locations of personnel and data become practically irrelevant" (1995, p. 214). However, despite this absence of spatial localization, it is possible to divide corporations and universities into components because members of a department or division will tend to share tasks and responsibilities that are distinct from those shared by members in other departments. Moreover, because the responsibilities of departments differ, members of single departments will tend to cooperate more with each other than with members of other departments. Haugeland's points about interfaces and replacement still hold. If one wants to contact someone in learning support, one must go through a secretary who keeps track of where the members of the department are; and it will be easy to tell who in a given office is working in learning support and who is not by the kind of work the person is doing. Furthermore, if one wanted to fire the staff of learning support and replace them with new members, one could do so without interfering with the operations of other departments.

As I remarked, I have left out some of the subtleties in Haugeland's discussion of decomposition. However, the point is developed well enough, I hope, to make intuitive the significance of interfaces in a decision about how to carve a system into components. Interfaces are like joints, or, in Haugeland's words, points of interactive contact, and the more clearly articulated a joint is, the more motivation there is for construing the parts connected at the joint as separable—as distinct components. Furthermore, the more separable (though, as I stressed above, not necessarily in the sense of *spatially* separable) two components are, the less intense is their interaction, the less tight their coupling. The resistor again makes this point. Because its interface with other components is limited to just two wires, its operation is almost completely unconstrained by what goes on around it. Compare the resistor to a connecting rod between a piston and a crankshaft: "[t]he different parts of a connecting rod interact so intensely, for example, that they always move rigidly together; by comparison, its interactions with the piston and the crankshaft are 'looser,' allowing independent rotation about a common axis" (1995, p. 215).

These ideas about components can be applied to a decision about whether Shakey's "mind" can be partitioned off from its body. Is the relationship between Shakey's "mind" and body like that between the resistor and the other components of a television, or is it more like the relationship between the connecting rod and the piston and crankshaft? In answering this question, Haugeland would have us examine the interface between the parts of Shakey that do the sensing and acting and the part responsible for thinking. In fact, the interface between Shakey's body and brain is quite well defined. Shakey's sensors construct an image of the world, and this image is sent, via cable, to Shakey's brain. Like the resistor, Shakey's brain does its job in nearly complete isolation from the rest of the system of which it is a component. The processing that occurs in Shakey's brain is cut off from the world and Shakey's body—it is unconstrained by the properties of Shakey's body except insofar as these properties influence the messages sent to it through the cable. Just as the *source* of electrical current that enters the resistor is irrelevant to how the resistor affects this current, so the source of information that enters Shakey's offline computer is irrelevant to what the computer does with this information. For these reasons, Haugeland would claim that the interface between Shakey's body and brain is clearly articulated, and thus Shakey's body and brain are distinct components. For our purposes, this is another reason for viewing Shakey's "mind" as disembodied.

The robots that have crawled from Brooks's lab mark an illuminating departure from the sense-think-act style of robotics that Shakey epitomizes (see Clark 1997 and Haugeland 1995 for detailed discussion of Brooks's robots). Brooks says of his robots there is "no clear distinction between a 'perception subsystem,' a 'central system' and an 'action system' . . . no single place where 'perception' delivers a representation of the world in the traditional sense" (1991b, p. 147). Rather, the better way to decompose Brooks's robots is in terms of layers of activity, or skills, each of which "connects perception to action directly" (ibid., p. 148). One such layer might do nothing but halt a robot if an object is detected dead ahead; another causes the robot to wander about in randomly generated directions; another causes the robot to set a heading for a distant location. Naturally, because a robot cannot carry out conflicting activities simultaneously, the activity layers must have the ability to suppress each other. If a robot is heading for a distant location and confronts an object in its path, the layer in charge of halting will come to the fore, preventing a collision. As Brooks puts it, each robot "is a collection of competing behaviors. Out of the local chaos of their interactions there emerges, in the eye of an observer, a coherent pattern of behavior. There is no central purposeful locus of control" (1991b, p. 149). In contrast to Shakey, in which there exists a clear interface between body and brain, Brooks's robots exhibit no such interface. Mind and body do not constitute separate components within Brooks's robots.

I have isolated two senses in which the conception of mind in standard cognitive science is disembodied. Functionalist theories of mind that equate minds with programs advocate body neutrality, meaning that the kind of body an organism possesses makes no causal difference to the kind of mind it may possess. Two minds are formally equivalent if they consist in the same pattern of relations between inputs, other states, and outputs, where these inputs and outputs are described generally so as not to bind them to any particular kind of body. The second sense of disembodiment, which I shall call *envatment*, conceives of the mind as a kind of way station. The mind is a junction to which sensory inputs are sent and then processed. From this junction emerge instructions for bodily movements. This is the picture of mind that invites talk of brains in vats, for it is consistent with this view that one can describe what the mind does without mentioning the body. All that matters for the brain's function is that it receives sensory signals—whether it is a body that collects these or whether they are generated by a computer or mad scientist makes no difference to what the brain does. The brain might as well exist in a vat.

6.2   The Claims of Embodiment

The best way to understand how researchers in EC have reacted to body neutrality and envatment is to examine their work. I mentioned just briefly Brooks's work in robotics, which is perhaps the most widely cited work throughout the EC research program. Brooks's work is appealing not only because it offers such a clear contrast to the standard way that cognitive scientists have understood the connection between perception and action but also because it actually implements these suggestions in robots that show a surprising versatility in natural environments. However, there is better work to consider if the goal is an evaluation of ST, and it is to an examination of that work that I turn in the next chapter. However, before doing so, it pays to say more precisely how evidence against body neutrality and envatment might present a difficulty for ST and support for EMT.

I hope it is already fairly clear why challenges to body neutrality or envatment might have some bearing on the plausibility of ST. If there is evidence that conflicts with body neutrality, this is evidence against ST and in support of EMT, for it is evidence of a need to specify particular facts about the body in an account of mind. Recall Block's (1978) point that any movement away from body neutrality is a movement toward mental chauvinism. But, of course, chauvinism is just what EMT is about. Just as male chauvinists might claim that only men ought to have certain entitlements, and religious chauvinists might believe that only, say, Christians, will have eternal life, so proponents of EMT believe that only humanlike bodies will have humanlike minds. Thus, evidence that calls into question the plausibility of body neutrality ought to cause discomfort to advocates of ST. Likewise, evidence that calls into question the mind's envatment seems to favor EMT insofar as envatment makes it possible to ignore facts about the body that houses the mind. Belief in the possibility of envatment encourages belief in ST, for it lulls one into thinking that a mind somehow just springs forth from a brain, regardless of the sort of container in which the mind is floating.

As I have already noted, ST is consistent with the claim that properties of the body have some kind of influence on mental properties. This influence might take several forms. Clearly happenings in or to the body—digesting a bratwurst, stubbing one's toe, sitting for too long on a bicycle saddle—can lead to the occurrence of various mental states. However, EC is not about these kinds of body-to-mind influences. In questioning body neutrality and envatment, EC researchers are not heralding what everybody already knows, that is, that stimuli to the body can produce mental states. As I read EC research, there seem to be at least three claims that might serve as responses to body neutrality and envatment. Often these claims are mixed together in ways that make them difficult to appraise. Worse, a researcher who presents evidence in favor of one of these claims sometimes ends up treating this evidence as support for another. In fact, each of the following claims is distinct from the others, and thus evidence for one may not support the others. The three claims are these:

(1) *Embodied Thought*:   The body contributes to or influences cognitive activities to an extent that cognitive science has not adequately appreciated. These contributions may take several forms, and some of these forms are clearly of more interest than others. Most trivially, it is often necessary for the body to move about or position itself in such a

way as to make various cognitive activities possible. Of more interest, perhaps the processing of information actually starts in the body, just as digestion actually starts in the mouth. Depending on the extent to which these actions and properties of the body affect cognition, differences in body plan could make differences to the nature of thought. In short, if the assumption of body neutrality is wrong, then one must concede that the kind of body an organism possesses makes a difference to the kind of mind it possesses. Furthermore, if this evidence calls into question the propriety of the sense-think-act conception of minds, this might lead one to reject the idea of minds and bodies as distinct components, which, in turn, elevates the importance of bodies in thought. I will have more to say about this in (3) below.

(2) *Embodied Conceptualization* (after Glenberg 1997):   The content of the mind—the manner in which the mind conceptualizes the world—is a function of body type. Organisms that differ in body type will conceive the world differently and will think differently. The basic categories an organism develops in order to think about the world are a function of how its body interacts with the world, and thus differences in body type will result in differences in how and what an organism thinks or is capable of thinking.

(3) *Extended Mind* (after Clark and Chalmers 1998):   The division between mind and body is impossible to maintain. The mind is extended in such a way that it permeates or "bleeds into" the body, and, perhaps, also the environment. It is thus impossible to individuate the mind without mention of body as well. In Haugeland's (1995) terms, mind and body are not separate components. This claim resists both views of disembodiment. If there is no clean interface between bodies and minds, if the two cannot be distinguished as separate components within a single system, then of course differences in bodies will entail differences in mind, and just as obviously, minds cannot exist as simply brains in vats.

There are now a lot of balls in the air to juggle. I have described two senses of disembodiment—body neutrality and envatment—and three claims that EC theorists make in response: embodied thought, embodied conceptualization, and extended mind. I have also said just a little about how these three responses to the two senses of embodiment might be made to work against ST and so in favor of EMT. In the following chapter I consider research that EC theorists cite in support of embodied thought, embodied conceptualization, and extended mind and attempt to show how, in responding to body neutrality or envatment, this work also presents difficulties for ST.

7
Embodied Minds

It is now time to begin a discussion of embodied cognition research with an eye toward its implications for the separability thesis. In the previous chapter I mentioned three claims that receive support among embodied cognition theorists—embodied thought, embodied conceptualization, and extended mind—and also noted that it is not uncommon to find aspects of these claims run together. In an effort to make the clearest case for each of these claims, I have decided to use them to structure discussion of the research rather than the other way around—rather, that is, than examining some body of work and trying to say which of the three claims the work might support. Accordingly, I have divided this chapter into three main sections, one for each claim, and, where appropriate, have subdivided a section to discuss distinct research projects. I should add as a word of caution, however, that some of the work presented as support for one claim might also support another, and that whereas a particular researcher might take his or her work to support one claim, I might interpret it as better evidence of another.

7.1 Embodied Thought

I have argued that viewing the mind as a computer program has fostered a belief in body neutrality, that is, a belief that the mind can be understood without reference to specific properties of the body in which it is "being run." In turn, body neutrality encourages acceptance of ST, for if the properties of the body do not enter into an explanation of how the mind works, then it is natural to suppose that the mind can be "run" in all sorts of bodies. In this section I consider evidence suggesting that there are many cognitive capacities that rely on particular bodily properties, that is, properties peculiar to certain kinds of bodies, in order to do their job. This evidence challenges the body neutrality assumption, for it suggests that minds cannot be understood without an appreciation of the properties of the particular kind of body that contains them. A fortiori, the evidence points away from ST, for it supports the idea that the human mind is uniquely suited to the human body: properties of mind therefore predict properties of body.

An analogy captures the force that this evidence has against ST. Imagine that you find yourself having to pilot an airplane. Knowing nothing about how to fly, you are nevertheless undaunted because you have in your possession an instruction manual for the operation of a submarine. However, it is not long before you realize that these instructions are of little help. The steps involved in maneuvering a submarine differ substantially from those involved in keeping an airplane aloft. Of course, there might be a few instructions that transfer (perhaps there are similarities in the steps involved in adjusting altitude), but, for the most part, trying to fly an airplane as if it were a submarine is almost certain to shorten your flight. Similarly, the human mind is intimately tailored to the human body. If it were possible to insert a human mind into a body that differed substantially from a human one—a body with just one eye, or that walked on six legs, or that had ears on its knees—then the mind could not "keep the body aloft." The body would crash just as certainly as would your airplane.

This analogy takes us some way in understanding the sense in which thought is embodied, but the analogy is not perfect. Indeed, the reason for its breakdown casts perhaps even more light on the sense in which thought is embodied. The problem with the analogy is this: submarine instructions can be contained in a manual that might easily be removed from the sub. The job they do—providing information about how to operate a sub—does not depend on the existence of a submarine. Of course the instructions might be easier to understand when sitting in the captain's chair of the submarine, surrounded by the apparatus that the manual describes. Nonetheless, the presence of the sub does not change the information that the instructions contain. Destroy the submarine and the instructions in the manual remain unchanged.

In contrast, the evidence I shall present below tells a story about the relationship between the mind and the body that differs from that which connects the submarine to the instructions for its operation. The body in many ways "preprocesses" the information that the brain receives and in other ways affects how the brain manages information. The body is more than simply a shell for the mind, more than a vessel that the mind pilots. The body is profoundly involved in mental operations. Not only is the human mind as suited to the human body as submarine instructions are suited to submarines; but, in addition, the mind depends on the participation of the body in order to execute its various tasks.

The first examples of what I have called embodied thought are obvious on even casual reflection. Consider the fact that human beings have two eyes. In the present context, the significance of two eyes is this. Two eyes, at a given distance apart, present to the brain information about disparity. Because each eye projects an image onto a retina and most objects at a distance of roughly 10 m and closer project to slightly different coordinates on each retina, the brain has a means by which to calculate the relative depth of objects. The squirrel looks closer than the tree, which in turn looks closer than the fence, because the retinal image of the squirrel appears on the temple sides of each retina whereas the image of the fence appears on the nasal sides of each retina, with the tree's image nestled between the two. Thus the brain uses the fact that the images appear at different coordinates on each retina to calculate the relative depth of the objects. But—and this is the crucial point— the brain's processing makes use of disparity information from *two* eyes. Were there more eyes than two, or fewer, or if the distance between the eyes differed, the processes in the brain that compute depth from disparity would be either useless or in need of significant recalibration.

Returning to the analogy I bruited earlier, we can suppose that the procedures for computing depth are analogous to the instructions that would steer a submarine. Just as submarine instructions would fail to keep an airplane aloft, the perceptual procedures that translate disparity information from two eyes into information about relative depth would not serve their function if fed information from a creature with more or fewer eyes than two. Moreover, the inadequacy of the submarine analogy is also illustrative here. The submarine instruction manual contains the same information whether the submarine it describes exists, but the processes that produce depth perception are incomplete without disparity information from two eyes. Just as submarine instructions do not work for airplanes, the instructions by which the human brain computes relative depth do not work in creatures with eye configurations other than those in a human being. This is the sense in which depth perception is embodied. The procedures by which human beings perceive depth—a fact about human psychology—are contingent on a fact about human bodies—that they contain two and only two eyes. One cannot maintain body neutrality, as some functionalists have suggested, and at the same time describe the psychological stages of human depth perception. The processes involved in human depth perception are intelligible only once one recognizes a fact about human bodies.

Beyond the fact that some aspects of human visual experience require the presence of two eyes is the fact that visual processing depends in certain ways on movements of the head and body. This is most obvious in the case of parallax (Churchland, Ramachandran, and Sejnowski 1994). Movement of one's body or head will make nearer objects appear to move against more stable-appearing distant objects. The tree in front of you will appear to move side to side against the fence behind it as you sway your head to and fro. In addition to stereopsis, this is a powerful cue to the relative distances of objects. Moreover, it would be a distortion to think of these body and head movements as simply an *aid* to vision that can just as easily be partitioned off from the processes of vision "proper." These motions are a genuine stage in visual processing, as much a part of vision as the detection of disparity or the calculation of shape from shading. True, we can perceive depth without moving our bodies and head, but likewise we can perceive depth without detecting disparity and we can perceive shape without the benefit of shading. Nevertheless, the human visual system takes advantage of information that comes from parallax, just as it takes advantage of information from disparity and shading. It is possible to see without these sources of information, but this shows only that the human visual system collects information that is in many contexts redundant. It does not show that head and body motion is not a part of vision. But, of course, to grant that human beings see, in part, by moving their bodies and heads, is to provide yet another reason to be wary of the functionalists' stance of body neutrality. Not only does the human visual system work in tandem with the human body—a body that moves in idiosyncratic directions and speeds and with particular degrees of freedom—but in many situations it cannot work without it. Human vision needs a human body.

What goes for vision is just as true for our other perceptual abilities. The human auditory system relies on the presence of two sources of sound input. Were human beings to have just one ear or more than two, the instructions for sound localization would have to change. The human auditory system is calibrated to the distance between human ears so that it can interpret correctly what the interaural time differences mean about the source of sound. Likewise, the fact that sounds of various frequencies pass through a head of a particular size and density provides the auditory system with other important information about the direction of the sound source. Organisms with heads much smaller than human heads, like insects and birds, cannot rely on their head size to provide sound source location. Thus the cricket's ears "are located as far apart as possible, on the tibiae of the front legs" (Robert, Miles, and Hoy 1996, p. 30). Furthermore, cricket ears as well as bird ears are connected to each other by an internal air passage, so that each ear is stimulated by pressure both from the external sound source and by pressure created within the air passage by tympanic movements in the opposite ear. Depending on whether an organism's ears are pressure receivers, as human ears are, or pressure-difference receivers, as cricket and bird ears are, subsequent steps in sound localization will differ. As Chiel and Beer observe, "body structure creates constraints and opportunities for neural control" (1997, p. 553). Having a small head places different demands on the neural processing of sound.

Just as is true of vision, the psychology of auditory perception begins at the periphery—with facts about where the ears are placed relative to each other, the distance between them, and the density of the matter that separates them. These facts all make a difference in how an organism hears. More specifically, they contribute information the absence of which would degrade an organism's auditory capacities. The moral from the above discussion of human vision applies here as well: the psychology of human hearing cannot be separated from facts about human bodies.

At this point one might be tempted to dismiss the above discussions of embodiment in vision and audition. After all, one might reason, it is obvious that the sensory equipment with which an organism is endowed makes a difference to the kind of information it can detect and so, accordingly, makes a difference to the kind of perceptual processing it subsequently undertakes. I fear that the skeptical reader will not be much comforted by the reminder that I already noted that some of the preceding might appear obvious. However, first, the point I draw from my comments about eyes and ears goes beyond the obvious claim that perceptual processes are tailored to bodily structures. The point is deeper— that psychological processes are *incomplete* without the body's contributions. Vision for human beings is a process that includes features of the human body—human beings see by using two eyes and moving their bodies about in a certain way. Human beings who lack two ears cannot localize sound as well as human beings who are binaurally blessed. So, the point is not simply that perceptual processes fit bodily structures. Perceptual processes *depend on and include* bodily structures. This means that a description of various perceptual capacities cannot maintain body neutrality, and it also means that an organism with a non-human body will have nonhuman visual and auditory psychologies.

But, second, the role of the body in cognition extends beyond its contributions to perceptual activity. There is evidence that the state of the body's viscera and musculoskeletal system not only biases perception, memory, and attention, but also influences a human being's ability to make sophisticated decisions. This evidence is prominent in Antonio Damasio's work on the neurobiology of emotions (1994, and also Bechara et al. 1997). Indeed, Damasio's famed somatic marker hypothesis is in essence the claim that states of body, including those of the viscera and musculoskeletal system, "mark" various choices as good or bad, thereby helping to winnow the field of options one faces and so facilitate decision-making processes. However, because Damasio's work supports both the ideas of embodied thought and extended mind, and, to a lesser extent, embodied conceptualization, I shall not pursue a discussion of his work here, but will instead treat it below in my discussion of extended mind.

7.2 Embodied Conceptualization

The claim behind embodied thought concerns how the mind does what it does—how it perceives, attends, recognizes, reasons, and so on. These processes, evidence from embodied cognition research suggests, cannot be divorced from the body—they function because of work that takes place in the body. But the claim of embodied thought is silent on the effect the body has on the *content* of what is thought. On the face of it, the idea that the properties of our body significantly influence what we think—how we categorize the objects around us, what we remember, what we can and cannot say—is, I think, far more remarkable than the claim of embodied thought. Many who are ready to accept the idea that a person's conception of the world is shaped by family, religion, culture, history, nationality, and so on, might balk at the possibility that one's body might actually play a prominent role in this shaping as well. Yet this is just the claim that some investigators of embodied cognition propose.

In this section I discuss three branches of research that converge on the idea that many of the concepts an organism possesses are reflections of the kind of body it has. Accordingly, if one wishes to understand how an organism conceives of its world, one cannot maintain a stance of body neutrality. More to the point, facts about what an organism thinks or is capable of thinking predict facts about its body. Insofar as this is true, it is reason to favor the embodied mind thesis over the separability thesis.

7.2.1 The Body in the Turing Test

Although not directly concerned with issues of embodiment, French's (1990) discussion of the Turing Test is a useful entryway into the claims of embodied conceptualization. What has come to be called the Turing Test is a procedure that Alan Turing (1950) proposed as a means by which to decide whether a computer is intelligent. The test is simple: an interrogator asks questions, via teletype, of a person and a computer.

After several minutes the interrogator must guess which of the two conversations he has had is with a person and which with a computer. Turing suggested that if the interviewer is unable to distinguish the person from the computer at better than chance, then the computer is intelligent. Thus intelligence is defined operationally as the ability to convince an interrogator that he or she is speaking to a person.

My interest here is not in whether the Turing Test is in fact an apposite operational definition of intelligence. Rather, it is in French's argument that the Turing Test fails as a test of intelligence in general and instead can at best test for a specifically human style of intelligence. As French remarks, "the Turing Test could be passed only by things that have experienced the world as we have experienced it, and this leads to the central point of the present paper, namely, that *the Test provides a guarantee not of intelligence but of culturally-oriented* human *intelligence*" (1990, pp. 53–54).

In barest outline, French's argument is this. Intelligence is built on a subcognitive scaffolding—a low-level cognitive structure comprising an associative network of "highly overlapping activatable representations of experience" (1990, p. 57). Human beings are mostly unconscious of this associative network, never having been explicitly taught the associations that it includes, nor having tried explicitly to learn them. The only feasible way one could obtain the kind of subcognitive associative network that human beings possess would be to experience the world as a human being. Yet, despite being a *sub*cognitive network, it has a manifest presence in conscious decision making. Because computers do not and cannot experience the world in a human way, an interviewer who knows how to reveal aspects of the subcognitive architecture would be able easily to distinguish the computer from the human being. However, this does not mean that a computer cannot have its own brand of subcognitive scaffolding and, on this basis, some kind of intelligence. Thus, the Turing Test tests for the wrong kind of thing: it indicates only whether a computer has *human* intelligence, not intelligence *simpliciter*.

French provides various illustrations of the subcognitive associations that he claims underlie human intelligence. Some of these associations become visible through the application of a lexical decision task. Human experience with the world results in associations of varying strength between concepts. So, for instance, a human being raised in the United States is more likely to think "pepper" when hearing the word "salt" than she is to think "lion." The lexical decision task draws on this fact. In this task, subjects must decide whether a given string of letters is a word. Psychologists have discovered that if the test string is preceded by a strongly associated word then this reduces the time it takes a subject to make a correct judgment. "If, for example, the item 'butter' is preceded by the word 'bread,' it would take significantly less time to recognize that 'butter' was a word than had an unassociated word like 'dog' or a nonsense word preceded it" (1990, p. 57). Presumably, French argues, a computer would not perform as a typical American on a lexical decision task "because there is no a priori way of determining associative strengths . . . between *all* possible concepts" (ibid., his italics). Here French is making the assumption that between any two concepts a human being possesses there is some degree, however slight, of association, where the degree of association is a function of a variety of circumstances, such as education and culture. However, because this associative network is immense and often unpredictable, reflecting the idiosyncrasies of human experience, there is virtually no way to program a computer so that it will faithfully produce humanlike results in a lexical decision task. Human performance on the task requires human experience.

A second example helps to reveal the pervasiveness of subcognitive associations. French describes a rating game in which players must rate the suitability of a given neologism for a particular object. Unlike the lexical decision task, the rating game seems to require conscious deliberation, thus avoiding suspicions one might have about the lexical decision task's usefulness as a test for intelligence. Here is what the players in this game see:

On a scale of 0 (completely implausible) to 10 (completely plausible), please rate:

• "Flugblogs" as a name Kellogg's would give to a new breakfast cereal
• "Flugblogs" as a name of a new computer company
• "Flugblogs" as the name of big, air-filled bags worn on the feet and used to walk on water

- "Flugly" as the name a child might give its favorite teddy bear
- "Flugly" as the surname of a bank accountant in a W. C. Fields movie
- "Flugly" as the surname of a glamorous female movie star

French imagines an interrogator armed with many of these neologisms, and expects that for each rating question there will be a typical response. Most English speaking human beings living today will rate "Flugblogs" as an implausible name for a cereal and as a more plausible name for air-filled bags. Similarly, it is hard to imagine "Flugly" as the surname of a glamorous movie star, but not much of a stretch to suppose that a child might choose it as a name for a teddy bear.

Whereas a human being's responses in the rating game are reliably predictable, the kind of subcognitive associations on which the results depend are, French sensibly claims, not programmable in practice. A computer that has not experienced the world in the way that a contemporary Westerner has will easily be found out through its performance on the rating game. English speaking human beings reject "Flugblog" as a name for a cereal because, perhaps, "The initial syllable 'flug' phonetically activates (unconsciously, of course) such things as 'flub,' 'thug,' 'ugly,' or 'ugh!,' each with it own aura of semantic connotations. 'Blogs,' the second syllable, activates 'blob,' 'bog,' and other words, which in turn activate a halo of other semantic connotations. The sum total of this spreading activation determines how we react, at a conscious level, to the word" (1990, p. 59). The "aura of semantic connotations" is precisely what the computer will not have in anything like a contemporary American's way—and so the computer will not rate neologisms as a contemporary American would.

We now come to the relevance of French's discussion of the Turing Test to the idea of embodied conceptualization. The lexical decision task and the rating game expose subcognitive associations that human beings have developed as a consequence of their immersion in a particular culture. However, there are undoubtedly also subcognitive associations that human beings share as a consequence of having the kinds of bodies they do. Another of French's examples makes this point:

Consider, for example, a being that resembled us precisely in all physical respects except that its eyes were attached to its knees. This physical difference alone would engender enormous differences in its associative concept network compared to our own. Bicycle riding, crawling on the floor, wearing various articles of clothing (e.g., long pants), and negotiating crowded hallways would all be experienced in vastly different ways by this individual. . . . The moral of the story is that the physical level is *not* disassociable from the cognitive level. (1990, p. 62, his italics)

The associative network that underlies human cognitive abilities depends, in part, on how human beings interact with the world, and this interaction, in turn, depends on the properties of the body that is engaged in these interactions. An organism that has eyes on its knees is likely strongly to associate concepts like *crawling* and *torture*, whereas human beings are more likely to develop a strong association between *crawling* and *diapers*.

Although French did not intend his objection to the Turing Test to stand also as a challenge to ST and in support of EMT, it seems to do just this. Indeed, because I have been presenting ST's competition, the embodied mind thesis, as a claim about what we could predict about bodies given only information about minds, the Turing Test is a version of the thought experiment I introduced in the previous chapter. Suppose that the Turing Test is reconfigured so that the interrogator communicates not with a human being and a computer, but with a human being and an extraterrestrial being. The job of the interrogator is to guess which conversation is with the human being and which with the ET. EMT predicts that if the ET's body is very different from a human body then these differences will manifest themselves psychologically and so the right questions will enable the interrogator to distinguish the human being from the ET. One can imagine, for instance, that human beings and ETs would perform very differently on the lexical decision task. Perhaps the ET is built in the way French describes—its body is human in form except for the position of the eyes, which are on its knees. Presumably the ET would be quicker to recognize "agony" as a word when primed with "crawling" than would a human being, whereas the human being would recognize more readily "baby" as a word when similarly primed. Likewise, whereas a human being might rate "crawlshion" as a plausible name for a kind of knee pad that cushions your knees as you garden, the ET might insist that "crawlshion" is more plausibly the name of protective eyewear.

Of course, these differences in performance on tests like the lexical decision task and the rating game might appear to be very localized, but I am inclined to believe that they are differences that would in fact ramify in myriad ways. These are differences that prevent the human being and the ET from seeing the world in the same way. It is not *what* they see that would differ, but *how* they see it. The human being sees the knee-high thistle as a pretty purple flower, the ET sees it as a dangerous obstacle; the human being sees wading as an opportunity to cool off, the ET as a reason to remove contact lenses; when annoyed by the bright sun, the human being thinks "baseball hat," the ET thinks "baggy shorts." Owing to their anatomical differences and the vastly distinct networks of associations that these differences would produce, the ET and the human being would conceive the world in profoundly incongruent ways.

In terms I introduced earlier, we may say that French's discussion of the Turing Test calls into question the thesis of body neutrality. To suppose that a computer could trick the interrogator is to accept that intelligence is body-neutral. Likewise, only if the claim of body neutrality were true would it make sense to suppose that an ET and a human being could perform similarly on the reconfigured Turing Test. But, the body neutrality thesis is implausible. Many of the associations an organism develops depend on the characteristics of its body, and because these associations permeate higher-level cognitive functioning, an interrogator should have an easy time distinguishing human beings from both computers and ETs. French's complaints about the Turing Test, then, provide a solid reason for rejecting the thesis of body neutrality, and, hence, they remove whatever support body neutrality provides to ST.

7.2.2 The Metaphorical Mind

Lakoff and Johnson's work on metaphor (1980a,b, 1999)[1] complements French's observations about the role of subcognitive associations in cognition. Like French, Lakoff and Johnson believe that the concepts through which we experience the world derive much of their texture from the culture in which the possessor of the concepts is immersed. Also, however, they suggest that the meanings of at least some concepts derive from the properties of one's body. As Lakoff and Johnson put it, "What is important is not just that we have bodies and that thought is somehow embodied. What is important is that the peculiar nature of our bodies shapes our very possibilities for conceptualization and categorization" (1999, p. 19). It is this claim that challenges the thesis of body neutrality and so also ST. As I did in my discussion of French, I shall first sketch the reasoning that leads Lakoff and Johnson to this conclusion and then flesh it out with some examples.

"The essence of metaphor," on Lakoff and Johnson's view, "is understanding and experiencing one kind of thing or experience in terms of another" (1980a, p. 5; 1980b, p. 455). Metaphor is, for instance, understanding what an argument is by reference to one's understanding of war, or understanding what love is by reference to one's understanding of a journey. Arguments, of course, are not war, and love is not a journey. This is why the statements "Argument is war" and "Love is a journey" are metaphors. However, these metaphors are extremely significant in how one conceives of arguments or love. Metaphors provide structure to the concepts they elucidate. Focusing on "Argument is war," Lakoff and Johnson note the following expressions of this metaphor in everyday language:

· Your claims are *indefensible.*
· He *attacked every weak point* in my argument.
· His criticisms were *right on target.*
· I *demolished* his argument.
· I've never *won* an argument with him.
· You disagree? Okay, *shoot!*
· If you use that *strategy*, he'll *wipe you out.*
· He *shot down* all of my arguments. (1980a, p. 4; 1980b, p. 454, their italics)

In claiming that metaphor structures one's understanding of a concept, Lakoff and Johnson mean more than simply that the metaphor helps one to grasp its meaning. In fact, the metaphor shapes the very meaning of the concept. "The metaphor is not merely in the words we use—it is in our very concept of an argument" (1980a, p. 5; 1980b, p. 455). Included in our concept of an argument are concepts associated with war. If, in arguing, we could not describe the person with whom we were arguing as an opponent, if we could not see ourselves as waging an attack or as standing our ground, if we could not claim victory or rally our defenses, then we could not conceive ourselves as engaged in argument. What we do when we argue is "structured by the concept of war" (1980a, p. 4; 1980b, p. 455). Were some other metaphor used to structure our concept of argument, say, "Argument is a dance" or "Argument is a tree," we would have a very different conception of argument than the one prominent in our culture. Indeed, as Lakoff and Johnson observe, it would be difficult to conceive members of some alien culture as arguing if their concept of argument were structured by the "Argument is a dance" metaphor. This does not show that arguments *are* war—arguments are war only metaphorically—but it shows instead that metaphors contribute to the meaning of a concept.

In virtue of contributing to the meaning of a concept, a metaphor adds a kind of systematicity to the concept. The "Argument is war" concept makes possible certain descriptions and actions but forecloses on others. It allows one to impose the inferential structure of war onto discussions of argument (Lakoff and Johnson 1999, p. 66). So, for example, in allowing "Argument is war" to structure how we think about arguments, we can draw on the vocabulary of battle to describe a particular argument. We can make sense of claims like "she withstood his barrage" and "he brought out his heavy artillery." We can infer that the argument is coming to an end if we learn that one side has inflicted lethal damage on the other. Likewise, the metaphor makes other ways of talking about argument inadmissible. In arguing, one can beat down an opponent, but one cannot cover him in kisses; one can deflect her blows, but one cannot show her a good time. Again, that some ways of describing an argument make sense whereas other ways do not does not mean that argument is war. It means that the "Argument is war" metaphor has permeated how we think about arguments—it has become part of how we understand the concept of an argument.

Crucially, Lakoff and Johnson believe that just about all conceptual thought involves metaphor: "metaphor pervades our normal conceptual system. Because so many of the concepts that are important to us are either abstract or not clearly delineated in our experience (the emotions, ideas, time, etc.), we need to get a grasp on them by means of other concepts that we understand in clearer terms..." (1980a, p. 115). There are, however, some concepts that we are able to understand without the benefit of metaphorical elaboration. These concepts are fundamental in the sense that they can be understood without reference to other concepts. Rather, we understand the fundamental concepts through "direct physical experience" (ibid., p. 57). Take, for instance, the spatial concept *up*. We understand the meaning of *up* as a result of our spatial experience. "We have bodies and we stand erect. Almost every movement we make involves a motor program that either changes our up-down orientation, maintains it, presupposes it, or takes it into account in some way" (ibid., p. 56; 1980b, p. 476). Similarly, our spatial experience underlies our understanding of concepts like *front-back, in-out, near-far*, and so on. And, in addition to these spatial concepts, the class of basic concepts also includes those dealing with force: "pushing, pulling, propelling, supporting, and balance" (1999, p. 36). Our familiarity with these concepts depends on the kinds of bodies we have and the kinds of actions we take with them. We know the basic concepts through our experience with bodies that orient up and down, that have a front and back, that move in and out of places, that approach and retreat, that push and pull; through our bodily experience we can develop a direct understanding of various spatial concepts.

It follows from Lakoff and Johnson's hypothesis about the development of basic concepts that were an organism to have a body that differed in salient ways from a human body then it would develop a distinct set of basic concepts. Thus, Lakoff and Johnson say, "[i]magine a spherical being living outside of any gravitational field, with no knowledge or imagination of any other kind of experience. What could UP possibly mean to such a being?" (1980a, p. 57; 1980b, p. 476). Similarly, Lakoff and Johnson observe, "The concepts *front* and *back* are body-based. They make sense only for beings with fronts and backs. If all beings on this planet were uniform stationary spheres floating in some medium and perceiving equally in all directions, they would have no concepts of *front* and *back*" (1999, p. 34). Of course, these organisms might possibly develop concepts of *up* and *front*, but their understanding of these concepts would be in terms of other basic concepts. *Up*, for one of these beings, would be understood in terms of some other concepts, just as (most of us) might understand concepts like *weightlessness* in terms of what it is like to swim underwater or bounce on a trampoline.

To summarize so far, Lakoff and Johnson argue (1) that most of our concepts are structured by other concepts. It is this structuring of one concept in terms of another that is the essence of metaphor. Moreover, (2) when one concept structures another it also contributes to the structured concept's meaning in various ways (it "prepares" the concept for particular inferences but not others, facilitates the concept's use in some contexts while impeding it in others, etc.). However, (3) concepts must be grounded in some way—they cannot all be structured in terms of each other. It is through experiences in the environment, interactions between the environment and a particular kind of body, that a small class of concepts is understood directly. Thus, (4) basic concepts are those that are known directly through bodily interactions with the world. We comprehend these basic concepts through the use of our bodies, through the orientations and movements that we make with our torsos, heads, arms, hands, and legs. So, (5) were our bodies to differ, so too would the basic concepts we derive from our interactions with the environment. This summary takes us close to the conclusion of Lakoff and Johnson's that bears on the thesis of body neutrality, that is, to the claim that "the peculiar nature of our bodies shapes our very possibilities for conceptualization and categorization" (1999, p. 19). Left to show is (6) basic concepts do in fact structure our nonbasic concepts. If Lakoff and Johnson can show this, they will have established that the nature of our bodies shape how we conceive the world.

Lakoff and Johnson cite many examples of concepts that receive structuring from basic concepts. For instance, consider the metaphors "Happy is up" and "Sad is down." These metaphors use a basic concept to structure a nonbasic concept. The nature of this structuring is apparent in the following: "I'm feeling up. That boosted my spirits. My spirits rose. You're in high spirits. Thinking about her always gives me a lift. I'm feeling down. I'm depressed. He's really low these days. I fell into a depression. My spirits sank" (1980a, p. 15; 1980b, p. 462). Of course, one would like to know why happiness is structured in terms of the concept *up* and sadness in terms of *down*. Lakoff and Johnson speculate that "Drooping posture typically goes along with sadness and depression, erect posture with a positive emotional state" (1980a, p. 15; 1980b, p. 462). If this speculation is correct, it suggests that organisms that didn't have bodies like our own would develop other metaphors to characterize happiness and sadness. *Happy* and *sad* would be structured in other ways and would thus assume different meanings.

As a second example, consider the metaphor "Foreseeable future events are up (and ahead)." This metaphor receives expression in the following ways: "The up-and-coming events are listed in the paper. What's coming up this week? I'm afraid of what's up ahead of us. What's up?" (1980a, p. 16; 1980b, p. 463). Lakoff and Johnson's explanation for why *up* should structure *foreseeable future events* is, again, speculative, but not implausible: "Normally our eyes are in the direction in which we typically move (ahead, forward). As an object approaches a person (or the person approaches the object), the object appears larger. Since the ground is perceived as being fixed, the top of the object appears to be moving upward in the person's field of vision" (1980a, p. 16; 1980b, p. 463). Insofar as Lakoff and Johnson's speculation is correct, it suggests that if our eyes faced toward the side rather than the front, or if we moved in a direction other than that toward which our eyes pointed, we would structure *foreseeable future events* with some concept other than *up*. Moreover, insofar as metaphors contribute to the meaning of a concept, *foreseeable future events* would have a different meaning for organisms that do not structure it in terms of *up*.

I do not wish to deny the speculative nature of Lakoff and Johnson's descriptions of how nonbasic concepts become rooted in bodily experiences. Moreover, it is consistent with their position that members of different cultures ground similar concepts in different kinds of bodily experiences. Thus, Lakoff and Johnson note, "some cultures orient the future in front of us; others orient it in back" (1980b, p. 462). This suggests that there may be many nonbasic concepts that are structured by different basic concepts across cultures. Perhaps the metaphor "happy is down" prevails in some cultures. Nevertheless, the point that bears on an evaluation of the thesis of body neutrality concerns the basic concepts—those derived from the interactions of a particular kind of body with an environment. Whereas human beings across cultures could, in virtue of having the same kind of bodies, develop the same or a similar repertoire of nonbasic concepts, it is credible that organisms with very different bodies and thus very different kinds of interactions with their environments would derive a different repertoire of basic concepts. Moreover, because these differences in basic concepts would send ripples across the pools of nonbasic concepts, it is credible that beings with human bodies and beings with nonhuman bodies would develop very different classes of nonbasic concepts. In short, they would conceptualize the world differently, which is just what the thesis of embodied conceptualization claims. And, if the body makes a difference to the kinds of concepts an organism develops, then minds predict facts about bodies, which is just what the embodied mind thesis claims.

7.2.3   The Body in Language

So far my discussion of embodied conceptualization may appear more evocative than convincing. The discussion has suffered from a lack of experimental evidence. French's claims about the body's role in shaping the meaning of one's concepts are, I think, sensible, but, of course, they are completely unsupported by experimental evidence. To date, no computer comes close to passing the Turing Test for any significant length of time, and so French's argument awaits final confirmation. Similarly, whereas Lakoff and Johnson might find experimental evidence to support their claim that members of different cultures develop different conceptualizations of the world as a result of using different metaphors to structure their concepts, they tend to steer clear of direct discussion of experimental findings, preferring to keep discussion at a more abstract level (although Lakoff and Johnson 1999 is more detailed in this regard). In any event, there are no experimental findings involving "a spherical being living outside of any gravitational field," and so there is no empirical support at all for the suggestion that were the properties of one's bodies to differ so too would the meanings of one's concepts.

Beginning with conceptual tools he developed in "What Memory Is For" (1997), the psychologist Arthur Glenberg and his students have applied an embodiment perspective to their research on memory and language comprehension. Unlike both French and (to a lesser extent) Lakoff and Johnson, Glenberg buttresses his claims about embodied conceptualization with experimental evidence. For these reasons, discussion of

Glenberg's work is perhaps more compelling than the work I have so far discussed. Here I shall describe some of the theory behind Glenberg's work and then discuss the experimental work he and his students have performed in order to draw attention to the body's role in language comprehension.

Glenberg's approach to memory and language comprehension owes a significant debt to J. J. Gibson's (1966; 1979) groundbreaking work on perception. In this work, Gibson insisted that perception is an active process, in which sensory systems "pick up" information about the environment through the discovery of invariants in the structured stimulation they receive. Thus, for instance, when one is approaching an obstacle like a wall, the light reflecting from the wall's surface is structured in such a way that it will produce a spreading field on the retina. The speed of the flow of light from the center of the retina increases as distance to the wall decreases, thus carrying information about the distance of the obstacle. This fact about "optical flow" is invariant—it is a characteristic of optical flow regardless of the speed at which the perceiver approaches the wall and the distance of the perceiver to the wall. Given its invariance, it serves to specify an impending collision. Similarly, Gibson believed, movement through the environment would reveal all sorts of other invariants, allowing an organism to perceive the environment in a successful (i.e., life-sustaining) way.

Most important and controversial was Gibson's idea that the detection of invariants could carry information about the *affordances* of features in the environment, that is, objects, surfaces, other animals, and so on. "Affordance" is Gibson's term for that which is offered to an organism by things in its environment. This idea of *offering* makes the meaning of affordances relative to the properties of the perceiver. A chink in the wall affords a hiding place for a mouse or a spider, but not a squirrel. The lake affords a supporting surface for a water bug, but not a cow. A stick might afford many things to a primate—a weapon, a cane, a tool for knocking fruit from the tree—while affording a place to perch for a bird. The affordance of an object or surface or place is, according to Gibson, the value or meaning of these things for a particular perceiver. Moreover, these affordances are perceived directly via the detection of the same sort of information that specifies an impending collision or the

direction of movement. The invariants in the stimuli that indicate affordances are more complex than those that indicate motion or distance,
but, Gibson thought, they are present in the structured stimulation that
reaches an organism nonetheless.

Although I have a great deal of sympathy for Gibson's theory of perception, it is not my goal here to defend the theory or, in particular, his
claim that affordances can be specified directly in stimulus information.
I mention Gibson's work here only because it helps to set the stage for
a discussion of Glenberg's research. Indeed, whereas Glenberg accepts
Gibson's idea that the world is perceived in terms of affordances, he need
not and does not endorse Gibson's views about how an organism detects
these affordances. For Glenberg, the ability to perceive affordances
marks a starting place:

My proposal is that perceptual systems have evolved to facilitate our interactions
with a real, three-dimensional world. To do this, the world is conceptualized (in
part) as patterns of possible bodily interactions, that is, how we can move our
hands and fingers, our legs and bodies, our eyes and ears, to deal with the world
that presents itself? [*sic*] That is, to a particular person, the meaning of an object,
event, or sentence is what that person can do with the object, event, or sentence.
(1997, p. 3)

My interest now is in examining Glenberg's extension of this claim about
perception to the area of language comprehension. In particular, I will
focus on those aspects of Glenberg's research suggesting that language
comprehension cannot be a body-neutral psychological capacity. The
nature of one's body influences how one understands language and,
insofar as language is a reflection of thought, the structure of one's body
shapes how one thinks about the world.

Glenberg's account of language comprehension, what he calls the
indexical hypothesis, is offered in contrast to recent theories of language
comprehension, such as latent semantic analysis (LSA) (Landauer and
Dumais 1997) and hyperspace analogue to language (HAL) (Burgess and
Lund 1997; Burgess 1998) that, roughly, define the meaning of a word
as a vector in a high-dimensional space. The dimensions of the space are
cooccurrences of words. Thus, in the case of HAL, the closeness of word
1 to another word 2 in a string of text (in this case consisting of 300
million words of 70,000 types) is assigned a value. Adjacency between
the words is valued at 10, a one-word separation between the two words

reduces the value of the connection to 9, a two-word separation to 8, and so on. The 70,000 words are plotted against each other, in a matrix consisting of 70,000 rows and columns. The meaning of each word is then represented by a vector through this matrix, where rows display co-occurrence values of words that precede a given word and columns show the co-occurrence values of words that follow a given word. Words are similar in meaning depending on how similar their vector values are. Hence, "street" and "road" will, on this analysis, be more similar in meaning than, say "street" and "hat" because the co-occurrence values of "street" with other words is much more similar to the co-occurrence values of "road" with these same words than are the co-occurrence values of "hat" with these words.

LSA encodes the meaning of words in a similar manner, although the focus for LSA is word co-occurrences within particular contexts (e.g., encyclopedia articles). As Landauer and Dumais describe their view, "[I]n essence, and in detail, it assumes that the psychological similarity between any two words is reflected in the way they co-occur in small subsamples of language" (1997, p. 215). Landauer and Dumais then extend their account of word meaning to talk about the meaning of sentences and passages. A sentence can be assigned a particular vector value by averaging the vectors of the words it contains, and the coherence between sentences in a passage can be assigned a value as the cosine of the angle in a multidimensional space between the vectors of the sentences in the passage (Glenberg and Robertson 2000, p. 381).

Glenberg objects to such analyses of meaning, arguing, along with Harnad (1990) and in the spirit of Searle (1980), that theories like LSA and HAL cannot constitute anything like a complete account of meaning, because there is nothing about frequencies of word co-occurrences that serves to affix meanings to words. So, for instance, one can imagine a person who speaks no Chinese familiarizing herself with the relationships that Chinese symbols bear to each other. She may, on this basis, even be able to recognize uncommon or incorrect uses of particular Chinese symbols. Nevertheless, Glenberg would argue, this kind of knowledge does not suffice to provide knowledge of the meaning of the symbols. One can know all the facts that define the LSA vector of a word without thereby knowing the meaning of the word.

Whether Glenberg's alternative indexical hypothesis succeeds as an answer to the so-called symbol grounding problem is of less concern to me than his claim that language comprehension depends on a speaker's recognition of affordances. One way to read Glenberg's work is as a challenge to a body-neutral account of language comprehension and in support of a body-*dependent* account. Theories of language comprehension like HAL and LSA are body-neutral because they allege that understanding a sentence consists (at least in large part) in one's exposure to the associations between words in a number of contexts. No mention or recognition is awarded to the role of the body in language comprehension. In contrast, if Glenberg and his collaborators can show that language comprehension rests in part on a speaker's ability to derive affordances from the referents of a sentence's words, then they will have shown that one's ability to understand sentences depends, at least in part, on the properties of one's body. A theory of language comprehension that denies or ignores the importance of the specific properties of one's body to one's ability to learn a language cannot be adequate. Thus, language comprehension cannot be body-neutral.

Glenberg and Robertson (2000) conduct several experiments that at once cast doubt on HAL and LSA theories of language comprehension and support the idea that language comprehension is sensitive to the kind of body one has. In one experiment they examine people's ability to understand innovative denominal verbs, that is, "verbs that are made out of nouns," (p. 391). So, for example, the nouns "bicycle" and "toilet paper" can be used as verbs, as they are in the following sentences: "John bicycled to town" and "Ray toilet papered the front yard." However, these uses of denominal verbs are familiar. What, Glenberg and Robertson (2000) ask, are the significant factors involved in understanding innovative denominal verbs, such as those appearing in the sentences "The newsboy porched the newspaper," and "My sister Houdini'ed her way out of the locked closet" (these examples are from Clark and Clark 1979)?

According to a theory like HAL or LSA, a novel word should be assigned a meaning that is comparable to other words with a similar vector—a similar collection of associations with other words in a given context. "For instance, if the system encountered a novel unknown word which happened to have very similar patterns of contextual usage to ROAD and STREET's patterns, then the system's vectors for the new word would be similar to the vectors for ROAD and STREET" (Glenberg and Robertson 2000, p. 392). A subject who encounters the innovative denominal verb "porched" ought, according to LSA, assign to it a meaning that reflects the associations the word "porch" bears to other words in many contexts. Accordingly, Glenberg and Robertson infer, LSA entails that sentences that place an innovative denominal verb in roughly the same contexts ought to be judged as equally sensible. Indeed, because LSA has a quantitative means of representing the coherence between sentences in a paragraph (the cosine of the angle in multidimensional space between the vectors corresponding to sentences in a paragraph), it is easy to create sentences that, according to LSA, ought to be judged by subjects as equally sensible.

Consider now Glenberg and Robertson's (2000) first experiment with innovative denominal verbs. Subjects would read stories that were followed by a critical sentence containing a denominal verb (see table 7.1). The subject's task was to judge the sensibility of the critical sentence and to write a paraphrase of the sentence. Some of the sentences subjects saw contained conventional denominal verbs, like "drummed," that occurred in normal contexts (e.g., "He drummed his fingers against the table"). Some contained semi-innovative denominal verbs like "booked" (e.g., to reserve a table) that occurred in atypical contexts and conveyed an unconventional meaning (e.g., "She booked the leg," where "booked" is intended to mean something like "to balance a table by putting a book under one of its legs"). Finally, a third group of sentences contained innovative denominal verbs that, presumably, subjects would never have previously encountered. Moreover, denominal verbs in the semi-innovative or innovative categories would be combined with either an afforded or a nonafforded context. The afforded context suggested a context in which the referent of the noun from which the denominal verb was created could be used in a way to accomplish a goal anticipated in the story. The nonafforded context included many of the same words as those contained in the afforded context, but suggested a goal that was somehow in conflict with the affordances of the referent of the noun from which the denominal verb was derived. Crucially, "the Afforded

Table 7.1
Stimuli Glenberg and Robertson (2000) used in their first experiment with innovative denominal verbs.

Conventional verb (slimed), Afforded
Kenny sat in the tree house and patiently waited. He clutched the jar of green ooze in his hand, and watched the approaching school bus move closer to his house. The teenage girl stepped off and walked towards the tree house unaware of the little boy above her taking the cap off the jar. Kenny waited until she was directly beneath him, and an evil grin spread across his face. Then, Kenny slimed his sister. (.21)

Semi-innovative verb (booked), Afforded
Lori loved her new table, until she noticed that everything she placed on it slid off to the left. The left back leg was lower than all the others. She could not imagine how to fix the slant. Then she spotted a pile of hard-covered books in the corner. She booked the leg. (.61)

Semi-innovative verb (booked), Nonafforded
Lori was having a really bad day. She could not find her textbook and she was late for class. Frantically, she ran over to the table where there was a pile of books. On the way, she banged her leg on the chair. She booked the leg. (.62)

Innovative verb (magazined), Afforded
Sebastian was perusing the latest issue of *Newsweek* when he was disturbed by a most annoying buzzing noise. He looked around the room to determine the source of this disturbance, and saw that a fly was patrolling the vicinity. Its incessant buzzing was making Sebastian insane. He had no choice but to terminate with extreme prejudice. So, he rolled up his *Newsweek* and waited patiently. When the fly came to rest on the coffee table in front of Sebastian, he recognized his opportunity. He magazined it. (.45)

Innovative verb (magazined), Nonafforded
Sebastian was perusing the latest issue of *Newsweek*. He became disturbed as he read an article about rising rates of home invasions in his vicinity. Sebastian decided to follow the advice of a security expert quoted in the magazine by purchasing a home security alarm. The salesman at the electronics store thought Sebastian was insane when he insisted on having the alarm installed that very day, but agreed when Sebastian threatened to terminate the sale. The alarm woke Sebastian when it began buzzing one evening.
He recognized his opportunity.
He magazined it. (.42)

Table 7.2
Sensibility ratings. From Glenberg and Robertson (2000). Standard errors are in parentheses.

	Sensibility rating	Paraphrase
Conventional verbs		
Afforded	5.67 (.12)	.99 (.01)
Semi-innovative verbs		
Afforded	3.78 (.27)	.96 (.02)
Nonafforded	2.29 (.21)	.13 (.03)
Innovative verbs		
Afforded	4.12 (.24)	.96 (.02)
Nonafforded	2.06 (.16)	.32 (.03)

and Nonafforded contexts were written so that the LSA cosines between these contexts and the critical sentence were approximately equated" (ibid., p. 393). This is why LSA predicts that subjects' sensibility judgments should be roughly equal regardless of whether the critical sentences occurred in afforded or nonafforded contexts.

Glenberg and Robertson found that, contrary to the predictions of LSA, subjects judged the sensibility of critical sentences containing innovative denominal verbs to be significantly higher in the afforded contexts than in the nonafforded contexts (see table 7.2). Semi-innovative verbs followed the same pattern of being judged more sensible in afforded than in nonafforded contexts, although relative to innovative denominal verbs, semi-innovative verbs were judged to be slightly less sensible in afforded contexts and slightly more sensible in nonafforded contexts. Similarly, paraphrases of the critical sentences containing innovative and semi-innovative verbs in the afforded conditions expressed the meanings that Glenberg and Robertson intended, whereas in the nonafforded conditions subjects were far less likely to express the meanings that Glenberg and Robertson intended for the sentences containing innovative or semi-innovative denominal verbs. It is worth repeating at this point that, if the sensibility of the sentences were determined only through the kind of abstract vector analysis of word meanings that theories like LSA promulgate, subjects should have judged sentences in the afforded and nonafforded conditions as equally sensible. On what, then, does the

Table 7.3
Sample Stimuli from Kaschak and Glenberg (2000).

Rachel worked for a scientist in a research firm. As part of her duties, she was required to bring the scientist's mail to his office so he could open it after lunch. On this particular day, Rachel encountered three large boxes among the mail addressed to the scientist. The boxes were way too big for her to carry.

Affordance manipulating sentence:
In the corner of the room, though, Rachel noticed an office chair with four *good/missing* wheels.

Critical sentence
Rachel *brought/chaired* the scientist his mail.

subjects' real performance depend? What is it about the afforded condition that enhances the subject's ability to comprehend language?

Before trying to answer these questions, I would like to look at another experiment conducted by Kaschak and Glenberg (2000). In this experiment, Kaschak and Glenberg created stories that anticipated transfer situations, that is, situations in which an agent in the story would be required to transfer an object from one place to another (see table 7.3). The penultimate sentence of the story contained an "affordance manipulating sentence," which would contain an object that either afforded transfer (e.g., a chair with good wheels) or that did not afford transfer (e.g., a chair with missing wheels). The final sentence in the story, the critical sentence, would contain either a conventional verb of transfer (e.g., "brought") or an innovative denominal verb (e.g., "chaired"). The dependent variable in the experiment was the time required for subjects to read the critical sentence. Kaschak and Glenberg were careful to counterbalance the affordance manipulating sentences with the critical sentences, so that afforded and nonafforded versions of the affordance manipulating sentence would appear just prior to sentences containing either conventional verbs of transfer or innovative denominal verbs.

Kaschak and Glenberg (2000) found that reading times for critical sentences containing innovative denominal verbs were significantly lower in the afforded contexts than they were in the nonafforded contexts. Reading times for the critical sentences containing conventional verbs of transfer were, as they predicted, only slightly faster in the afforded conditions. As in the earlier experiment, the data suggest that subjects' language comprehension differs depending on whether the innovative denominal verb they encounter is matched with an afforded or nonafforded context.

Of course, there are elements of Glenberg et al.'s research that are likely to make philosophers uneasy. In particular, Glenberg and his colleagues take themselves to be providing evidence against one theory of "human meaning" and in favor of another. However, they do not address a number of topics that philosophers concerned with meaning see as essential to any such theory, for example, a distinction between sense and reference, a distinction between the meaning of words and the meaning of sentences, and an account of the relationship between meaning and truth. Yet, there is an interpretation of Glenberg et al.'s work that makes attention to these philosophical concerns unnecessary. More specifically, Glenberg et al.'s work can be taken to confirm the idea of embodied conceptualization—and so counter the idea of body neutrality—regardless of its success as a theory of meaning (in the philosophers' sense of theory of meaning). Here is what I have in mind.

Glenberg et al.'s work, whether it satisfies the concerns a philosopher brings to issues of meaning, reveals a real effect. Subjects reliably judge as more sensible sentences containing innovative denominal verbs in some contexts than they do in other contexts. Moreover, the best predictor of whether a given innovative denominal verb will be one that enters into a sensible sentence seems to be whether the verb suggests an action that a human being can undertake in order to achieve a particular goal. Thus, for instance, whether one judges the sentence "She booked the leg" to be sensible depends on whether one can imagine oneself performing an action with a book to accomplish some goal, such as stabilizing a table. Similarly, whether one can understand the sentence "Rachel chaired the scientist his mail" depends on whether one can imagine oneself doing something with a chair that would result in the delivery of mail. But, to say that sensibility judgments depend on a subject's ability to *imagine* him- or herself doing some kind of action is just to say that the judgments depend on how one understands the manner in which an agent with a body of a particular sort can interact with an object with certain properties so as to bring about some outcome. If a subject were led to believe that Rachel were two inches tall, or weighed only five pounds, or had no appendages with which to grasp, then, quite clearly, the suggestion that she *chair* the scientist his mail would be no less perplexing than the suggestion that she *tennis ball* the scientist his mail, or *shingle* him his mail, or *grass* him his mail.

Making sense of language, Glenberg et al.'s work suggests, depends in part on a kind of perspective-taking. From the perspective of someone with a humanlike body, wheeled chairs are something that can be pushed, and so it is a relatively easy affair to make sense of an innovative denominal verb like "chaired" in a context that suggests transfer. Bodies like ours permit the use of chairs for some purposes but not others. Bodies like ours can push chairs, but cannot swallow them; we can sit on chairs but cannot balance them on our heads; we can use them to ward off lions, but not to reach the tops of tall trees. All of these facts about chairs are contingent on facts about human bodies. Likewise, the perspective from which a human being judges the sensibility of a sentence is one that reflects these facts. One need not have a full account of meaning, in the philosopher's sense of meaning, to accept Glenberg's claim that language comprehension involves an appreciation for the affordances of objects. The essential point is that an ability to understand sentences seems, at least in many cases, to incorporate an organism's knowledge about how its body might interact with objects in its environment. Differences in body will, presumably, create differences in one's ability to understand sentences, and from facts about sentence comprehension one could predict facts about body.

7.3   Extended Mind

The focus of this chapter so far has been on the assumption of body neutrality. If gross morphological and anatomical features of an organism's body do not play a significant role in how or what an organism thinks, then it might seem natural to suppose that a humanlike mind can be embodied in many different ways, just as ST asserts. On the other hand, if the properties of an organism's body determine or contribute profoundly to how and what it thinks, then there is reason to favor EMT. There is reason, that is, to believe that it might be possible to predict properties of an organism's body from knowledge of its psychology. It was for the purpose of calling into question the assumption of body neutrality that I examined work supporting the idea of embodied thought and embodied conceptualization. According to these theses, the body's doings constitute a link in various cognitive processes, and insofar as cognitive processes have evolved to incorporate the kind of information that particular bodies can provide, cognition will be sensitive to properties of the body and so cannot be body neutral. Similarly, because gross morphological and anatomical features have a pervasive impact on the kinds of concepts one develops to wrestle order and organization into the world, conceptualization cannot be body neutral but must be understood relative to properties of particular bodies.

In this final section I shift my focus to the claim that minds are envatted. This, recall, is sometimes offered as another reason to think that ST is plausible. The envatted mind is a mind that, as we saw Haugeland (1995) putting it in the previous chapter, has a clearly defined interface with the body. Minds would be envatted if their realization constituted a component in the larger body. For the mind to be envatted, it must be *contained*. It must have clearly defined borders in the same way that a resistor in a television set has clearly defined borders. It is containment that makes the thesis of envatment coherent, for it makes possible the suggestion that while the body is "over there" doing its thing, the mind might be somewhere else, receiving signals from the body via radio or cable connections and, in turn, sending signals to the body through similar channels. Similarly, it is containment that makes it clear why envatment might support ST. If the mind can be separated from the body, then it can be "hooked up" to different kinds of bodies, just as the same resistor might be made to operate in different kinds of appliances, or Shakey's STRIPS program might be put in charge of analyzing input from different kinds of robots.

Just to emphasize a point I made in my earlier discussion of Haugeland, containment does not require spatial localization. Thus, a department of learning support services in a university can be a component of the university even if its members are spread throughout other departments. In saying that learning support services is contained, or is a component, it is important only that there be some way of distinguishing it from other components. Because the members of learning support work on a common set of problems that other members of the university do not, cooperate and meet more with each other than they do with people not in their department, and so on, it makes sense to conceive of learning support services as a single unit despite its spatial integration with the rest of the university. Moreover, learning support services might have a clearly defined interface in its interactions with other departments. Perhaps it is possible to make appointments with members of learning support services only through a learning support service receptionist. This, in effect, cuts off professional communication between the learning support person and the philosopher next to whom she sits unless the philosopher has scheduled an appointment through the appropriate channels.

Similarly, even though the brain does seem spatially localized, it is not for this reason that one might think of the mind as envatted. The mind could still count as envatted if the biological parts that realize it were spread out across the body. The reasons for conceiving it as envatted in such a circumstance are parallel to those that justify calling learning support services a single department. If the parts that realize the mind all work toward the solution of similar problems, communicate with each other more than they do with other parts of the body, receive and send information from and to the body through clearly articulated channels, and so on, then the mind can be envatted despite not have a spatially localized realization.

I now wish to consider two lines of argument that make envatment seem an unlikely hypothesis. The work I shall examine attacks a necessary condition for envatment: that the mind be cleanly separable from the rest of the body. The first reason to doubt the clarity of the separation between mind and body comes from neurological evidence Damasio (1994) presents. The second reason proceeds from a view of mind that philosophers such as David Chalmers, Andy Clark, and Rob Wilson have propounded.

7.3.1   The Mind beyond the Brain

Of the many issues Damasio explores in his book *Descartes' Error* (1994)—the effect of emotions on rationality, the construction of a sense

of self, neurobiological accounts of behavior, and more—I will be prin-
cipally interested in those parts of his work that highlight the role of the
body in reasoning. Sometimes Damasio says things in support of embodied thought, as in his discussion of how the state of one's body affects
decision making and other cognitive functions. More often, however,
Damasio is concerned with establishing his claim that "body and brain
form an indissociable organism" (1994, p. 88). It is this claim that makes
Damasio a proponent of what, following Clark and Chalmers (1998), I
call *extended mind*.

Damasio's case for extended mind follows a route that Haugeland
(1995) would applaud. As I just recounted, envatment suggests that the
mind and body can be separated, that is, can be construed as separate
components that communicate only through some well-defined interface.
As we saw in my discussion of Shakey, the interface between Shakey's
body and brain is so well defined that the distance between them can
easily be stretched with no loss in Shakey's abilities. Considerations of
transmission speed aside, whether Shakey's brain is in the room next to
Shakey's body, is in the building across the street, or is halfway around
the planet makes no difference to its operation. If the performance of a
human mind could be maintained once whatever it is that realizes it were
removed from the body, then this would be reason to suspect that the
interface between human bodies and brains is as clean as it is between
Shakey's body and brain.

In fact, as Damasio argues at length, the mind is not realized simply
in the brain, nor is it a spatially spread but easily distinguishable component like the department of learning support services. Rather, its realization is integrated throughout the body. Damasio begins his discussion
of this integration with the claim that the brain evolved for the purpose
of maintaining the body (1994, pp. 229, 230); and, accordingly, one
function of the brain "is to be well-informed about what goes on in the
rest of the body" (ibid., p. 90). Whether this assumption is correct is
really not important to the story that follows, for the details of the story
are true regardless of the historical events that led human brains to move
to fixation in the human population. However, the conjecture is plausible given the extent and nature of the connections between brains and
bodies. Moreover, Damasio points out that the distinctively human

neocortex considered by many to be the "seat of reason" is built not just *on top* of the older subcortical area of the brain that regulates many of the involuntary but life-sustaining actions of the body (breathing, digestion, homeostasis, heartbeat), but also "*from* it and *with* it" (ibid., p. 128). This is a peculiar way to describe the relation between the neocortex and the subcortical parts of the brain, but it makes much more sense when one appreciates the tangle of connections and feedback loops between the neocortex, the subcortical regions of the brain, and the body.

Subcortical areas of the brain, such as the brain stem, hypothalamus, and parts of the limbic system (the cingulate gyrus and amygdala), play a significant role in the biological regulation of the body. The hypothalamus in particular regulates the production of hormones through its control of various endocrine glands. These glands, under instructions from the hypothalamus, release chemicals into the bloodstream and in this way control such things as body metabolism and immunity (Damasio 1994, p. 118). The hypothalamus and the limbic system together are in charge of controlling the delicately balanced biochemical processes that keep bodies alive. Yet control of these chemical processes depends not only on instructions that initiate from the brain, but also on the complex chemical activity in the body.

As an illustration of the intricacy of these connections between brain and body, Damasio explains that the pituitary gland releases chemicals to control the hormone secretions of the thyroid and adrenal glands (all parts of the endocrine system). Controlling the pituitary gland is the hypothalamus, which in turn is under the control of the limbic system and the neocortex. The release of hormones into the bloodstream acts on both the endocrine glands from which they were secreted and on the pituitary and hypothalamus, as well as on other areas of the brain. Unlike the resistor, which operates in relative isolation from that which goes on in the rest of the television, the activities of different areas of the brain are severely constrained by not just various chemical and neural transmissions from other parts of the brain and body, but also by their own transmissions. The operation of the pituitary gland, for instance, depends in part on the chemicals surrounding it and the neural impulses coming from the neocortex. But the chemicals surrounding the pituitary and the impulses coming to it from the neocortex and hypothalamus depend in part on what the pituitary is doing (1994, pp. 118–119).

But now add to the complexity of this picture the fact that those parts of the brain that are in charge of the body's biological regulation are also integral to mental functioning: "The hypothalamus, the brain stem, and the limbic system intervene in body regulation *and* in all neural processes on which mind phenomena are based, for example, perception, learning, recall, emotion and feeling, and . . . reasoning and creativity. Body regulation, survival, and mind are intimately interwoven" (1994, p. 123). It is this conception of the relation between body and mind that stands behind Damasio's remark that the neocortex does not simply rest on top of the older body-regulating areas of the brain but arose from and with it. "The neocortex becomes engaged along with the older brain core, and rationality results from their concerted activity" (ibid., p. 128). Mental processes are not the deliverances of simply the brain, but a brain that is at once intimately enmeshed with a body. The influences the brain and body impose on each other permeate each to the extent that it can no longer make sense to talk about there being a "what the brain does" that stands in coherent contrast to a "what the body does." As Damasio puts it, "mind derives from the entire organism" (ibid., p. 225).

The significance for envatment of the brain's broad reach into the body and, conversely, of the body's penetration into the workings of the brain is not lost on Damasio. He is aware of the philosopher's brain in a vat thought experiment. He remarks:

It might be argued that if it were possible to mimic, at the level of the dangling nerves, realistic configurations of inputs as if they were coming from the body, then the disembodied brain would have a normal mind. Well, that might be a nice and interesting experiment "to do" and I suspect the brain might indeed have *some* mind under those conditions. But what that more elaborate experiment would have done is create a body surrogate and thus confirm that "body-type inputs" are required for a normally minded brain after all. And what it would be unlikely to do is make the "body inputs" match in realistic fashion the variety of configurations which body states assume when those states are triggered by a brain engaged in making evaluations. (1994, p. 228, his italics)

In fact, I believe Damasio's reply here is confused. His response seems simultaneously to affirm the possibility that a brain could be removed from the body without disrupting the inputs it receives from the body while also denying that the brain would function in its normal manner. If the inputs to the brain in the vat were exactly what they are to a brain in a body, what explains why the envatted brain would have *some* mind, but not a normal mind? More confusingly, Damasio then asserts at the end of the passage that it would hardly be possible to do just what he imagines it *is* possible to do at the start of the passage, namely, mimic the inputs that a brain in a body actually receives. Either it is possible to mimic the inputs to the envatted brain precisely or it is not. If it is, why wouldn't the brain perform normally? If it is not, then this is just to deny the coherence of the thought experiment.

Although Damasio's reply to envatment is unsatisfying, I believe that the neurological evidence he brings to light about the relation between the body and the brain does bear on the tenability of the thought experiment. The point Damasio fails to appreciate in his response to envatment is that even if it is possible to remove the brain from the body while retaining the brain's connections to the body, this does not suffice to show that the *realization* of the mind is a well-defined component of the body. Whether it is a well-defined component depends on the nature of its connections with the rest of the body, and it is in this context that Damasio's discussion of the intimacy and complexity of brain–body interaction comes to the fore. As I understand the neurological facts Damasio presents, the mind is realized in a complex of processes spread across brain, viscera, and other parts of the body. Accordingly, the proper response to envatment is that it *is* impossible, or that if it is possible this is only because the entire organism has been envatted.

I mentioned at the beginning of this discussion of envatment that for the idea of a brain in a vat to have the kind of significance that advocates of ST attribute to it, it is necessary to think of the mind as realized entirely by the brain. Recall that the thesis of envatment supports ST on the assumption that *minds* can be separated from bodies. If the human mind stands in the same relation to the human body that Shakey's mind stands in relation to its robotic body, then it is conceivable that facts about mind do not carry information about the bodies with which they are associated. If minds and bodies can be independent of each other, one might suppose that a mind can be wedded to a variety of kinds of bodies. It turns out, however, that (assuming Damasio's description of the brain–body relationship to be accurate) there is no simple, clean connection between the realization of the mind and the rest of the body. The thesis of envatment begs the question in its assumption that because brains can be removed from bodies the realization of the mind can be removed from bodies. More precisely, it begs the question in its assumption that what realizes the mind is a well-defined organ. Accordingly, envatment is impossible not because of any logical incoherence, but just because the realizer of the mind does not happen to constitute a precisely defined component of the body.

Granting Damasio's description of the ties between brain and body, I hope it is clear why ST seems less likely than EMT. ST assumes that it is possible to talk about mental properties in abstraction from bodily properties. It is this abstraction that makes tenable the idea that the same kind of mind might be inserted into different kinds of bodies. But, it is just such an abstraction that Damasio's work challenges. It is not simply processes in the brain that create a mind, but processes taking place in the skin, in the stomach, and in other visceral organs. Hence, an abstract characterization of brain processes cannot suffice to capture the elements by which a physical organization realizes a mind. Because the processes that realize the mind cannot be neatly separated from those occurring in the rest of the body, the nearest abstract description of processes from which minds emerge must include happenings in the body as well.

7.3.2 The Mind Outside the Body

Recently, some philosophers (e.g., Clark and Chalmers 1998; Wilson 1994; 1999; 2004) have promoted the idea that the use of various props external to the body extend the mind into the environment, and, if this were true, the idea of envatment would become problematic. These philosophers are, in essence, applying Richard Dawkins's idea of an extended phenotype to the individuation of minds. Dawkins (1982) argues that the decision to define an organism's phenotype from the "skin in" is arbitrary. Just as genes encode information that results in a spider's having eight legs, so genes also encode information that results in the morphology of a spider's web. The morphology of the web is as much a consequence of genetic coding as other more familiar elements of a spider's phenotype, and thus to deny that a web is part of the spider's phenotype simply because it is "outside" the spider is, Dawkins thinks, an indefensibly arbitrary claim about phenotypic extent. Indeed, it appears question begging to deny that the spider's web is part of the spider's phenotype if one does so for the reason that it is outside the spider. Whether the web is outside the spider depends, of course, on where one draws the boundaries of the spider, which, in turn, depends on how one individuates phenotypes.

In a similar spirit, Clark, Chalmers, and Wilson explore the idea that minds extend beyond the brain and indeed beyond the skin. Clark and Chalmers (1998) offer the following example to motivate the idea of extended mind. Inga has a normal memory and among the information it contains is the fact that the Museum of Modern Art is on 53rd St. Deciding that she would like to see an exhibit she has heard about, Inga thinks for a moment, remembers that MoMA is on 53rd St., and off she goes. Otto, on the other hand, suffers from Alzheimer's disease and relies on a notebook to store information that he is now unable to retrieve from memory. Otto too hears about the exhibit at MoMA and he too forms a desire to attend. He looks at his notebook, sees written there the fact that MoMA is on 53rd St., and off *he* goes. Clark and Chalmers argue that there is no principled difference between Inga and Otto's belief about MoMA's location despite the fact that Inga's belief is inside her head and Otto's is in his notebook. Every reason for thinking of Inga's nonoccurrent beliefs as part of her cognitive system is also a reason to think of the statements in Otto's notebook as a part of his cognitive system: "The information in the notebook functions just like the information constituting an ordinary non-occurrent belief; it just happens that this information lies beyond the skin" (1998, p. 13).

As I noted, Clark and Chalmers's suggestion that minds extend beyond brains and bodies conflicts with the possibility of envatment. If minds leak into environments then an envatted brain would constitute at best only part of a mind. Envatting the entire mind would require a vat of unknown proportions—one capable of encompassing not only an individual's body but perhaps vast regions of the world, including other individuals. However, unlike the argument against envatment that Damasio's work suggests—an argument that turns on empirical facts about the brain's relation to the rest of the body—Clark and Chalmers's argument is entirely conceptual. This, of course, is not to say that it is unsound or weak, but, because its force does arise from a particular conception of what minds are, the argument tempts the following sort of response.

One could accept Clark and Chalmers's claim that the information in Otto's notebook is functionally identical to the information in Inga's head, but at the same time one could deny that this fact by itself makes the information in Otto's notebook a belief. That is, one might insist that there is more to being a mental state than being functionally identical to a mental state. Certainly it is true for many nonmental properties that functional considerations do not suffice to individuate them as the kind that they are. Artificial kidneys, despite their functional identity to real kidneys, are artificial for all that. Likewise, a critic of Clark and Chalmers could insist that there is more to being a mental state than being functionally identical to a mental state. This seems to be the view of philosophers like Ned Block and John Searle, who, as we have already seen, devise thought experiments that, they think, count against a purely functional account of mental states. Of course, Clark and Chalmers are free to respond that if one denies that functional criteria suffice for defining mental states, one should be ready to supply and justify the missing ingredients.

However, perhaps this burden shifting is unfair. Perhaps it is just a feature of what we mean by "minds" that they do not extend beyond the skin of an organism. Clark and Chalmers would no doubt gape at the audacity of this suggestion. It is, as they point out, simply arbitrary to insist that the mind stops at the skin. It is precisely at this point, however, that the superiority of the earlier argument against envatment shows itself. I argued that envatment is not possible if that which realizes the mind, as a matter of neurophysiological fact, cannot be separated from the body. This is not a consequence of the concept *mind*, at least not on its face, but rather a consequence of empirical facts about the rich and entangled integration of the brain with the rest of the body. Clark and Chalmers's point, on the other hand, boils down to a question of semantic policy. How do we choose to use the word "mind"? Can mental states be outside one's head or not? It seems to me that this question by itself is not very interesting. Some, like Clark and

Chalmers, will answer in the affirmative. Others might appreciate the considerations that Clark and Chalmers raise in their favor but, nevertheless, persist in their view that minds simply cannot extend beyond bodies. In the end, however, the disagreement exposes less about what minds are than it does about how people choose to talk about minds.

In contrast to Clark and Chalmers's defense of the extended mind, which, I have argued, ultimately rests on decisions about how to use the word "mind," Wilson (2004) develops the idea of what he calls "wide" minds from his examination of the realization concept. In chapter 2 I introduced some of the ideas on which Wilson's case rests. The first idea involves a distinction between the core and noncore parts of a realization. The total realization of a kind will contain a core part as well as noncore parts, where the difference between these is one of salience or importance. Talk of salience or importance of course introduces an observer-relative condition, and Wilson accepts this, claiming that the concept of realization has an "epistemic dimension" (ibid.). To illustrate these ideas, Wilson notes that the circulatory system has various parts— "such as the heart, the arteries, the capillaries, the arterioles, the venules, and the blood" (ibid.). These parts will realize a property, such as that of having a blood pressure of 120 over 80. The most salient realizer of this property is the state of the arteries and heart. However, the arteries and the heart cannot realize the blood pressure without the rest of the circulatory system. Thus, for Wilson, the arteries and heart constitute the core realization of the blood pressure, whereas the parts of the circulatory system that provide "back up" constitute noncore parts of the blood pressure's realization. Together, the arteries, heart, and rest of the circulatory system compose the total realization of the blood pressure.

I have some misgivings about Wilson's account. For one thing, it is not clear that it is correct to describe the circulatory system as *realizing* blood pressure. Why not think of the circulatory system as *causing* a particular blood pressure? Insofar as realization is supposed to be a synchronic relation of determination and causation is typically a diachronic relation, Wilson's example is vulnerable to doubts that it marks a genuine case of realization. Indeed, it certainly sounds more natural to describe the heart and arteries as among the *causes* of a particular blood pressure than it does to say that blood pressure is realized by the heart and arteries. Second, Wilson's concession that the distinction between core and noncore parts of a realizer depends on epistemic and context-relevant considerations does not answer the harder questions about how these considerations ground particular distinctions between core and noncore parts. Relative to which epistemic concerns and contextual features ought one to define the heart and arteries as core parts of a realization while assigning capillaries, arterioles, venules, and blood to the less significant noncore part?

Misgivings aside, Wilson uses in an interesting way the distinction between core and noncore parts of a realization. Specifically, the distinction lays ground for a further one between *entity-bounded* and *wide* realizations:

Entity-bounded realization: a total realization of a property whose non-core part is located entirely within the individual in which the property is instantiated;

Wide realization: a total realization of a property whose non-core part is not located entirely within the individual in which the property is instantiated. (Wilson 2004, with slight revisions)

Entity-bounded realization is the sort philosophers more commonly recognize. The core and noncore parts of the realization of pain, for instance, are completely internal to the individual who experiences the pain. On the other hand, given externalist intuitions of the sort I discussed in chapter 2, it is plausible that at least some mental states (e.g., beliefs about water, beliefs about arthritis) have realizers whose noncore parts are external to the subject. Molecularly identical twins might have beliefs of different types because of their relationships to different natural or social features of their environments. It is this possibility, *inter alia*, that moves Wilson to claim that the mind is extended: some mental states are realized (in part) in things external to a subject.

Wilson's case for wide minds is more cautious than Clark and Chalmers's. In particular, Wilson need not agree with Clark and Chalmers's claim that Otto's belief about MoMA resides in a notebook. This, as I mentioned, seems ultimately to rest on a stipulation: anything that has the functional role of a belief is a belief. One who doubts that functional role is all there is to belief will not feel compelled to accept this claim. On the other hand, one can deny that a notebook can contain beliefs while maintaining nevertheless that the contents of a notebook might constitute *part* of the total realization of some beliefs. Otto's belief that MoMA is on 53rd St. must be realized somewhere, and, however one distinguishes the core from the noncore parts of a belief's realization, it is not unreasonable to suppose that at least part of the realization of Otto's belief is not in his head.

In the end, I think Wilson's work on extended mind provides a persuasive reason to question envatment. Wilson's account leaves open important questions, especially those involving the distinction between core and noncore parts of a total realization, but I think that despite these questions he gives a sound basis to accept that the mind ain't *all* in the head (or body!). Insofar as this is true, it means that a science of the mind will have to look beyond the brain for a more complete understanding of psychology. Notice, however, that this criticism of envatment is not so clearly a defense of EMT. It may be true that minds are extended, or wide, in Wilson's sense, but this does not imply that from properties of minds it is possible to predict properties of bodies.

Still, the possibility of extended minds suggests a related and provocative idea. Throughout this book I have been arguing that it is possible to predict properties of the brain and body from knowledge of mental properties; but perhaps it is also possible to predict properties of the world from mental properties. Perhaps anything with a humanlike mind must live in a humanlike natural and social world. Although not conceived in these terms, research in embodied cognition by people like Clark (1999, 2001), Hutchins (1995), and Wilson (2004) promotes such a view. For these thinkers, much of what is distinctive about the human mind resides in the props and tools (the "scaffolding") with which human beings surround themselves in an effort to increase their cognitive reach. If one buys the argument that the notepads, calculators, charts, and so on that have been designed for the purpose of extending cognitive abilities are in fact properly construed as a feature of human cognitive architecture—as part of the realization base of human cognition—then one might wish to take seriously the following hypothesis. To have a humanlike mind involves far more than having a humanlike brain and body. It also entails living in the kind of environment that human beings have constructed—an environment cluttered with the artifacts that help make human cognitive capacities what they are.

7.4 Summary

The length of this chapter recommends a brief summary. The goal of the chapter has been an examination of work in embodied cognition that might help to adjudicate between two competing hypotheses. ST, on the one hand, holds that properties of mind do not carry information about properties of body. EMT, on the other hand, holds that properties of mind reflect properties of the body, and so from facts about mind it is possible to predict facts about body. One might be tempted by ST if one thinks that minds are like programs, capable of being run on a variety of kinds of hardware. On this view, it is possible for a psychologist to explain the mind while retaining a stance of body neutrality. Alternatively, the idea that minds are essentially brains in vats also encourages belief in ST.

Research in embodied cognition suggests negative responses to both body neutrality and envatment. Work in perception reveals that properties of the body actually play a crucial role in perceptual processes. Thus, an explanation of perceptual processes cannot proceed without attention to the body's contribution. Work on metaphor and language comprehension also casts doubt on body neutrality. The metaphors by which we render the world in familiar terms, as well as our ability to use and comprehend novel linguistic forms, are body dependent. Finally, envatment is a coherent conception of the mind only insofar as the mind is contained in the brain and the brain constitutes a component that can be separated from the rest of the body. But the brain is not the locus of the mind. The mind emerges from complex interactions between the brain and the body, and, perhaps, artifacts external to these things as well. All this suggests that the smallest vat capable of holding a mind would have to be quite large indeed.

In short, as embodied cognition research continues to amass, the seams that have traditionally divided mind from body begin to fade. The fallout from EC no doubt has larger consequences for how we must think about minds than simply a rejection of ST. However, I hope the contents of this chapter have gone some way to making a case against the ideas of body neutrality and envatment that support ST.

8

Final Thoughts

As I noted in the preface, despite the naturalistic turn that has dominated philosophy of mind in recent years, the dogma of the ghost in the machine continues to haunt most discussions of the mind–body relationship. Both the multiple realizability thesis and the separability thesis encourage a view of mind as an entity that, as Ryle put it, must somehow be harnessed to the body. The claim that minds are multiply realizable suggests that there are no particular physical properties necessary for minds. The claim that minds and bodies are independent, that the properties of the mind can be investigated in isolation from those of the body, suggests that the mind is like the occupant of a house.

In describing MRT and ST as naturalized descendants of the dogma of the ghost in the machine, it is not my intention to ridicule them. Unlike ghosts, whose presence cannot be empirically determined, MRT and ST offer testable predictions about the mind–body relationship. If MRT is true, we should not be able to predict properties of the brain from properties of the mind. Similarly, if ST is true, we should not be able to predict properties of the body from properties of the mind. It is because MRT and ST make predictions that they can be tested against their competitors: the mental constraint thesis and the embodied mind thesis.

I should note that although this approach to thinking about MRT and ST may be new, it is not without some precedent. As Gary Hatfield (1999) has shown, investigations of neurophysiology have for a long time been guided by psychological facts. From the fact that we see just one world despite having two eyes, Newton predicted in 1704 that the nerve fibers from the two eyes must partially decussate (i.e., cross) at the optic chiasma. In the 1870s, Hering, observing that afterimages have a color

228   Chapter 8

complementary to that which caused them (a yellow stimulus causes a blue afterimage, red causes green, etc.), speculated that the neurophysiology of color must have an opponent organization. Newton and Hering obviously believed that mental properties forced particular physical solutions, and they were right.

In the preceding chapters I have scoured a variety of fields—neuroscience, brain evolution, perceptual theory, interactive vision, cognitive psychology, embodied cognition—in an effort to discover what, if any, predictions can be made about brains and bodies from facts about human psychology. I have also discussed and developed ideas about multiple realizability, constraints, convergence, and embodiment that, I think, must come into play in an evaluation of MRT and ST. The conclusions I have reached are necessarily speculative and sketchy, for there is in fact no discipline that has dedicated itself to testing the predictions of MRT and ST. Indeed, it is perhaps the most novel contribution of this book to suggest that these ideas, because they are empirical hypotheses about the mind–brain/mind–body relationship, can be tested. In any event, I have had to make do with research that, although intended for other purposes and for the support of other hypotheses, can, with some exertion, be made applicable to an assessment of MRT and ST.

Although I cannot stress enough that firm convictions about the relative likelihoods of MRT and ST against their competitors must await further empirical research, I predict that as this research accumulates, we will find that the human mind is far more intimately harnessed to the human brain and body than either MRT or ST envisage. The more we come to understand the brain, the more we will come to see as no accident that the human mind is realized in the way that it is. Similarly, as embodied cognition research progresses, the traditional boundaries between mind and body will either continue to fade or will require extensive realignment. In short, my bet is that the mind is far more incarnate than most philosophers, and certainly most laypersons, have appreciated.

Of the many holes and gaps in my study of MRT and ST, perhaps the most conspicuous is my failure to address consciousness and qualia. Can conscious states be multiply realized? Are there different ways to realize the acidic, bitter taste one experiences when licking the positive and negative poles of a nine-volt battery? Does humanlike consciousness require a humanlike body? Is the human experience of red distinct from the avian experience of red in virtue of differences in human and bird bodies? I think the reason these questions seem so much harder than questions about perception and cognition is that, on the one hand, it is more difficult to provide functional descriptions of consciousness and qualia. The task analyses by which R-properties are identified and so realizations distinguished must have a functional description to serve as their guide. But, what are the functional characteristics of a red experience? I cannot begin to imagine how to provide a task analysis the experience of red. Notice that Hering's work on the opponent organization of color vision did not lead to the discovery of the neural realization of color experience, but rather showed why the relations between color experiences are as they are. That is, one can know quite a lot about the opponent processes in color vision without knowing how the experience of color is realized.

But, on the other hand, it is perhaps more difficult to answer questions about the multiple realizability of consciousness and qualia simply because we do not know enough about the properties of brain states. Speculation about whether a kind is multiply realizable boils down to what one knows about the capacities of realizing kinds. Given my knowledge of physical materials, I can imagine many different kinds of mousetraps that would capture mice effectively. In contrast, given my general ignorance about compounds, elements, and electrical conductivity, I can barely imagine one way to build a semiconductor. If I knew more about these things, perhaps I could devise a thousand distinct kinds of semiconductors. The point is that because it is an empirical matter whether a kind is multiply realizable, our ability to determine whether some kind is multiply realizable will hinge on how well we understand the world, how familiar we are with nature's constraints. Perhaps one day we will understand properties of brain states well enough to answer questions about the realization of consciousness and qualia with as much aptness as Newton showed in his discovery of the partial decussation at the optic chiasma.

Notes

Chapter 1

1. "SETI" is an acronym for the Search for Extraterrestrial Intelligence project. However, as I will soon explain, my interest is less in whether there might be humanlike minds on other planets than it is in whether, here on Earth, there could have evolved humanlike minds that are realized in nonhumanlike ways.

2. Of course, it is a historical contingency that the initial conditions include some things and not others, but here I wish to distinguish initial conditions from conditions that arise from initial conditions.

3. Putnam eventually forsakes the Turing machine in favor of the broader notion of a probabilistic automaton, which assigns particular probabilities to transitions between states (Putnam 1967).

4. For this simplified description of a solar cell I am relying on Macaulay (1988, 1998).

5. In evolutionary biology, "homologous" means "similar due to common ancestry." As I will soon argue, Block and Fodor must mean "analogous" in this context, i.e., similar *despite* the fact the trait evolved independently in the two lineages leading to the two descendants.

6. See also Sober (2000), who marshals the same reasoning in an argument bearing on the other minds problem.

Chapter 2

1. For further discussion of this point see Burge (1979); Egan (1992, 1995); Shapiro (1993, 1997); and Wilson (1992, 1995, 2004).

2. But see also Lycan (1981).

3. Here I mean *why* in the sense of *what it's "good" for* or *what its purpose is*. There is another sense of *why* that is important to my project. In asking why the mind evolved the properties it did the answer might involve constraints that made it impossible that it evolve other properties than those that it did.

4. First-class levers are those in which the fulcrum is between the load and the effort, e.g., a common balance scale. Third-class levers are those in which the effort is between the fulcrum and the load, e.g., a hammer.

5. However, as we shall see in chapter 5, Batterman and I end up with very different views about what to count as multiple realizations.

Chapter 3

1. McGhee (1999) gives a good introduction to the theory and application of morphospaces.

2. These parameters are: (1) the shape of the generating curve, defined as the cross-sectional outline of a hollow tube as it coils about a fixed axis; (2) the position of the generating curve relative to the axis of coiling; (3) the exponential rate of increase of the generating curve; and (4) the exponential rate of translation of the curve along the axis (Raup 1962, p. 150).

3. This assumes that the dimensions represent quantitative values.

4. Amusingly, William Paley (1805) considered the possibility of a watch that could produce others of its kind. Paley believed that the discovery of such a device should "increase beyond measure our admiration of the skill which had been employed" in its construction. He was no doubt correct.

5. Of course, it is still possible that forces like genetic drift allow the trait to move to the more optimal state.

6. I owe much of the following discussion to Kemp's (1982) classic treatment.

7. The loops of Henle are U-shaped structures located in the kidney's nephrons. They provide a surface area for water-reabsorption.

8. I recognize that despite the multiple realizability of time-keeping devices, it may be true that 90 percent of time-keeping devices are of a single kind. If one knows this, then one can make a good prediction about the kind of timepiece being used. No doubt one can believe that a kind is multiply realizable without believing that the multiple realizations are equally distributed in a population. Hence, for my characterization of multiple realizability to work, I must assume that the advocate of multiple realizability believes just that multiple realizations of a kind are possible and has no beliefs about the distribution of these realizations.

9. For pinhole eyes—the simplest sort of image-forming eye, consisting simply of a cup into which light enters through a narrow aperture without the focusing benefit of a lens—a bigger aperture comes at the cost of *increased* blurriness. However, make the aperture too small and the image, though sharp, will not be sufficiently bright to be useful.

10. Dawkins (1996) too compares photons to raindrops.

Chapter 4

1. This suggests another problem in drawing clearly the distinction between universal and historical constraints. It might be considered a universal constraint that, given some contingent event in the past—the evolution of trait Y—an organism must then evolve some other trait, X, if it is to display some particular capacity. The evolution of X is necessary for the capacity, but, suppose, only given Y's presence. The fact that the situation can be described as either a universal or historical constraint in some contexts does not affect the use I make of the distinction.

2. Below I will address the correlation between intelligence and brain size.

3. As with topographic maps, there is evidence that modular designs have evolved independently in several lineages (Kaas 2000b).

Chapter 5

1. This is how Batterman (2000) interprets Fodor.

2. In fact, I'm not sure whether Fodor finds macroregularities as beguiling as he suggests in this passage. Unlike Kim, he's quite comfortable with the possibility of macroregularities, and I think he would agree with most of what I have to say in response to Kim. Apologies to Fodor if I have misread him here.

3. Thanks to Batterman (2000) for making this passage known to me.

4. This is a position I also defended in my (2000). I've since changed my mind.

5. Of course, there would be available some uninteresting generalizations, e.g., "All eyes are made of atoms."

Chapter 6

1. Compare to Wilson's (2002) six views of embodiment.

2. This isn't quite right. There is no need to assume that all human beings start life with the same initial mental "settings." However, this does not affect the main point here. Minds are formal systems if they contain well-defined tokens that are modifiable in well-defined ways so that any system that can be interpreted as having the same tokens modified in the same ways would count as an instance of the same mind.

3. To be fair to Block, he's pretty clearly talking about the logical rather than nomological possibility of alternatively embodied minds. The point I am making in this paragraph is better directed toward someone who allows the *nomological* possibility that minds can be connected to bodies that differ significantly from the human body.

4. However, many functionalists would be willing to accept the claim that minds are multiply realizable if there is variation in the brain that produces them despite similarities in the body. For discussion of neural plasticity see chapter 2.

Chapter 7

1. I am here discussing only a small piece of Lakoff and Johnson's much larger research program. Nevertheless, it seems clear that the piece I am discussing can stand on its own, and so it is possible to accept these findings without endorsing other claims they make, particularly regarding their objections to metaphysical realism and an objective account of truth. For critical discussions of some of their work, see Murphy (1996) and Glucksberg and McGlone (2000).

References

Allen, C., and Bekoff, M. (1995). "Function, Natural Design, and Animal Behavior: Philosophical and Ethological Considerations." *Perspectives on Ethology* 11: 1–46.

Allman, J. (1999). *Evolving Brains*. New York: W. H. Freeman.

Aristotle. (1941). *Physics: Bk. II: Ch. 9*. In R. McKeon (tr.) *The Basic Works of Aristotle* (New York: Random House).

Arnold, S. (1992). "Constraints on Phenotypic Evolution." *American Naturalist* 140: S85–S107.

Batterman, R. (2000). "Multiple Realizability and Universalizability." *British Journal for the Philosophy of Science* 51: 115–145.

Bechara, A., Damasio, H., Tranel, D., and Damasio, A. (1997). "Deciding Advantageously before Knowing the Advantageous Strategy." *Science* 275: 1293–1295.

Bechtel, W., and Mundale, J. (1999). "Multiple Realizability Revisited." *Philosophy of Science* 66: 175–207.

Bickle, J. (1998). *Psychoneural Reduction: The New Wave*. Cambridge, Mass.: MIT Press.

Block, N. (1978). "Troubles with Functionalism." In W. Savage (ed.), *Perception and Cognition: Minnesota Studies in the Philosophy of Science*, vol. 9, pp. 261–325. Minneapolis: University of Minnesota Press. Reprinted in Block (1980a), pp. 268–305.

Block, N. (1980a). *Readings in Philosophy of Psychology*, vol. 1. Cambridge, Mass.: Harvard University Press.

Block, N. (1980b). "Introduction: What Is Functionalism?" In Block (1980a), pp. 171–184.

Block, N., and Fodor, J. (1972). "What Psychological States Are Not." *Philosophical Review* 81: 159–181. Reprinted in N. Block (1980a), pp. 237–250.

Brooks, R. (1991a). "New Approaches to Robotics." *Science* 253: 1227–1232.

Brooks, R. (1991b). "Intelligence without Representation." *Artificial Intelligence* 47: 139–159.

Burge, T. (1979). "Individualism and the Mental." In P. French, T. Uehling, and H. Wettstein (eds.), *Midwest Studies in Philosophy*, vol. 4, pp. 73–121. Minneapolis: University of Minnesota Press.

Burgess, C. (1998). "From Simple Associations to the Building Blocks of Language: Modeling Meaning in Memory with the HAL Model." *Behavior Research Methods, Instruments, and Computers* 30: 188–198.

Burgess, C., and Lund, K. (1997). "Modelling Parsing Constraints with High-Dimensional Space." *Language and Cognitive Processes* 12: 177–210.

Causey, R. (1972). "Attribute-identities in Microreductions." *Journal of Philosophy* 69: 407–422.

Cherniak, C. (1995). "Neural Component Placement." *Trends in Neuroscience* 18: 522–527.

Chiel, H., and Beer, R. (1997). "The Brain Has a Body: Adaptive Behavior Emerges from Interactions of Nervous System, Body, and Environment." *Trends in Neuroscience* 20: 553–557.

Churchland, P. M. (1981). "Eliminative Materialism and Propositional Attitudes." *Journal of Philosophy* 78: 67–90.

Churchland, P. S., Ramachandran, V., and Sejnowski, T. (1994). "A Critique of Pure Vision." In C. Koch and J. Davis (eds.), *Large-Scale Neuronal Theories of the Brain*, pp. 23–60. Cambridge, Mass.: MIT Press.

Clark, Andy (1997). *Being There: Putting Brain, Body, and World Together Again*. Cambridge, Mass.: MIT Press.

Clark, Andy (1999). "Where Brain, Body, and World Collide." *Journal of Cognitive Systems Research* 1: 5–17.

Clark, Andy (2001). "Reasons, Robots, and the Extended Mind." *Mind and Language* 16: 121–145.

Clark, Andy, and Chalmers, D. (1998). "The Extended Mind." *Analysis* 58: 7–19.

Clark, Austen (1993). *Sensory Qualities*. Oxford: Clarendon Press.

Clark, E., and Clark, H. (1979). "When Nouns Surface as Verbs." *Language* 55: 767–811.

Clarke, P., and Whitteridge, D. (1976). "The Projection of the Retina, Including the 'Red Area,' onto the Optic Tectum of the Pigeon." *Quarterly Journal of Experimental Physiology* 61: 351–358.

Cohen, J., Dunbar, K., and McClelland, J. (1990). "On the Control of Automatic Processes: A Parallel Distributed Processing Model of the Stroop Effect." *Psychological Review* 97: 332–361.

Conway Morris, S. (1998). *The Crucible of Creation: The Burgess Shale and the Rise of Animals*. New York: Oxford University Press.

Copeland, J. (1993). *Artificial Intelligence: A Philosophical Introduction.* Oxford: Blackwell.

Cummins, R. (1975). "Functional Analysis." *Journal of Philosophy* 72: 741–765.

Dagan, D., and Camhi, J. (1979). "Responses to Wind Recorded from the Cercal Nerve of the Cockroach *Periplaneta Americana*: II. Directional Selectivity of the Sensory Nerves Innervating Single Columns of Filiform Hairs." *Journal of Comparative Physiology* A 133: 103–110.

Damasio, A. (1994). *Descartes' Error: Emotion, Reason, and the Human Brain.* New York: Avon Books.

Dawkins, R. (1982). *The Extended Phenotype.* San Francisco: Freeman.

Dawkins, R. (1996). *Climbing Mount Improbable.* New York: W. W. Norton.

Dawson, M. (1998). *Understanding Cognitive Science.* Malden, Mass.: Blackwell.

Dennett, D. (1981). "True Believers: The Intentional Stance and Why It Works." In A. F. Heath (ed.), *Scientific Explanation*, pp. 53–75. Oxford: Clarendon Press.

Dennett, D. (1991). "Real Patterns." *Journal of Philosophy* 88: 27–51.

Denton, C. (1981). "Topography of the Hyperstriatal Visual Projection Area in the Young Domestic Chicken." *Experimental Neurology* 74: 482–498.

Dowling, J. (1998). *Creating Mind: How the Brain Works.* New York: W. W. Norton.

Dretske, F. (1988). *Explaining Behavior: Reasons in a World of Causes.* Cambridge, Mass.: MIT Press/Bradford.

Egan, F. (1992). "Individualism, Computation, and Perceptual Content." *Mind* 101: 443–459.

Egan, F. (1995). "Computation and Content." *Philosophical Review* 104: 181–203.

Elbert, T., Pantev, C., Wienbruch, C., Rockstroh, B., and Taub, E. (1995). "Increased Cortical Representation of the Fingers of the Left Hand in String Players." *Science* 270: 305–307.

Enç, B. (1976). "Identity Statements and Microreductions." *Journal of Philosophy* 73: 285–306.

Enç, B. (1983). "In Defense of the Identity Theory." *Journal of Philosophy* 80, 279–298.

Enç, B. (2002). "Indeterminacy of Function Attributions." In A. Ariew, R. Cummins, and M. Perlman (eds.), *Functions: New Essarys in the Philosophy of Psychology and Biology*, pp. 291–313. New York: Oxford University Press.

Feigl, H. (1958). "The 'Mental' and the 'Physical.'" In H. Feigl, M. Scriven, and G. Maxwell (eds.), *Concepts, Theories, and the Mind-Body Problem:*

Minnesota Studies in the Philosophy of Science, vol. 2, pp. 370–497. Minneapolis: University of Minnesota Press.

Fernald, R. (1997). "The Evolution of Eyes." *Brain, Behavior, and Evolution* 50: 253–259.

Finger, T. (1978). "Gustatory Pathways in the Bullhead Catfish, II, Facial Lobe Connections." *Journal of Comparative Neurology* 180: 591–706.

Finlay, B., Darlington, R., and Nicastro, N. (2001). "Developmental Structure in Brain Evolution." *Behavioral and Brain Sciences* 24: 263–308.

Fodor, J. (1968). *Psychological Explanation*. New York: Random House.

Fodor, J. (1974). "Special Sciences (Or: The Disunity of Science as a Working Hypothesis)." *Synthese* 28: 97–115. Reprinted in Fodor (1981), pp. 127–145.

Fodor, J. (1980). "Methodological Solipsism as a Research Strategy in Cognitive Psychology." *Behavioral and Brain Sciences* 3: 63–73. Reprinted in Fodor (1981), pp. 225–253.

Fodor, J. (1981). *RePresentations: Philosophical Essays on the Foundations of Cognitive Science*. Cambridge, Mass.: MIT Press.

Fodor, J. (1997). "Special Sciences: Still Autonomous after All These Years." *Philosophical Perspectives* 11: 149–163.

Fodor, J., and Pylyshyn, Z. (1988). "Connectionism and Cognitive Architecture: A Critical Analysis." *Cognition* 28: 3–71. Reprinted in J. Haugeland (1997), pp. 309–350.

French, R. (1990). "Subcognition and the Limits of the Turing Test." *Mind* 99: 53–65.

Futuyma, D. (1998). *Evolutionary Biology*, third ed. Sunderland, Mass.: Sinauer.

Gibson, J. J. (1966). *The Senses Considered as Perceptual Systems*. Prospect Heights, Ill.: Waveland Press.

Gibson, J. J. (1979). *The Ecological Approach to Visual Perception*. Boston: Houghton-Mifflin.

Gillett, C. (2002). "The Dimensions of Realization: A Critique of the Standard View." *Analysis* 62: 316–323.

Glenberg, A. (1997). "What Memory Is For." *Behavioral and Brain Sciences* 20: 1–55.

Glenberg, A., and Robertson, D. (2000). "Symbol Grounding and Meaning: A Comparison of High-Dimensional and Embodied Theories of Meaning." *Journal of Memory and Language* 43: 379–401.

Glucksberg, S., and McGlone, M. (2000). "When Love Is Not a Journey: What Metaphors Mean." *Journal of Pragmatics* 31: 1541–1558.

Godfrey-Smith, P. (1993). "Functions: Consensus without Unity." *Pacific Philosophical Quarterly* 74: 196–208.

Goldstein, E. (1989). *Sensation and Perception*, third ed. Belmont: Wadsworth.

Gould, S. J. (1989a). *Wonderful Life*. New York: W. W. Norton.

Gould, S. J. (1989b). "A Developmental Constraint in Cerion, with Comments on the Definition and Interpretation of Constraint in Evolution." *Evolution* 43: 516–539.

Gould, S. J., and Lewontin, R. (1979). "The Spandrels of San Marco and the Panglossian Paradigm: A Critique of the Adaptationist Programme." *Proceedings of the Royal Society of London* B 205: 581–598.

Gregory, R. (1991). "Origins of Eyes: With Speculations on Scanning Eyes." In J. Cronly-Dillon and R. Gregory (eds.), *Vision and Visual Dysfunction*, vol. 2, pp. 52–59. New York: Macmillan.

Haldane, J. W. S. (1928). "On Being the Right Size." In J. W. S. Haldane, *Possible Worlds*, pp. 20–28. New York: Harper Press.

Harnad, S. (1990). "The Symbol Grounding Problem." *Physica D* 42: 335–346.

Hartline, H., Wagner, H., and Ratliff, F. (1956). "Inhibition in the Eye of Limulus." *Journal of General Physiology* 39: 651–673.

Hatfield, G. (1991). "Representation in Perception and Cognition: Connectionist Affordances." In W. Ramsey, S. Stich, and D. Rumelhart (eds.), *Philosophy and Connectionist Theory*, pp. 163–195. Hillsdale, N.J.: Lawrence Erlbaum.

Hatfield, G. (1999). "Mental Functions as Constraints on Neurophysiology: Biology and Psychology of Vision." In V. Hardcastle (ed.), *Where Biology Meets Psychology: Philosophical Essays*, pp. 251–271. Cambridge, Mass.: MIT Press.

Haugeland, J. (1981). "Semantic Engines: An Introduction to Mind Design." In J. Haugeland (ed.), *Mind Design*, pp. 1–34. Cambridge, Mass.: MIT Press.

Haugeland, J. (1995). "Mind Embodied and Embedded." In L. Haaparanta and S. Heinämaa (eds.), *Mind and Cognition: Philosophical Perspectives on Cognitive Science and Artificial Intelligence, Acta Philosophical Fennica* 58: 233–267. Reprinted in J. Haugeland (1998), pp. 207–237.

Haugeland, J. (1997). *Mind Design II*. Cambridge, Mass.: MIT Press.

Haugeland, J. (1998). *Having Thought: Essays in the Metaphysics of Mind*. Cambridge, Mass.: Harvard University Press.

Hendry, S., Hsiao, S., and Brown, M. (1999). "Fundamentals of Sensory Systems." In M. Zigmond, F. Bloom, C. Landis, J. Roberts, and L. Squire (eds.), *Fundamental Neuroscience*, pp. 657–670. San Diego: Academic Press.

Hooker, C. (1981). "Towards a General Theory of Reduction. Part I: Historical and Scientific Setting. Part II: Identity in Reduction. Part III: Cross-Categorical Reduction." *Dialogue* 20: 38–59, 201–236, 496–529.

Hutchins, E. (1995). *Cognition in the Wild*. Cambridge, Mass.: MIT Press.

Jerison, H. (1973). *Evolution of the Brain and Intelligence*. New York: Academic Press.

Kaas, J. (1997). "Topographic Maps Are Fundamental to Sensory Processing." *Brain Research Bulletin* 44: 107–112.

Kaas, J. (2000a). "The Reorganization of Sensory and Motor Maps after Injury in Adult Mammals." In M. Gazzaniga (ed.), *The New Cognitive Neurosciences*, second ed., pp. 223–236. Cambridge, Mass.: MIT Press.

Kaas, J. (2000b). "Why Is Brain Size So Important?" *Brain and Mind* 1: 7–23.

Kandel, E., Schwartz, J., and Jessell, T. (2000). *Principles of Neural Science*, fourth ed. New York: McGraw Hill.

Karten, H., and Shimizu, T. (1989). "The Origins of Neocortex: Connections and Lamination as Distinct Events in Evolution." *Journal of Cognitive Neuroscience* 1: 291–301.

Kaschak, M., and Glenberg, A. (2000). "Constructing Meaning: The Role of Affordances and Grammatical Constructions in Sentence Comprehension." *Journal of Memory and Language* 43: 508–529.

Kemeny, J., and Oppenheim, P. (1956). "On Reduction." *Philosophical Studies* 7: 6–19.

Kemp, T. S. (1982). *Mammal-like Reptiles and the Origin of Mammals*. New York: Academic Press.

Kim, J. (1992). "Multiple Realization and the Metaphysics of Reduction." *Philosophy and Phenomenological Research* 52: 1–26.

Kim, J. (1998a). *Mind in a Physical World*. Cambridge, Mass.: MIT Press.

Kim, J. (1998b). *Philosophy of Mind*. Boulder: Westview Press.

Kirschfeld, K. (1976). "The Resolution of Lens and Compound Eyes." in F. Zettler and R. Weiler (eds.), *Neural Principles in Vision*, pp. 354–370. Berlin: Springer.

Kitcher, P. (1984). "1953 and All That: A Tale of Two Sciences." *Philosophical Review* 93: 335–373.

Knudsen, E. (1980). "Sound Localization in Birds." In A. Popper and R. Fay (eds.), *Comparative Studies of Hearing in Vertebrates*, pp. 289–322. New York: Springer-Verlag.

Lakoff, G., and Johnson, M. (1980a). *Metaphors We Live By*. Chicago: University of Chicago Press.

Lakoff, G., and Johnson, M. (1980b). "Conceptual Metaphor in Everyday Language." *Journal of Philosophy* 77: 453–486.

Lakoff, G., and Johnson, M. (1999). *Philosophy in the Flesh: The Embodied Mind and Its Challenge to Western Thought*. New York: Basic Books.

Land, M. (1991). "Optics of the Eyes of the Animal Kingdom." In J. Cronly-Dillon and R. Gregory (eds.), *Vision and Visual Dysfunction*, vol. 2, pp. 118–135. New York: Macmillan.

Land, M., and Fernald, R. (1992). "The Evolution of Eyes." *Annual Review of Neuroscience* 15: 1–29.

Landauer, T., and Dumais, S. (1997). "A Solution to Plato's Problem: The Latent Semantic Analysis Theory of Acquisition, Induction, and Representation of Knowledge." *Psychological Review* 104: 211–240.

Lewis, D. (1969). "Review of Putnam," excerpted from "Review of Art, Mind, and Religion." *Journal of Philosophy* 66: 23–35. Reprinted in Block (1980a), pp. 232–233.

Lewis, D. (1978). "Mad Pain and Martian Pain." Reprinted in Block (1980a), pp. 216–222.

Lycan, W. (1981). "Form, Function, and Feel." *Journal of Philosophy* 78: 24–50.

Macaulay, D. (1988, 1998). *The New Way Things Work*. New York: Houghton Mifflin.

Marr, D. (1982). *Vision*. San Francisco: Freeman.

Martin, R. D. (1990). *Primate Origins and Evolution: A Phylogenetic Reconstruction*. Princeton: Princeton University Press.

Maynard Smith, J., Burian, R., Kauffman, S., Alberch, P., Campbell, J., Goodwin, B., Lande, R., Raup, D., and Wolpert, L. (1985). "Developmental Constraints and Evolution." *Quarterly Review of Biology* 60: 265–287.

McClelland, J., and Rumelhart, D. (1986). "A Distributed Model of Human Learning and Memory." In J. McClelland, D. Rumelhart, and the PDP Group (eds.), *Parallel Distributed Processing*, vol. 2, pp. 170–215. Cambridge, Mass.: MIT Press.

McGhee, G. (1999). *Theoretical Morphology: The Concept and Its Applications*. New York: Columbia University Press.

McMahon, T., and Bonner, J. (1983). *On Size and Life*. New York: Scientific American Books.

Miller, G. (1956). "The Magical Number Seven, Plus or Minus Two: Some Limits on Our Capacity for Processing Information." *Psychological Review* 63: 81–97.

Millikan, R. (1984). *Language, Thought, and Other Biological Categories*. Cambridge, Mass.: MIT Press.

Morell, P., and Norton, W. (1980). "Myelin." *Scientific American* 242: 88–118.

Murphy, G. (1996). "On Metaphoric Representation." *Cognition* 60: 173–204.

Nagel, E. (1961). *The Structure of Science*. New York: Harcourt Brace.

Neander, K. (1991). "The Teleological Notion of 'Function.'" *Australasian Journal of Philosophy* 69: 454–468.

Newell, A., and Simon, H. (1976). "Computer Science as Empirical Inquiry: Symbols and Search." *Communications of the Association for Computing Machinery* 19: 113–126.

Nilsson, D. (1989). "Vision Optics and Evolution." *BioScience* 39: 298–307.

Oppenheim, P., and Putnam, H. (1958). "Unity of Science as a Working Hypothesis." In H. Feigl, M. Scriven, and G. Maxwell (eds.), *Minnesota Studies in the Philosophy of Science*, vol. II, pp. 3–36. Minneapolis: University of Minnesota Press. Reprinted in R. Boyd, P. Gasper, and J. D. Trout (eds.), *The Philosophy of Science* (Cambridge, Mass.: MIT Press, 1991, pp. 405–427).

Ott, M., and Schaeffel, F. (1995). "A Negative Powered Lens in the Chameleon." *Nature* 373: 692–694.

Packard, A. (1972). "Cephalopods and Fish: The Limits of Convergence." *Biological Review* 47: 241–307.

Paley, W. (1805). *Natural Theology*. London: Rivington.

Pascual-Leone, A., and Torres, F. (1993). "Plasticity of the Sensorimotor Cortex Representation of the Reading Finger of Braille Readers." *Brain* 116: 39–52.

Pettigrew, J., and Konishi, M. (1976). "Neurons Selective for Orientation and Binocular Disparity in the Visual Wulst of the Barn Owl (*Tyto alba*)." *Science* 193: 675–678.

Place, U. T. (1956). "Is Consciousness a Brain Process?" *British Journal of Psychology* 47: 44–50.

Polger, T. (2002). "Putnam's Intuition." *Philosophical Studies* 109: 143–170.

Putnam, H. (1960). "Minds and Machines." In S. Hook (ed.), *Dimensions of Mind*, pp. 148–179. New York: New York University Press. Reprinted in Putnam (1975a), pp. 362–285.

Putnam, H. (1967). "Psychological Predicates." In W. Capitan and D. Merrill (eds.), *Art, Mind, and Religion*, pp. 37–48. Pittsburgh: University of Pittsburgh Press. Reprinted as "The Nature of Mental States," in Putnam (1975a), pp. 429–440.

Putnam, H. (1975a). *Mind, Language, and Reality: Philosophical Papers*, vol. 2. New York: Cambridge University Press.

Putnam, H. (1975b). "Philosophy and Our Mental Life." In Putnam (1975a), pp. 291–303.

Putnam, H. (1975c). "How Not to Talk about Meaning." In Putnam (1975a), pp. 117–131.

Putnam, H. (1975d). "The Meaning of Meaning." In K. Gunderson (ed.), *Language, Mind, and Knowledge: Minnesota Studies in the Philosophy of Science*, vol. 9, pp. 131–193. Minneapolis: University of Minnesota Press. Reprinted in Putnam (1975a), pp. 215–271.

Putnam, H. (1988). *Representation and Reality*. Cambridge, Mass.: MIT Press/Bradford.

Pylyshyn, Z. (1980). "The Causal Power of Machines." *Behavioral and Brain Sciences* 3: 442–444.

Radinsky, L. (1987). *The Evolution of Vertebrate Design*. Chicago: University of Chicago Press.

Ramsey, F. (1931). "General Propositions and Causality." In *The Foundations of Mathematics and Other Logical Essays*, pp. 237–255. New York: Harcourt Brace.

Raup, D. (1962). "Computer as Aid in Describing Form in Gastropod Shells." *Science* 138: 150–152.

Raup, D. (1966). "Geometric Analysis of Shell Coiling: General Problems." *Journal of Paleontology* 40: 1178–1190.

Resnik, D. (1995). "Developmental Constraints and Patterns: Some Pertinent Distinctions." *Journal of Theoretical Biology* 173: 231–240.

Richardson, R. (1979). "Functionalism and Reductionism." *Philosophy of Science* 46: 533–558.

Ridley, M. (1986). *Evolution and Classification: The Reformation of Cladism.* New York: Longman.

Ringo, J. (1991). "Neuronal Interconnection as a Function of Brain Size." *Brain, Behavior, and Evolution* 38: 1–6.

Robert, D., Miles, R., and Hoy, R. (1996). "Directional Hearing by Mechanical Coupling in the Parasitoid Fly *Ormia ochracea.*" *Journal of Comparative Physiology A* 179: 29–44.

Rosenberg, A. (1985). *The Structure of Biological Science.* Cambridge: Cambridge University Press.

Ryle, G. (1949). *The Concept of Mind.* London: Hutchinson.

Schaffner, K. (1967). "Approaches to Reduction." *Philosophy of Science* 34: 137–147.

Schmidt-Nielsen, K. (1990). *Animal Physiology: Adaptation and Environment,* fourth ed. New York: Cambridge University Press.

Searle, J. (1980). "Minds, Brains, and Programs." *Behavioral and Brain Sciences* 3: 417–424.

Shapiro, L. (1993). "Content, Kinds, and Individuation in Marr's Theory of Vision." *Philosophical Review* 102: 489–514.

Shapiro, L. (1994). "Behavior, ISO Functionalism, and Psychology." *Studies in History and Philosophy of Science* 25: 191–209.

Shapiro, L. (1997). "A Clearer Vision." *Philosophy of Science* 64: 131–153.

Shapiro, L. (2000). "Multiple Realizations." *Journal of Philosophy* 97: 635–654.

Sharma, J., Angelucci, A., and Sur, M. (2000). "Induction of Visual Orientation Modules in Auditory Cortex." *Nature* 404: 841–847.

Shoemaker, S. (1981). "Some Varieties of Functionalism." *Philosophical Topics* 12: 93–120.

Shoemaker, S. (1999). "Self, Body, and Coincidence." *Proceedings of the Aristotelian Society* (supplemental vol.) 73: 287–306.

Shoemaker, S. (2001). "Realization and Mental Causation." In C. Gillett and B. Loewer (eds.), *Physicalism and Its Discontents*, pp. 74–98. Cambridge: Cambridge University Press.

Sklar, L. (1967). "Types of Inter-Theoretic Reduction." *British Journal for the Philosophy of Science* 18: 109–124.

Smart, J. J. C. (1959). "Sensations and Brain Processes." *Philosophical Review* 68: 141–156.

Sober, E. (1992). "Learning from Functionalism—Prospects for Strong Artificial Life." Reprinted in M. Boden (ed.), *The Philosophy of Artificial Life*, pp. 361–378. (New York: Oxford University Press, 1996). Originally, in C. Langton, C. Taylor, J. Farmer, and S. Rasmussen (eds.), *Artificial Life II* (Redwood City, Calif., 1992, pp. 749–766).

Sober, E. (1993). *Philosophy of Biology*. Boulder: Westview Press.

Sober, E. (1999a). "Testability." *Proceedings and Addresses of the APA* 73: 47–76.

Sober, E. (1999b). "The Multiple Realizability Argument against Reductionism." *Philosophy of Science* 66: 542–564.

Sober, E. (2000). "Evolution and the Possibility of Other Minds." *Journal of Philosophy* 97: 365–386.

Sternberg, S. (1969). "Memory Scanning: Mental Processes Revealed by Reaction-Time Experiments." *American Scientist* 57: 421–457.

Stich, S. (1983). *From Folk Psychology to Cognitive Science*. Cambridge, Mass.: MIT Press.

Turing, A. (1950). "Computing Machinery and Intelligence." *Mind* 59: 433–460.

Ulinski, P. (1980). "Organization of Retinogeniculate Projection in Pond Turtles, *Pseudemys* and *Chrysemys*." *Neuroscience Abstracts* 8: 260.

Ulinski, P. (1984). "Design Features in Vertebrate Sensory Systems." *American Zoologist* 24: 717–731.

Vogel, S. (1998). *Cats' Paws and Catapults*. New York: W. W. Norton.

von Melchner, L., Pallas, S., and Sur, M. (2000). "Visual Behaviour Mediated by Auditory Cortex Directed to the Auditory Pathway." *Nature* 404: 871–876.

Walsh, D., and Ariew, A. (1996). "A Taxonomy of Functions." *Canadian Journal of Philosophy* 26: 493–514.

Went, F. (1968). "The Size of Man." *American Scientist* 56: 400–413.

Williams, G. (1966). *Adaptation and Natural Selection: A Critique of Some Current Evolutionary Thought*. Princeton: Princeton University Press.

Wilson, M. (2002). "Six Views of Embodied Cognition." *Psychological Bulletin and Review* 9: 625–636.

Wilson, R. (1992). "Individualism, Causal Powers, and Explanation." *Philosophical Studies* 68: 103–139.

Wilson, R. (1994). "Wide Computationalism." *Mind* 103: 351–372.

Wilson, R. (1995). *Cartesian Psychology and Physical Minds: Individualism and the Sciences of the Mind.* New York: Cambridge University Press.

Wilson, R. (1999). "The Individual in Biology and Psychology." In V. Hardcastle (ed.), *Where Biology Meets Psychology: Philosophical Essays,* pp. 357–374. Cambridge, Mass.: MIT Press.

Wilson, R. (2001). "Two Views of Realization." *Philosophical Studies* 104: 1–30.

Wilson, R. (2004). *Boundaries of the Mind: The Individual in the Fragile Sciences: Cognition.* New York: Cambridge University Press.

Wright, L. (1973). "Functions." *Philosophical Review* 82: 139–168.

Index